A Frightening Love: Recasting the Problem of Evil

# A Frightening Love: Recasting the Problem of Evil

Andrew Gleeson
*Flinders University of South Australia, Australia*

palgrave
macmillan

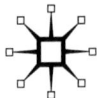

First published 2012 by
PALGRAVE MACMILLAN

Palgrave Macmillan in the UK is an imprint of Macmillan Publishers Limited, registered in England, company number 785998, of Houndmills, Basingstoke, Hampshire RG21 6XS.

Palgrave Macmillan in the US is a division of St Martin's Press LLC, 175 Fifth Avenue, New York, NY 10010.

Palgrave Macmillan is the global academic imprint of the above companies and has companies and representatives throughout the world.

Palgrave® and Macmillan® are registered trademarks in the United States, the United Kingdom, Europe and other countries.

ISBN: 978–0–230–24975–2

This book is printed on paper suitable for recycling and made from fully managed and sustained forest sources. Logging, pulping and manufacturing processes are expected to conform to the environmental regulations of the country of origin.

A catalogue record for this book is available from the British Library.

A catalog record for this book is available from the Library of Congress.

10  9  8  7  6  5  4  3  2  1
21 20 19 18 17 16 15 14 13 12

Printed and bound in Great Britain by
CPI Antony Rowe, Chippenham and Eastbourne

*For my mother and father*

# Contents

# Preface

This book has six main themes:

1. Theodicy is a moral failure.
2. The distinction commonly drawn between the intellectual problem of evil on one hand, and the personal or existential problem of evil on the other, is spurious.
3. The problem of evil rightly configured is existential. It is a struggle inside our hearts between the apparently rival claims of God's *love* on one side, and *morality*, claiming our allegiance in the name of the victims of evil, on the other.
4. There is no single, universally correct resolution to the problem. Both belief in the face of evil and disbelief on account of it can be justified. Moreover one individual can rightly be bound by conscience to the first stand and another to the second: the universalisability of judgements fails for the problem of evil.
5. God is not a moral agent or an efficient causal force. He is love itself, visible to us in the instantiations of love in the world. This position cannot be reached by metaphysical argument, but is the truth we can recognise if we are sufficiently free of the blinding effects of evil in our lives.
6. This position rejects any view which seeks to give an account of God's reality which can be understood independently of our religious lives and experiences. Such views insinuate an objectifying sense of reality (such as we find in science, but not only there) as if it were the single, univocal sense, when in fact it is only one sense among others. There is also moral reality, and there is what I call 'existential reality'. Talk about these realities gets its sense from the human encounter with them. God's reality as love itself is an existential reality.

Overall the book is a case study in the dissociation of a certain way of doing philosophy from its subject matter. Some philosophers of religion do not pay sufficient attention to actual religious life. Theodicists do not pay sufficient attention to moral life. Both say in the philosophy seminar room things they would never countenance in their personal lives. When in the book I criticise these things I am not criticising the people who say them. Quite the opposite. The point is not about the philosophers themselves but about the dissociation of their philosophising from their lives, and thus relies on the assumption that their lives are *not* like their philosophies. It is the same sort of dissociation we see in other areas of philosophy: for example, in radical scepticism about the senses. It occurs because philosophers subscribe to a certain conception of what serious thought is, a conception which treats actual human lives and responses as external to thought, even as hindrances to it. The conception aspires to what is sometimes called the 'Archimedean point' or the 'view from nowhere'. More than anything that conception of thought is my target. So, really, this is a work of meta-philosophy.

My inspiration for the book came during an advanced course on the problem of evil I first taught at Åbo Akademi, in Turku, Finland, in December 2006, and then at the University of Adelaide in 2007. A draft was written in the second half of 2008 and early 2009. Early versions of Chapter 3 were read to the Adelaide University Philosophy Club, and to the first annual conference of the Australasian Philosophy of Religion Association, held in Canberra in 2008. That chapter is forthcoming in the *Heythrop Journal*. Many of the book's mature arguments were discussed by a class of senior students at Rhodes University, South Africa, in April–May of 2009, where I also presented material to a staff seminar. The typescript was refined and completed during 2010 and 2011.

I am grateful for comments I received from many people on the occasions mentioned above and in personal correspondence and conversation. I especially thank David Cockburn, Garrett Cullity, John Gill, Joe Mintoff and Craig Taylor, all of whom, especially John, provided written comments on various parts of the book. I also benefited from discussion with them and with Nick Trakakis, Chris Walsh and Francis Williamson. The work of Raimond Gaita inspired the meta-ethical themes of the book, especially the material on the forms of thought in Chapter 4. I thank Lars Hertzberg for arranging the Turku trip. I am especially grateful to the philosophy department at Rhodes University for hosting my visit there so warmly. It was a return, after several years, to a splendid place of fine students, colleagues and friends.

Your maxims are proverbs of ashes,
    Your defences are defences of clay.

# 1
# The Greater Good

## 1. Ivan Karamazov's challenge

In Dostoevsky's *The Brothers Karamazov*, Ivan Karamazov lays down a powerful challenge to the very idea that, charged with responsibility for the evil in his creation, God could earn an acquittal before the tribunal of morality. Ivan concentrates his argument on the suffering of children. Here is one of his examples:

> This poor child of five was subjected to every possible torture by those cultivated parents. They beat her, thrashed her, kicked her for no reason till her body was one bruise. Then they went to greater refinements of cruelty – shut her up all night in the cold and frost in a privy, and because she didn't ask to be taken up at night (as though a child of five sleeping its angelic, sound sleep could be trained to wake and ask) they smeared her face and filled her mouth with excrement, and it was her mother, her mother, did this! And that mother could sleep, hearing the poor child's groans!

Addressing his pious brother, Alyosha, Ivan uses the example to drive home his objection to all attempts to justify the ways of God to man:

> Can you understand why a little creature, who can't even understand what's done to her, should beat her little aching heart with her tiny fist in the dark and the cold, and weep her meek unresentful tears to dear, kind God to protect her? Do you understand that, friend and brother, you pious and humble novice? Do you understand why this infamy must be and is permitted? Without it, I am told, man could not have existed on earth, for he could not have known good

and evil. Why should he know that diabolical good and evil when it costs so much? Why, the whole world of knowledge is not worth that child's prayer to 'dear, kind God'! (Dostoevsky 1912, pp. 247–8)

The challenge – its urgency enhanced by the unspeakable evils of the twentieth century – has haunted much thought about God and evil since Dostoevsky's time. Among some it has helped feed a profound scepticism about the traditional project of 'theodicy', the attempt to give an account of God's reasons for creating the world that will earn him moral exoneration. According to Nick Trakakis (2008, p. 167), this scepticism is so widely taken for granted among theologians and continental philosophers that they rarely explicitly defend it. In contrast, while passing acknowledgement is often paid to Ivan Karamazov in setting the scene for 'the problem of evil', the vast bulk of philosophical discussion of that topic within the Anglo-American analytic school of philosophy has failed to take his argument, and similar anti-theodical ideas, seriously.[1]

This is very strange, since these ideas could hardly be more relevant. The core of the challenge is its straight-out, unblinking denial that any good, however great, is worth certain sorts of (actual) human suffering, especially the suffering of children. This is not to be committed to a moral absolutism against doing evil in *any* circumstances. Doing or allowing such serious evil for the sake of greater goods is here to be understood as doing it for the sake of taking a good situation, or at least not a bad one, and making it better. It is to be contrasted with doing or allowing such evil for the sake of avoiding catastrophe, as in moral dilemmas. It is not a catastrophe if God does not create at all or if he creates only a world of inanimate matter and insentient vegetation. The latter situation is good and the former is at least not bad. This non-absolutist understanding is all that is needed for the challenge to theodicy, so that is how I shall construe it.

So if Ivan Karamazov is right, then on the face of it at least, any argument which seeks to exonerate God by appealing to some good that evil is the inescapable means to or price of – evil which the good, in some way, counts for more than – is undermined. This captures not only those theodicies which explicitly appeal to justifying greater goods (greater than the evil paid for them) but also at least the main contemporary version of that defence of God which seeks to deflect responsibility for evil from him to his creatures by appeal to free will – that version due to Alvin Plantinga (1974a). For as we shall see Plantinga's 'free will defence' also relies on greater goods (free will itself being chief among those goods). The thought that the evils of the world are such that *no* greater good *could* vindicate God, so that the strategy of appealing to such goods is misguided, has rarely been raised. The thought that the very idea of a moral vindication for God misrepresents him (as being a bigger version of a moral agent like us) is rarely found in the analytic literature on the problem of evil.

Mainstream theodicy standardly postulates that despite all the evil it contains the world is redeemed by the greater good in it, so long as the evil is a necessary condition for the good and a post-mortem compensation is provided for the innocent victims of evil. The evil need not be a necessary condition for the good in the sense of being a means to it (as with suffering giving rise to virtue). It may be that the evil is an incidental consequence (an unavoidable cost) of the good. This is so with free will, the good on which many theodicists place the most weight. Thus a maliciously cruel act may not produce the greater good of forgiveness in its victim – it may bear no good fruit of its own – but it is a consequence of giving creatures free will that God (as opposed to us) cannot avoid (short of withdrawing the free will) if some creature chooses it. The account can be complicated by requiring that a certain number of other greater goods – from the standard retinue: rational agency, moral responsibility and personal growth, compassion and love, reconciliation with God in an everlasting post-mortem beatitude – must be realised in addition to free will to secure a good great enough to justify creating a world with actual-world levels of evil in it. Thus, Alvin Plantinga offers a logically possible scenario (as the lynchpin to his defence of God against an 'atheological' argument from evil) which requires not only that free will exist but also that creatures 'freely perform more good than evil actions' in order for a world to be 'more valuable, all else being equal, than a world containing no free creatures at all' (1974a, p. 30).

Theodicy rests on the assumption that good can come of evil and redeem the world containing that evil. Of course it is true that there are sometimes benefits from suffering, both to the victim and to others. There is sometimes a degree of consolation in remembering, for example, that the organs of a lost loved one have helped another to live. It is true and important that controlled adversity can build character. And far beyond all that, some people have seriously confessed that their sufferings (up to a certain limit, arguably) have been a blessing to them, though this is a matter to be handled with great care. But for all this, the 'good from evil' line of thought has serious limitations when it is appealed to as a form of *justification* for the creation of a world containing that evil. Would and should those thus consoled or otherwise benefited take the further step of agreeing with the theodicist that God is morally justified in creating a world with these evils if he did so for the sake of the goods? Because we are sometimes licitly grateful for the good consequences some evil can entail, it by no means follows that we are right to start viewing the evil as an acceptable price to pay for that good when it is unavoidable.

We are talking about serious evils, not discomforts and inconveniences. The former, unlike the latter, are what we might call 'existential evils', ones that threaten our capacity to see the world in a spirit of gratitude and love: the evils that can break our spirit. (The distinction is crucial; see Chapter 3.) Thus it is one thing to justify making children do their homework – or go to the dentist or wear embarrassing clothes to school so that the other children tease them (all examples to be found in the literature) – for the good it does them. But it is quite another to justify creating a world in which they suffer cancer, or are raped, tortured and murdered, because of the opportunities for moral and spiritual growth this presents them with,[2] and worse still to justify it partly on account of the moral opportunities it presents to others.[3] To reiterate, I am not denying that serious suffering, even horrendous suffering, is sometimes of spiritual benefit to people (just as, equally often at least, it crushes people entirely). Nor am I denying that a certain controlled degree of challenge and exertion is necessary for human maturation and fulfilment, especially in the young. What I am denying is that these truths can be used to morally justify creating a world with the sort of horrendous suffering that exists in our world, especially, as Ivan stresses, the suffering of children: not even if that suffering *always* produced spiritual benefits for everyone involved, including the victims (not, of course, that it does).

The claim that a given case of consolation or some other benefit from evil can justify the creation of that evil is itself a moral claim, and as subject to moral appraisal as anything else. Sometimes the claim is true – as with the discomfort and inconvenience demanded by homework and athletic training – and sometimes it is not. For example, it would be unconscionable to justify painful experiments on living and fully conscious children from the fact that this resulted in scientific discoveries which reduced the overall quantity of suffering – even if we compensated them afterwards (see the next section). Or to endorse John Harris's (1975) 'survival lottery', in which citizens are executed for their organs, which can keep alive and healthy a larger number of people – and not merely because in the actual world we might have secured these goods without the evils. Again, this is so even if a post-mortem world is available to compensate the victims.

If this is right, then how much more objectionable is it to create a world in which the suffering of children is considered an acceptable price for the standard set of greater goods, listed above, that theodicists trade in, especially given that in this case there is no plausibility in supposing God is acting to avoid a disaster? There is no legitimate redemption in the thought that the children suffered so that humans generally (including their tormentors) might have these goods, great as they are. 'Yes, we have our lives, our freedom, our health, our spiritual growth – *but at whose expense?* Do we have these things *decently?*' We must ask these questions. We cannot simply take for granted a hierarchy of goods and evils, with the greater goods always outweighing the evils, without asking whether it is decent to acquire the goods at the expense of the victims of the evil. It thus would miss the point entirely to respond to Karamazov's challenge by simply upping the quantity or quality of goods, as if the lives of children were a tradable commodity on sale to the theodicy able to bid the most good for them. Ivan says:

> Listen! If all must suffer to pay for the eternal harmony, what have children to do with it? Tell me, please? It's beyond all comprehension why they should suffer, and why they should pay for the harmony. ... I renounce the higher harmony altogether. It's not worth the tears of that one tortured child who beat itself on the breast with its little fist and prayed in its stinking outhouse, with its unexpiated tears to 'dear, kind God'! It's not worth it, because those tears are unatoned for. They must be atoned for, or there can be no harmony. But how? How are you going to atone for them? Is it possible? By their being avenged? But what do I care for avenging them? What do I care for a hell for oppressors? What good can hell do, since those children have already been tortured? ...I want to forgive. I want to embrace. I don't want more suffering. And if the sufferings of children go to swell the sum of sufferings which was necessary to pay for truth, then I protest that the truth is not worth such a price. (Dostoevsky 1912, pp. 250–1)

Ivan goes on to insist that *no* amount of post-mortem forgiveness and reconciliation or justice would justify the creation of such suffering. He declares that he does not want an eventual harmony at such a price and would 'rather be left with the unavenged suffering' (p. 251). I take it that he intends the eventual eternal harmony to include the child-victims.

But, he is claiming, what they have suffered cannot be justified by any future compensation or reward for them. The point is not an epistemic one about the likelihood of such harmony (or any other good) actually being achieved, but a moral one. The point is not that we humans cannot celebrate the great goods of this world, or even those of a next world if such there be, despite the evils they have entailed (though that celebration should not be unalloyed, without a sense of its cost). The point is that – *pace* theodicy – we cannot, on God's behalf, *morally justify* his creation of a world with such evils on the ground of the goods. It is shouldering the goods with a burden they cannot bear by putting them in a position where they are contaminated by the evils, so that it becomes a serious question whether we now can celebrate them decently at all. In a nutshell: *the lives of children are not for sale.* These questions must be faced. The failure of so much of the theodical literature to press them adequately is too often hidden behind an impersonal pseudo-objectivity of weighing goods and evils. But the point about contamination shows that the image of an economic exchange breaks down here. If I barter my oranges for your apples the apples are unaffected and I get what I wanted: perfectly good apples. But if God or a human being barters a child's life for some general good (and even if the child shares in that good) the good *is* affected and we get something that we did not bargain for: a moral burden.[4]

## 2. Compensation and consent

Karamazov's challenge is a powerful moral critique of theodicy. There are parents so infatuated with a cause they believe is for the general improvement of the world that they sacrifice their own child to it: we can see this in certain religious and political ideologies, of which the religious ones are able to hold out the prospect of a post-mortem compensation for the children. The ideologies blind these parents to the moral reality of their actions. It is not difficult to imagine their remorse if they were brought to their senses.

As we have seen, Ivan says it makes no difference if the children (and other victims, of course) share in the good they have been sacrificed for or are otherwise compensated. But many theodicists are unconvinced of that. In this section I shall look more closely at whether compensation changes the situation. Then I shall examine the appeal to victims' consent made by some theodicists. The discussion is important because it will reveal that Ivan's moral critique of theodicy (or a moral understanding of that critique) may not go deep enough.

It is a logical truism about compensation that normally it is not a moral justification of the evils it is for. If I negligently spill a damaging chemical into my neighbours' backyard, causing their garden to be killed, I am (at least) obligated to pay compensation, but it doesn't follow that the original negligence is thereby justified. Quite the opposite. It normally implies I have done wrong to someone and owe them the compensation in payment for the wrong. The point applies with particular force to theodicy, since the serious evils theodicy deals with would, in legal terms, be criminal wrongs rather than merely civil torts, and deserve *punishment* rather than compensation. True, governments sometimes award compensation to victims of natural disasters for which no human beings are responsible. But on a theistic view either God or some other non-human-created agent is responsible for these evils (either by act or omission) and government steps in because it is not practical to get such beings to pay up in a timely fashion. In some jurisdictions, government also pays compensation for industrial and other accidents, but again this is not because wrongdoing is assumed to be absent in all cases, but because it is judged, on grounds of efficiency or practicality, that the compensation is best treated as a public responsibility rather than a private one. Governments also pay compensation for compulsory acquisition of private property for public purposes, and this might look like the best model for the theodicist to adopt since it does not imply the government acts wrongly (government might also seem more analogous to God than a human individual). But the model is stretched beyond what it will bear if we apply it to serious evils. For example, the government cannot murder its citizens, or let them be murdered, in the name of a greater public good – not because it cannot be sure of securing the good, but because such an act would be a travesty of the conditions of justice that bind commonwealths together as a political community. (Governments can require us to fight just wars at risk to our lives; however, this is not a case of a greater good in the relevant sense, but a case of averting catastrophe.) The bottom line is that where compensation is owed this is because the agent who owes it does so on account of a wrong he or she has done. There are some exceptions to this, such as the ones noted here, but none for the sorts of terrible evils theodicy has to account for. But theodicy cannot admit that God has acted wrongly. (The suggestion that God is compensating victims for evils that *others* – non-human-created beings – have freely perpetrated, so that *he* is not the one who has acted wrongly, is one I shall come to below in Section 4.)

Theodicists would be ill advised to try to get out of this by construing the compensation as simply an outweighing future good. On this construction God creates a world with these evils, and is *justified* in doing so because of a 'bigger picture' that includes future outweighing goods to victims (as well as good for others and the world as a whole), so that while he has indeed created a world that inflicts *evil* on people, he is not guilty of doing them a *wrong*, of acting towards someone as he should not have acted. The greater goods might still be described as something owed to the victims, and thus even as a kind of compensation, but of a prospective sort: God owes the victims the future greater goods in order to *prevent* a wrong done to them (the wrong of inflicting the evils without the 'compensation') rather than to make up for an *existing* wrong. But this is simply to revert to the greater goods justification that the introduction of compensation was supposed to qualify in the name of justice and in the hope of escaping Karamazov's challenge. It is true that so long as that justification is applied *within* each individual life – each individual enjoys outweighing greater goods, so that their life is a good to them as a whole, as it is sometimes put – then the picture is not a purely consequentialist one in which some individuals are ruthlessly sacrificed for the greater good without further thought about them. But Ivan's objection is not simply to the injustice of some being sacrificed to a collective good. It is to the whole idea that serious evil may be inflicted, or be permitted to be inflicted, on people, especially children, for the sake of greater goods, even if the victims share in those goods. This is quite clear from his remarks on the 'eternal harmony'.

It is enormously tempting, though, for philosophers to feel that Ivan is taking too parochial a view. It is understandable that one might draw a line in the sand at sacrificing some for others, especially if the some are children. But, the thought would go, there is no injustice, no illegitimate abuse of people as mere means, if *within* an individual life some stage of it is, so to speak, sacrificed for the sake of a later stage. Nor indeed, more strongly, is there any injustice if some stage of an individual life is sacrificed for the sake of the greater good of the collective, so long as this is subject to the caveat that the individual life is 'good on the whole' – good on the whole to the individual concerned. In practice this means good in its later stages outweighing the evil of its earlier stages. God of course is able to ensure this and indeed able to deliver the incommensurate good of eternal happiness, a good great enough (the supporters of this line of thought believe) to outweigh, indeed overwhelm, any evil. Ivan needs to take a larger view of things and not let his emotions be overwhelmed by local events. To make it more explicit, the objection is (in effect) saying we need to take the point of view of an agent able to envisage and sympathise with every stage in a person's life: the point of view of an ideal observer. Or if not take that view our-selves – for perhaps that is an impossibility for limited beings like us – at least trust in the deliverances of someone who can: God.

I suspect this line of thought receives subterranean encouragement from presenting Karamazov's challenge – as I have done myself so far – as primarily *moral* criticism. That presentation is liable to distort its real force, at least to a philosophical audience. Many philosophers (by no means all) accept a picture of moral judgements as akin to theoreti-cal conjectures, one moral judgement inviting another in a speculative way that distances itself from (indeed may condescend to) actual, real-life human responses, including a philosopher's own responses, which are liable to be treated merely as data ('intuitions') against which to test a general account of morality: data which can in principle be over-ridden. And among the philosophers with this view, not a few naturally aspire to a God's-eye view of things, treating our human and mor-tal 'limitations' – of ignorance, but also of non-rational passions and attachments – as contingent encumbrances upon moral understanding. These philosophers need not be consequentialists, or at least not pure consequentialists (the caveat under discussion is already a departure from that), but to them it seems just obvious that this sort of abstrac-tion to a universal, Olympian viewpoint (not just in ethics but in any field of thought: the God's-eye view) is the proper form thought should take. They take the fact that it dispenses with the limited viewpoint we humans are capable of – a viewpoint that pays special attention to those we personally know and especially those we love – as a central merit, a release from insularity and prejudice.

But is it really? Taking the analogy of God to human parents, is it acceptable, or even morally possible, for good and loving parents to put children through Auschwitz (or permit it) for the sake of any greater good – even if the children share in the good or are otherwise com-pensated? The children of course will not willingly agree. But children are short-sighted and lacking in impulse control, so their judgement cannot be trusted, and for that reason we entrust them to parents and guardians who make decisions for them (so that we are already moving in the direction of an ideal observer, the theodicists might say). Alright, but what are we to make of parents who take the ideal observer's long view of things and *agree* to put their children through Auschwitz for the sake of some greater good on condition the children are granted eternal beatitude afterwards? Consider some different sorts of cases where we can at least understand, even if we do not approve of, parents inflicting, or permitting the infliction of, serious evils on their children, or finding that thinkable. We all understandably feel the pressure to do terrible actions in order to avert a disaster, whatever moral view we ultimately take about that. We can imagine Sophie Zawistowska, with the most painful reluctance, choosing to give up her daughter to the gas chambers to save her son, when (in the 1980 novel by William Styron) the Nazis demand she choose one child or lose both. We would not condemn her action. We understand why people make such choices between alternative disasters. But *ex hypothesi*, as I have pointed out, the case of God creating the world is not a matter of avoiding disaster. It is doing (or permitting) evil purely in order that *a greater good may come of it*: in order to make a good or not-bad thing better. This is what the ideal observer does not flinch from. In another kind of case, sometimes people murder or prostitute their children or commit other violations of them without any excuse of avoiding a greater evil, but simply because they are overwhelmed by frightening human passions of greed, hatred, cruelty and so on.[5] Again, *ex hypothesi* this is not what theodicists or anyone else supposes about God. Then there is the case of some religious believers, not all Christian, who love their children but who refuse certain life-saving medical treatments. In my judgement (except where the belief is purely superstitious) they do not do so for the instrumental reason of securing a future post-mortem good for their children or anyone else (even if they believe in such a thing, which not all may do) but because they regard the treatment itself as a kind of violation right now of something that gives life weight and significance.[6] But once more this is not the same as what theodicy – on the analogy of God's decision to create the world to parents' decision to have children – in effect invites parents to agree to. Theodicy – by claiming that a greater good justifies God in creating the world so long as the victims of evil are specially compensated with a life that is on balance good for them – implies that parents would be doing no wrong by their children to agree to a deal that sends their children to Auschwitz for the sake of the world's greater good, so long as the children share in that good, enjoying an eternal beatitude afterwards. In all these different cases we can make sense – though we may not approve – of parents agreeing to their children being subjected to terrible evil (even without a greater good or compensation), and the cases (even the evil passions case, at least in some versions) are consistent with the parents genuinely loving their children. But, in contrast, can parents who *genuinely love* their children, and are not subject to some corrupting passion, agree to release the children to terrible evil, not because of a dilemma or in the name of some important value they would otherwise violate, but just to make an already good world better (not, say, to relieve misery, but to turn a world in which people are on balance happy for three score years and ten into one in which they are perfectly happy for ever)? *Pace* the straightforward moral construal of Karamazov's challenge, the point now is not the moral one that the parents are acting immorally. The problem is the conceptual one of recognising them as genuinely loving human parents in the first place, or as ones free from the poisonous influence of some hidden passion. We would wonder over such parents in the way we sometimes wonder over psychopaths, only much more so – wonder, that is, how human they really are. By this I don't of course mean that we wonder about their biological classification, but rather how capable they are of normal human responses, not only of sympathy, but also of the hatred, malice and so on which so often overwhelm that sympathy. The problem is that unless faced with a dilemma or a violation of something deeply important to their sense of life's meaning, or disordered by the destructive passions mentioned before, *parents cannot bring themselves to agree to such things being done to their children*, whatever good the children (let alone anyone else) stands to gain. Of course the ideal observer will regard this as merely a psychological infirmity. But that is not how the parents can regard it. For them it constitutes a limit they cannot even consider trespassing. It is not as if they spend time weighing the pros and cons and finally coming down against it, as they might do with deciding whether to send their children to a certain school. What would we think of parents who discussed as a serious possibility sending their children to Auschwitz in hope of a later and greater good for the children, however certain that good? Absent the sort of circumstances I distinguished in the other cases, the claim that they love their children, or even that they humanly sympathise with them, is undone by their willingness to consider such an act, consideration that would put them closer to the category of the monstrous than the human. It is of no avail to say the parents might do this but of course unwillingly or sorrowfully. That makes sense in the dilemma or violation cases, but not here. The supposed unwillingness and sorrow are exposed as crocodile tears by the willingness to consider, let alone do, the deed. It would be either satire or horror. A race of beings who lived this way would no more be acting immorally when they did such things than are tigers or sharks when they attack and kill prey. This is why I say the criticism is deeper than moral criticism.

Human parents are not merely reluctant to agree to such things; it is beyond their ken to take it seriously. In a word, they find it *unthinkable* to treat their children in such a way. Tellingly, the idea of such things is advanced only in philosophy seminar rooms. None of the theodicists who attribute such a policy to God would consider it for a moment in their own lives, and not just because they cannot be sure of the consequences. It is something that does not – except, as I say, in the pretence of the academic seminar room – come within our consideration at all: it represents a boundary beyond which lies something deeply alien to us. So long as God is to be considered as a moral agent answerable to the same moral standards we are answerable to (as theodicists would have it) we cannot treat what is morally impossible for us as a virtue in God. There is an irony here that in the name of a certain morality and its picture of perfection, theodicy effectively denies God the parental love that Christianity makes central to his nature, and even the ordinary sympathy that is basic to human decency. In seeking to attribute *good* motives to God for creating a world where children suffer as some do, theodicy in fact makes him much more alien and frightening to us.

But – the advocates of the ideal observer might say – perhaps being human is second best. For all that we can't see it, or at least can't take it seriously, we would be morally improved if we were ideal observers. Well, perhaps so. But that just raises the question (a central question of this book): is morality so construed worth the cost? It asks us to purchase an omni-sympathy (if it really is sympathy) unrestricted by the contingent limitations of being human. But, as I have been arguing, those 'limitations' include the parental love – and wider human fellowship, but I shall focus on parental love – that finds handing your children over to torturers for the sake of some subsequent good (even conceiving them with that intention, to get a closer analogy with God) unthinkable. Here is a description of that love by Anne Manne in which she contrasts it with a recently popular philosophical incarnation of a quasi-ideal observation, 'care':

> *Care* is a very different word from *love*. Care is cool and careful, reasoned, a word which implies distance and limits. Love is not. Love is passionate, implacable, intense, unreasoned. It is love that children need, not just care. Children need most not trained, expert, professional care, but the passionate partiality of parental love. (1994, p. 23)

It is just because this love matters to us – and so being children or being parents are the momentous things they are to us – that the morality of the ideal observer is simply too cold and remote to make a universe we can be at home in. Do we really want to endorse an ethic that would require us to do things that, as we really are, are unthinkable? Everything that really matters to us would be gone. We do not want to live in such a world.

But perhaps some theodicists might be willing to allow us humans a lesser standard – a concession to our fallen condition perhaps – while holding God to a stricter one. We are not subject to the morality of the ideal observer, but God might be (after all he *is* the ideal observer). But that is profoundly untrue to the Christian understanding of God. To regard God as a sort of cosmic civil engineer or social planner – one of a particularly ruthless sort too, at least within individual lives – is the *antithesis* of the personal love that Christianity has always said God has for us: the same sort of deep and passionate attachment to his children that human parents have for their children (so that they cannot send them to Auschwitz for greater goods) and which in God's case went all the way to the Cross for his children. Such will be a central theme of this book.[7]

But, for all this, does the picture change if, in addition to requiring compensation for the victims of evil, we also require their *consent* to their sufferings as a second caveat in relation to the moral legitimacy of the project of creation for greater goods? Obviously there cannot be actual consent in advance of creation. But it is possible to appeal to a notion of hypothetical consent. Thus Alvin Plantinga (2004) has suggested that if (in addition to securing future goods for themselves, as well as for the collective and the cosmos) victims suffer only evils that they would have consented to in advance if they could have, and if they were fully informed and not subject to 'disordered affections', then God does no wrong in creating the world. God is in the clear if what we might call an 'ideal consenter' would agree to the deal. But an ideal consenter is just a version of the ideal observer, and so all the difficulties I have described return. The child will certainly not agree; it is terrified out of its wits. And if it did agree no parent would give that any weight. The parents will not agree on their own account either. What's it to any of them what an ideal observer thinks? They – we – are not ideal observers, so why should we care what beings from Mars think when they want us to do things that are beyond our pale? The ideal observer is *inhuman* in the worst sense of the word.

Many theodicists talk of providing the victims with a post-mortem greater good that is good *for* the victims themselves (Adams 1999; Tracy 1992; Stump 1990; Plantinga 2004). This appears to take the perspective of the victims themselves seriously. But appeal to the ideal observer simply undoes that: we do *not* consent, and if that is simply brushed aside because the ideal observer says we *should* consent, then how is *our* perspective being taken seriously, how is *our* autonomy being respected?[8] It is perhaps partly for this reason that Adams (1999) resorts to the idea of a putative future, post-mortem consent (of a very strong sort as we shall see in Chapter 2, where I discuss her theory). But this idea, though it seems to dispense with the ideal observer, covertly relies on it. Why should retrospective consent be superior to prospective? Why should it free God from moral criticism while the latter does not? (After all, at least under the conditions of human life, we would prefer the latter as more authoritative.) The important point is simply that whatever we might think in some remote (and frankly, fantastic) future it remains the case that we morally cannot *now* conceive children and send them to Auschwitz. To say that a future, retrospective consent would trump this when it comes to what we or God should do *just is* to abandon the human view in favour of the ideal observer's.[9] The human view flees with uncomprehending horror from the very idea of such a thing, including the idea that retrospective consent, even if forthcoming, would justify it. We flee from the idea that *anything* can justify this, including our own (or our children's) consent. The opinion that this is some sort of limitation or fault is not a thought that can be accommodated inside the human view. It belongs to the ideal observer's view. If God is to be genuinely the God of love Christians hold him to be, then they must say that, like us, he cannot even contemplate doing such things as theodicists suppose.

## 3. Plantinga and moral assumptions

It could be objected that while Karamazov's challenge might be relevant to *theodicy*, perhaps it will not be relevant to what has come to be called a *defence* of God against 'the argument from evil' to show he does not exist. A theodicy attempts to find 'morally sufficient reasons' (MSRs) which would exonerate God for creating the world, and which it is reasonable to believe may well be his actual reasons given what we know about the world (the theodicist need not insist they *are* his reasons). In contrast it is enough for a defence that an MSR be no more than a logical possibility, however outlandish given what we know about the world.

Thus a defence might be called a *possible* theodicy. But just for that reason, Dostoevsky's challenge is fully relevant to it. It makes no difference to the status of that challenge whether the MSR is the one God actually acts on or not, or whether it is known, or reasonably believed, to be the one he acts on, or whether it is a wild conjecture. A moral objection to a hypothetical course of action, or to a reason for a course of action, is not negated if the course, or the reason, is never realised.[10]

A theodicy, if successful, is adequate to meet the logical version of the problem of evil, which charges that there is an inconsistency in holding both that an omnipotent, omniscient and perfectly good God exists and that evil exists, or at least the kinds and levels of evil that exist in the actual world. Most theodicies also aspire to be adequate for the *evidential* version of the problem, which holds that actual-world evil renders the existence of God *improbable*. In contrast a defence is adequate only to the logical version. Karamazov's challenge is a logical version of the problem concerned with actual-world evil. Since it denies the pivotal moral assumption of mainstream theodicy – that greater goods can morally justify God in creating worlds in which children suffer as they do in ours – it knocks out the basic move that renders God and actual evil consistent with one another. So if the challenge succeeds (and there is no other way of meeting the argument from evil), then God and actual evil are inconsistent with one another and there is no need to consider the evidential version of the argument.

So far I have concentrated on theodicies and defences which, in one way or another, appeal to greater goods that outweigh the evil in the world. But there is another line of thought which on the face of it might seem very different. This says that God is not to be blamed for evil, since it entered (or enters) the world through the exercise of the (contra-causal, 'libertarian') free will possessed by human beings and perhaps other created agents. Hence Alvin Plantinga (1974a, 1974b) has famously argued that it is a logical possibility that the counter-factuals of creaturely freedom are such that God, if he created a world with free creatures at all, could only create a world wherein those free creatures did evil as well as good and the resultant world-wide balance of good and evil would in no case have been better than that in the actual world. Plantinga accounts for physical evil in this way as well as moral evil by assuming that some physical evils are due to evil human choices (as is evidently true) and that it is logically possible that others – naturally caused disease, injury and death – are the result of free acts of other created agents. So it is logically possible that God could not have *created* a world with free creatures and with a better balance of good and evil (all good and evil, physical and moral) than the one we actually have, despite the fact that such a world is *possible*. This may not be the best of all possible worlds, but it is possible that it is the best God could have created, or an equal best. Plantinga supports this by making the moral assumption that this world is better than a world without free will creatures, or no world at all, so long as the creatures freely perform more good than evil actions. If this is so, Plantinga concludes, God had a morally sufficient reason to create it, so that he did no wrong in creating it. The argument is one by possible counter-example. Given the logically possible scenario described above, it follows that the existence of God is consistent with the existence of the actual world's evil, and the logical version of the argument from evil is refuted. This argument is a defence rather than a theodicy since Plantinga merely affirms his speculation about the counter-factuals of creaturely freedom to be possible rather than true or known to be true – but possibility is all the argument needs. It has sometimes been claimed that with this argument Plantinga has solved the logical problem of evil once and for all.

I disagree. The argument depends on the assumption that this world is better than a world without free will creatures, or no world at all, and thus that God had a morally sufficient reason to create it. So in the end, Plantinga's version of the 'free will defence' is fundamentally a greater goods argument, rather than the radically different argument we might have expected. It depends on the assumption that a kind of greater good – free will, plus a positive balance of good creaturely acts over evil ones – outweighs actual-world evil and justifies the creation of that world. But of course it is not obvious that this assumption is true, to say the least. It runs smack bang into Karamazov's challenge. That God may, in the name of free will and a positive balance of good acts over evil, knowingly create a world where his creatures, especially children, will be subjected to the horrendous evils we find in this world is *exactly* what Karamazov's challenge challenges. Ivan Karamazov does not allow that *any* good, however much it outbalances the evils of our world, will justify God creating our world (always remembering that by a 'greater good' here we are talking about an improvement to an already good or not-bad situation, not the avoidance of disaster). Instead he asserts (in effect):

A. *No amount or kind of greater good morally justifies creating a world where children suffer as they do in this one.*

Plantinga needs to respond to Karamazov's challenge. In his classic publications setting out this defence to the logical version of the argument from evil, Plantinga (1974a, 1974b) does not engage with the challenge at all, despite the fact that he quotes Dostoevsky. More recently, in the development of his 'O Felix Culpa' theodicy, Plantinga (2004) does attempt to meet worries about his moral assumptions by introducing forms of compensation and consent as caveats on God creating the world for the greater goods of the incarnation, atonement and eternal beatitude. But as we saw in the previous section these do not meet Karamazov's challenge. Plantinga himself thinks that the incarnation, atonement and eternal beatitude themselves are not weighty enough to do so or he would not have introduced the caveats. The upshot is that he has no reply to one of his own worries about the 'O Felix Culpa' theodicy: that it portrays God as exhibiting something like Munchausen-by-proxy syndrome, a mental disorder 'in which parents harm their children and then rush them to the hospital in order to look heroic and get attention' (Plantinga 2004, p. 14).

Plantinga may respond by insisting that, since we are dealing here with the logical version of the argument from evil – under which it is claimed there is an inconsistency between *God exists* and *evil exists* – then it is not enough that A be true; it must be a necessary truth.[11] But A is a *moral* claim, and if it is true then surely it is necessarily true. It would be *ad hoc* for Plantinga to stipulate that the sort of necessity moral propositions have is not the right sort of necessity. After all, A expressly applies to every world (every relevant world, that is: every one in which children suffer as they do in this world) and truth in all (relevant) worlds *is* just the sort of necessity Plantinga works with.

The argument so far is enough to show that Plantinga has failed in his attempt to refute the logical version of the argument from evil. He might retreat to the position of Nelson Pike (1990) and contend that since his opponents have undertaken to prove God and evil are inconsistent, they bear an onus to establish that A is true: there is no onus on the theist to establish ~A. So long as Plantinga can show that they have failed to discharge that onus, their argument, though not shown to be incapable of success, can be said to be a failure to date. The longer this failure persists, he might add, the more reasonable it becomes to believe the argument cannot succeed. How forceful is this? Well, it all depends on what one counts as *establishing* A. If by establishing it one means showing that it is true, or at least very likely to be true, by considerations of the sort that dominate the literature of professional analytic moral philosophy – if one must find arguments that would command general agreement among such thinkers – then Plantinga can indeed compellingly claim that neither A nor anything like it has been established. The jury is still out in moral philosophy and so long as it is out the logical version of the argument from evil cannot be said to succeed, though neither can it be said *finally* to be a failure. If and when moral philosophers make progress in their subject perhaps the matter will one day be resolved.

So a common, arguably dominant, line of philosophical thought would go. That line of thought assumes a certain conception of moral philosophy as an academic subject, and with that a certain conception of moral thought and justification, one that assimilates these to the specialised techniques of the academic subject. Very similar assumptions are common in mainstream analytic philosophy of religion. The central argument of this book challenges these assumptions, mainly in the context of philosophy of religion (and the problem of evil in particular) but with inescapable forays into moral philosophy as well – and in any event, the basic line of criticism is the same. The ideal of legitimate persuasion in question would treat A as established only when arguments have been discovered, purporting to show it is true, or very likely to be true, which would satisfy people *in virtue of being properly informed, rational agents and regardless of all except their most minimal moral assumptions (and ideally none).* That is to say, this ideal of moral justification is one that aspires to an Archimedean point, a morally neutral vantage point or one as close to that as can be achieved. Now, I have stated this in a very strong form which any actual instance will only approximate to, but I have done so in order to bring out the *central tendency*, the direction of striving if you like, of this intellectual ideal. In practice most particular justifications are forced to include in their basic resources some minimal moral assumptions: *impartiality*, for example, is a very common one (sometimes claimed to be a logical feature of moral discourse, thus somewhat camouflaging its substantive moral content).[12] For present purposes though it is enough that straightforward appeals to conscience and humanity, devoid of philosophical underwriting, are not considered sufficient for moral justification (they are often dismissed as 'emotional'). My whole argument against theodicy has rested on just such appeals, supplemented by argument designed to remove misunderstandings and combat objections, but in no way seeking to provide a justification more fundamental than those appeals. Now if such appeals are not admitted as legitimate forms of justification, then Plantinga may well be right in saying that A has not yet been established. But he would say this at the risk of courting moral scepticism, for is there any moral position established to so high a standard? Certainly none that philosophers in general have reached a consensus on.[13]

On the other hand, if Plantinga admits appeals to conscience and humanity as in-principle sufficient justifications, then the whole nature of the debate changes fundamentally. The conception of thought and justification I shall attack in this book appeals predominantly to people's capacities for factual knowledge, instrumental rationality, logical reasoning, various technical skills and other qualities of this ilk, keeping other capacities, such as moral judgement, to a minimum. It treats considerations that are merely local, contingent, historical or individual as hindrances to thought, and it is often outrightly hostile to discussions that it sees as too moralising or literary or 'emotional'. In Chapter 4, where I describe this ideal of justification at length, I call it 'impersonal'. I shall argue that this conception of thought and justification is not merely set too high but that it actively distorts the nature of thought and of justification in these (and other) areas. The alternative conception of thought, which I call 'existential', forgoes the aspiration to neutrality, allows non-argumentative forms of justification and admits the relevance of what is contingent and individual. It fears that when we demand justification of too much, even of our most basic human responses, we risk undermining the forms of thought and justification that are actually within our reach. It moves in an intellectual world influenced more by art and literature than by science. On this alternative, the appeals to conscience and humanity by which I have, in this chapter, defended Ivan Karamazov's critique of theodicy are in principle perfectly legitimate. There is no need to be fazed by the fact that there are many intelligent and well-informed people they will fail to move. They do not stand in need of some deeper, neutral and argumentative sanction, something with which to box anyone into an intellectual corner using the narrower set of resources of the impersonal conception.

The present point is that if, in line with the existential conception of thought and justification, we admit the in-principle justificatory force of appeals to conscience and humanity, then Plantinga can no longer squarely say that A has not been established. I would say it is established by the existential appeal to conscience and humanity I have used. But there is no assessing this claim if one refuses to countenance the very idea of justification in these terms. The deeper moral of the failure of Plantinga's argument is that we should look seriously at the existential conception of thought. It will be one of the main themes of this book.

## 4. Free will theodicy, God and moral agency

It might be wondered whether Plantinga's argument is true to the spirit of the appeal to free will, the spirit which points out that God does not perpetrate moral evils; he at most permits them: *we* are to blame, not God! As I wrote above, one might have expected this to make for a different argument than one relying on greater goods. One might have expected an argument to the effect that since God's intentions were good – they were for an Eden, a world without evil – he is not to blame because human beings, exercising their gift of free will, have corrupted his plan. Free will features in the theodicies and defences considered so far as a justifying greater good. Presumably the alternative is some sort of principle to the effect that so long as God himself does not directly create evil – so long as all the evil in the world can be attributed to the free choices of created beings – then he is insured against blame for any evil in the world. But this is not right in such unqualified form. If God puts weapons – feet and fists and teeth for a start, then sticks and stones, and the resources from which humans can manufacture more serious weapons – in the possession, or within the reach, of creatures, then this can be justified only (if it is at all) if the good of doing so is great enough to warrant whatever risk there is of the creatures abusing their gifts. For example, God will not escape some responsibility for the evil in the world if he knew that the chances of creatures abusing these gifts amounted to a near certainty. That would be like giving nuclear weapons to North Korea. If North Korea uses them, then of course it bears the lion's share of blame, but the party irresponsible enough to give it the weapons must bear some blame: it is not good enough to say 'Well, the North Koreans nuked Seoul, not us.'

Still, perhaps there is something in the notion of goods that outweigh the risk of terrible evils (rather than the evils themselves) if we assume that the risk was something less than certain, and that God knew the risk and could not alter it without interfering with human freedom – I shall grant all that for the sake of argument.[14] This strategy is not obviously vulnerable to Karamazov's challenge. Whereas a good is contaminated by making *actual* human suffering a condition for it, this is not clearly so for making the *risk* of such suffering a condition for it. We non-culpably put our children's life and bodily integrity at risk every time we drive them as passengers in our car, and we do so for trivial goods that cannot possibly outweigh being a paraplegic, but which outweigh a certain low risk of becoming one. There are several serious metaphysical problems with this position, such as the mysterious subliming of human freedom as a 'contra-causal' phenomenon and the assumption that evil is only a contingent feature of human life. But we do not need to enter into these matters. The line of thought runs into other serious problems.

As I have already said, if God knew the Fall was a certainty, then surely he bears some of the blame. If he knew creating the world would certainly result in the Fall, and that there is no catastrophe which will ensue if he does not create (as there is not), it can no longer be said uncomplicatedly that he escapes all responsibility. If one creates a situation which one knows is *bound* to result in Ivan Karamazov's suffering children, then, at least without the excuse of averting catastrophe, surely one bears some responsibility for that suffering. Again, creation under these circumstances would be rather like giving nuclear weapons to North Korea. So it seems the theodicist must deny that God knew the Fall to be a certainty. Either he did not know its likelihood at all or he knew it to be less than certain. Suppose first that he had no idea how likely the Fall was. Then in creating the world God was knowingly putting tremendous power to do harm in the hands of creatures whose behaviour was *ex hypothesi*, unguaranteed, unknown and predictable only with luck. This case is like deciding to give nuclear weapons to a nation of which we know nothing: if we pass on the weapons and nuclear holocaust ensues, do we not bear a share of the responsibility? Why else do we think nations have a responsibility to abide by arms control measures? If Dr Frankenstein's creation, loaded up with an unpredictable free will gadget, turns on his maker and others, should the doctor be free of all responsibility? In deciding to create beings of such destructive potential, while being wholly ignorant of their likely behaviour, then (however unavoidable that ignorance) God did not merely *take a risk*; he acted *recklessly*. He played Russian roulette with the lives of children. From a moral point of view, calculated risks of disaster are one thing; wild plunges into the unknown quite another.

So suppose instead that God knew the probability of the Fall to be something less than certain (and does not know whether that low probability will be realised or not). There are two possibilities: that he knew the likelihood to be high and that he knew it to be low. Suppose first that he knew it to be high. Then he knowingly, willingly took an action with a high risk of disaster. Must he not then bear some responsibility for the outcome? Consider the nuclear weapons and Frankenstein cases again. So, finally, suppose he knew the likelihood to be low, vanishingly remote even. This is the scenario most favourable to the theodicist. It does not seem that God acted irresponsibly in taking such a remote risk.

If this is a logical possibility (as I grant for the sake of argument), then perhaps the logical problem of evil can still be solved. Call this argument the 'low-risk, free will theodicy'.[15]

D. Z. Phillips (2005, pp. 33–44) and, under his inspiration, Nick Trakakis (2008, pp. 168–71) have argued that even when God has done what he morally should do – which, according to theodicy, is that he must create a world of evils for the sake of greater goods – he nevertheless is tainted by evil and thus cannot be perfectly good. They liken his situation (under theodical assumptions) to moral dilemmas such as that of the fictional Sophie Zawistowska, mentioned back in Section 2, who was forced to choose whether to give up her son or her daughter to the Nazi death mills, on pain of both children being taken if she refused to choose. Whatever she did, she would be doing evil. Whatever she did, she would do wrong to someone, do something she should not do. As Phillips puts it, she must bear the consequences of her decision, whatever it is. Or, perhaps better, we might say she must bear the consequences of her tragic situation, her bad moral luck. And the consequences, on every alternative, mean that she is not free from evil-doing. (This does not mean that others can blame her, perhaps not even those whom by her actions she does evil to. But she may well blame herself, hold herself accountable before God, even knowing her action was not culpable by public, universalisable moral standards. Sophie could not live with the decision to give up her daughter's life and eventually took her own.) God, Phillips and Trakakis argue, is in the same structural situation. If he creates, he inflicts evil. If he does not, then he also does evil (by the lights of greater good theodicy) since he fails to realise the best state of affairs (or at least one better than not creating). So God must bear the consequences of his situation, and they include evil-doing, an evil-doing for which he is answerable. But that means, by the theodicists' own lights, that God cannot be free of evil as they claim; he cannot be 'perfectly good'. Perhaps their line of thought also applies to cases which are not dilemmas and where indeed it may be uncontroversial that the agent has acted rightly, or at least not wrongly. Consider a motorist who takes all appropriate precautions, whose driving is as safe as driving a car can possibly be, but who, nevertheless, hits and kills a young child who runs in front of the car. Here, if we admit the moral licitness of driving at all, we will surely agree that the motorist has not acted wrongly. Neither society, nor any spectator, nor even the victim, can hold the driver to account on the ground simply that they should not have gone driving that day – which would require holding all other safe drivers to account, whether they kill anyone or not (it would amount in fact to a moral prohibition on driving). If the motorist continues to drive (safely) they can defend this in obvious ways against the suggestion of wrongdoing. Yet quite consistently with all this, *the motorist has done evil all the same and that changes their moral condition.* In particular they have obligations towards the victim and the victim's family arising from the fact that they killed the child. Their moral relations to them are very different from those of a mere spectator. And, more than that, it is also morally required of the motorist that they feel some sort of horror at what they have done and even a kind of remorse. I say 'a kind' of remorse because while this remorse is remorse for killing the child, it does not involve an admission of *culpability* for that action. Rather the motorist should be remorseful in the sense of facing the pain of a lucid acknowledgement of the significance of what they have done (kill a child), of the evil in which this embroils them, and of the need, in the light of it, to (borrowing words from Trakakis) do penance and seek forgiveness from the family and from God. But while the driver is not culpable for killing the child (they are not a murderer), they *are* culpable if they fail to meet the obligations I have just been listing, obligations incurred by their non-culpable misfortune in killing the child: in the right circumstances at least, the family and even other parties could rightly criticise a frivolous insouciance or a proud defiance that refused to acknowledge a need to be remorseful in the sense I have gestured at. Now add to the case the assumption that the risk of a motorist hitting a child in the location was very remote (perhaps it was one of those child-free, gated retirement villages) and that the motorist in question knew this. Could the theodicist's case of God creating the world with a minute risk of evil be of a similar kind? If the cases are alike, then Phillips and Trakakis want to say that even though God cannot be blamed by other parties for creating the world – he is not culpable for its evil – neither is it true to say that he is 'perfectly good' as theodicists claim. On the contrary, like my motorist, he has done evil, or at least is deeply implicated in the evil-doing of others, and stands in need of making apology and penance and seeking forgiveness.

Some philosophers will reject this argument outright because they cannot accept the separation of remorse, apology, penance and forgiveness from culpability.[16] But since I agree with Phillips and Trakakis about this I shall not criticise their argument on this score. I think what they say about dilemmas is roughly right, and I extend it to non-dilemma cases of non-culpable evil-doing, such as that of my imaginary motorist. But the Phillips–Trakakis argument does not show that in the low-risk-of-evil theodicy scenario God has done something wrong in the sense of something he should not have done. They show only that he has done something which, like my motorist's accident, incurs various further responsibilities, such as apology and compensation. But it does not follow that he acted wrongly in creating the world, that he should not have done it. In the low-risk scenario it seems very implausible to say that, even in retrospect. Just as no one, not even my motorist's victims, can blame the motorist for driving under the envisaged conditions, no one can blame God for creating under the envisaged conditions – even though the bad moral luck both suffer puts them under specific responsibilities to victims of their actions. Thus theodicists can allow what Phillips and Trakakis say: that God is not perfect in the sense of being untouched by evil. That is something of a concession. But they can still maintain a good deal, perhaps most, of what they have traditionally claimed, namely that God is perfectly good in the sense that he does not *do* anything he should *not* do. He is not guilty of any *culpable* evil-doing. As a bonus it seems they can recover the concept of compensation from my Section 2 argument. Under the low-risk, free will theodicy (as opposed to greater good theodicy) God's owing compensation does not entail that God acted wrongly (that is, in a way he should not have) nor does it reduce to the standard greater good position vulnerable to Karamazov's challenge. This is because he is giving the compensation for what other, created agents have done, not what he has done.

To rebut the low-risk, free will theodicy we need to dig deeper. The argument I am now going to give against it is an argument which tells against theodicy in general, not just the version this section is devoted to. The gist is that creation is the prerogative only of a God who is not answerable to his creatures. To be answerable to human beings and their values, as theodicy assumes God to be, is to have a creaturely status, and for a creature to aspire to the divine act of creation is a blasphemy, and thus something no creature can morally do. So just in the act of creating the world the God of the theodicists presumes a status it is not entitled to. So theodicy, including the low-risk, free will theodicy, fails. Now I must spell this out.

The analogy between the low-risk, free will theodicy and the motorist case is misleading. Driving, flying, having surgery, taking medical drugs, being immunised: these are all activities with various degrees of usually low risk that we routinely undertake. They are acceptable to us not only because the risk is low, but also because they fall within a certain conception of human life, of what is appropriate to human circumstances and what is not. At the core of this conception is an ideal of humility, and thus conversely of pride or hubris. In theological terms, it is a conception of impiety, and thus of what it is to be *creature* rather than *Creator*. The ideal implies certain (admittedly vague) limits that a human being should not cross. This picture of human life has a distinctive Christian form, but it is far from confined to Christianity. The ancient Greeks famously made it the pervasive theme of some of their greatest works of drama and philosophy, such as the story of Oedipus and Plato's dialogue *Euthyphro*. In the modern era, though the picture is under serious attack, non-Christian and Enlightenment writers from Mary Shelley in *Frankenstein* and Robert Louis Stevenson in *Strange Case of Dr Jekyll and Mr Hyde* to H. G. Wells in *The Invisible Man* have told cautionary tales that depend on it. Oedipus, Dr Frankenstein, Dr Jekyll, Wells's invisible man: in each case we have men who overestimate their importance and abilities (in Oedipus's case at least, who throw their weight about with a knowing swagger) and bring disaster upon themselves, realising too late their hubris. As the proverb says, 'Pride goeth before a fall.' The modern examples are particularly relevant to the present argument, since they involve attempts by science to interfere with some of the most basic conditions of human life: our vulnerability to moral evil (Stevenson), our public visibility to others and the equality of power this helps enforce (Wells) and the origin of life itself (Shelley). These are all attempts, as we say, to 'play God', to press at the limits of our creatureliness and arrogate to ourselves the prerogatives of the Creator. The attempts bring disaster in their train, but it would be a mistake to think that disaster is the reason for accounting the attempts as pride and impiety (it is of course a reason to consider in deciding whether to make the attempt or not). That would reduce the moral of the stories to mere enlightened prudence. Perhaps the disasters can be avoided. Who knows what human technology can achieve? If we forecast that science cannot, without disaster, achieve the goals of Shelley, Stevenson or Wells, or create designer children, or 'trans-humans', then we may be in no better a position than those who said we would never fly in planes or walk on the Moon or transplant hearts. But what I think we can know is that if human ingenuity ever succeeded in making us invulnerable to physical and moral evil, if it freed us from all physical and mental limitations, or indeed succeeded in passing some admittedly vague point along the road to this – and is that not the ultimate goal of untrammelled technological ambition, taken to its logical conclusion? – then we would suffer another sort of disaster. We would enter an inhuman (trans-human?) world in which the concepts of pride and humility, of hubris and impiety, of morality and (I would argue) of compassion and love no longer existed.[17] This is a very different sort of disaster from the straightforwardly this-worldly sort. It will go quite unrecognised by denizens of the brave new world. It is recognisable only from within our present perspective, but it is no less real for that. Impiety then involves a dilemma. Either we fail in seeking the utopia of release from our creaturely subjection to evil and suffer a straight-forwardly worldly disaster, or we succeed, in which case we suffer a different sort of disaster, a spiritual one. The aspiration for this utopia, for release from our condition as creatures, is the gist of impiety and hubris. Due to the fact of this dilemma we can conclude – in contrast to the motorist case – that despite the element of bad moral luck involved in the (let's suppose) remote chance of the aspiration going pear shaped being realised, we nevertheless are guilty of a *culpable* wrong in pursuing that ambition. It is culpable because it is impious.

In aspiring to effect that release, human creatures blasphemously arrogate to themselves the exclusive prerogative of the Creator. But that means that if God himself is styled as a moral agent, as capable of acting from motives of love and compassion and so on, as capable of actions that can be assessed in principle as right or wrong (even if they are always right) and as exhibiting virtues such as humility as opposed to pride, then God himself is being styled as a creature living under sub-jection to evil – provided I am right in my assumption that these sorts of qualities are not possible without the mortal limitation of vulnerabil-ity to evil. But if God is a creature – *a* god rather than *the* God – then it too is arrogating to itself the exclusive prerogative of the Creator; it too is guilty of impiety and hubris in seeking to transcend its condition as a creature. But of course an anthropomorphic moral agent of just that sort, answerable to the same standards human beings are answerable to, is exactly what theodicy supposes God to be, including the low-risk, free will theodicy, which, if it can survive all other criticisms – I think it is certainly theodicy's best bet – still succumbs here.

Fortunately theodicy is mistaken in construing God as a moral agent. Moral notions, including those of pride and humility, have no appli-cation to God outside the human context of the incarnation, for he does not satisfy the conditions of limitation – mortality, vulnerability to physical and moral evil – which are necessary for the application of these concepts. But if God is not an agent performing loving acts, what is he? The answer – in line with perfectly orthodox Christian teach-ing – is that God *is* love. He is love itself. I expand on this answer in later chapters.

It is, in the end, my central objection to theodicy that it makes God subject to human moral judgement, and thus undermines his authority and abolishes the very distinction between creatures and their Creator. This is a point to which I shall return many times throughout the book. This is the view which the believer must take if they are to maintain faith consistently and decently in the face of the reality of evil. If God's moral agency is granted, the problem of evil is insoluble.

## 5. The impersonal and the existential problems of evil

Let us return now to greater good theodicy. Discussion of the problem of evil in mainstream analytical philosophy is for the greater part a debate over (usually metaphysical) facts and logic. Moral assumptions are made, but in most cases tacitly or so briefly the reader may scarcely notice them, and the debate quickly moves on to the apparently more tractable factual and logical issues. Thus Plantinga proposes (what he takes to be) logically possible factual scenarios about free will and non-human intelligent creatures, and he and his opponents debate the logic and metaphysics of counter-factuals about creaturely behaviour and divine foreknowledge of that behaviour. Thus Hick (1978), Swinburne (1998) and their ilk defend factual claims about the effects, or likely or possible effects, of evils on human character development, and the necessity of these evils for that development. Critics, such as Rowe (1979), appeal to the possibility of unredeemed evils (the fawn in the forest fire) and debate the strength of the inference from our not knowing of any actual good that redeems this to the conclusion that, probably, there is no such good. And so it goes. All this of course makes no sense unless certain moral assumptions are in place, crucially that the putative good states, if they exist, really do justify God in creating a world with the evil ones. But the assumption that they do justify that is rarely challenged and even more rarely defended. It is simply taken for granted. The radical-ness of Karamazov's challenge is that it focuses attention on this assumption – and issues such an unequivocal repudiation of it.

Indeed it would be a not very great exaggeration to say that much of this literature nearly reduces the moral assumptions to factual ones, by making them into quasi-quantitative judgements. Greater good theodicies share the assumption that God is to earn his acquittal before the tribunal of morality by creating a world in which the good (including compensation) 'counts for more' than the evil. I choose that expression as an attempt to be neutral between different accounts of how the good and the evil are to be compared. On the simplest version, it is a matter of cost/benefit analysis, of counting up the good and the bad, as if placing them on a pair of scales, and seeing which outweighs the other. Understandably, some theodicists have sought to distance themselves from this model. Perhaps the best known is Marilyn McCord Adams (1999, 2001), who develops a quasi-aesthetic account in which the good and evil combine in an 'organic whole' of such overall goodness that the evil is 'defeated'.

Most atheologians challenge only the factual assumptions of theodicy, or assumptions of logic and probability. If those factual assumptions are granted, and the underlying moral assumption left unquestioned, theodicy may well win the day. This neglect of Karamazov's challenge by the atheistic side seems particularly strange, given that on the face of things it favours them. Perhaps that goes to show how strong is the attraction of ruling philosophical ideas. In any event, if the approach embodied in greater good thinking (or in Adams's organicism) is rejected, both sides of the argument will have to think again: the whole nature of the problem, and of what serious thought about it consists in, needs to be radically reconsidered.

But how else *can* the argument go on? Dostoevsky's Ivan has shown the way with a challenge that might be appropriated by atheists. On the other side, how can the believer proceed if not armed with all the apparatus of greater goods and so on? My answer depends on the distinction I drew in Section 3 between two conceptions of thought, the *impersonal* on the one hand and the *existential* on the other. To recapitulate and expand, impersonal thought values discursive clarity and exactitude, logical reasoning, instrumental rationality, respect for facts, evidence and probability, and similar skills generally summed under the rubric of a properly informed, rational being, skills in which analytic philosophers receive specific professional training. It proceeds argumentatively and aspires (at the ideal limit) to a neutral vantage point. It admires the ideal of objectivity embodied in modern science, distrusts the local, individual and anecdotal, and is hostile to discussions it sees as moralising or 'emotional'. That is, it draws on just the sorts of resources I have been saying the mainstream literature on the problem of evil largely confines itself to.

I deny that serious thought about God and evil must or should be restricted to the impersonal in this sense. It is not true that the alternative means there is no serious, truth-regarding, 'cognitive' thought, no legitimate claims to truth or knowledge, that there will be only arbitrary and irrational preference, ill-disciplined emoting, propaganda and so on. The alternative existential conception does not aspire to neutrality, allows non-argumentative forms of justification – such as appeals to conscience or humanity, or to the influence of literature, art and personal example and experience – and thus admits the relevance of what is contingent and individual. It gives important scope to forms of individual judgement that are not reducible to technique. Chapter 4 will try to make this clearer. Here I offer *The Brothers Karamazov* as an example. Far from Ivan's horrifying examples – and, more importantly, his own responses of sorrow and anger to them – being a distraction from serious, 'intellectual' thought, they are, on the existential view, included in *the very stuff of it*. And if we ask how the examples and responses are to be appraised, we need to realise that the capacities integral to such appraisal are not merely those of factual information, rationality, logic and their kin (though of course they are essential) but include those that might be associated with the work of a (now old-fashioned) sort of moral-cum-humanistic literary critic: such things as courage, seriousness, honest self-examination and the power of moral imagination to envisage suffering, childhood, parenthood, love and what they mean. With these wider capacities comes a wider set of critical terms for appraising claims: not just truth and falsity of a straightforward factual sort, not just sound/unsound, valid/invalid, rational/irrational and so on, but sober *versus* sentimental or cynical, refreshing *versus* world-weary, passionate *versus* jaded, lucid *versus* self-deceived, serious *versus* flippant, and many more, all the concepts by which we appraise people, their lives and their moral stances when we are not philosophising in the professional sense. Thus, in Ivan's case, we might ask whether his attitude does not smack, to some degree, of histrionic self-dramatisation, of someone exaggerating evil in order to be in love with his own tears. If we think so, then we might have to examine whether our own response is tinged by cynicism or a comfortable innocence of profound suffering. And so on.

This does not mean our thinking remains confined to private and occasional observations (and an unrelieved, humourless self-dwelling and agonising is itself a vice). It is through comparison of cases, real and sensitively imagined, that we can reveal those responses which are most lucid and truthful, which are most free from the distortions of our ego. To think in this way requires a willingness for self-scrutiny, and for scrutiny of oneself by others, that is unfamiliar in standard academic practice. And that capacity is not likely to be nourished without attention to the treatment of these things in literature and art, and more importantly in life, with special attention to the testimony of those who have endured suffering. But these are precisely the existential modes of thought that are so rarely found in the analytic literature on the problem of evil, and indeed in many instances (I will give examples in the next two chapters) are actively excluded.

On the impersonal view genuine thought is anonymous, admitting in its substance (i.e. its arguments and conclusions, as distinct from its literary style) no essentially individual inflection. Just because of this impersonality, thought becomes a matter of expertise. Topics can be turned over to the experts, people professionally trained in the impersonal techniques of thought, who can reach our conclusions for us. This is not just an in-principle matter. The institutionalisation of thought in academic bodies, the credentialisation and academicising of more and more areas of life, the elevation of experts over laypeople in just about everything from cooking to sex, and the increasing claim of academic experts to influence public policy and professional practice (the explosive growth of applied and professional ethics): ours is the age of the expert. The coolly distant and objectifying tone of most philosophical discussion of the problem of evil, the scepticism and sometimes open disdain many philosophers have for any seriously personal idiom, manifests the same assumption.

In contrast the personal conception recognises that the problem of evil involves moral and existential questions which we cannot hand over to experts to resolve for us, any more than we can questions about whom we will marry or how we will treat our friends. An upshot of this, and one of the deepest differences between the two conceptions, is that the personal conception is consistent with the rejection of the assumption, sacrosanct to the first, and all but universal in the literature, that ideal thinkers think essentially alike, so that there is a single correct view about the problem of evil, the same for all of them, on which they will eventually converge if given enough time.[18] I personally reject that assumption for the problem of evil, and it is the alternative, existential conception of thought which opens the door to that rejection. On the view I shall defend, some people, without moral or intellectual fault, are required to believe in God despite evil, and others, equally without fault, are required to disbelieve on account of evil: and both parties can be right. God can be consistent with evil for me because of a moral-cum-existential stand that is true for me: despite evil, I *must* see the world as the creation of God's love. And he can be *in*consistent with evil for you because of a moral stand that is true for you: given evil, you *cannot* morally bring yourself to see the world that way. In short, I reject the universalisability of all moral and existential judgements. On this view, the problem of evil is a moral dilemma in that equally powerful cases can be made for God and against him, and people can be not merely justified in going either way, but morally *required* to. But that, of course, requires denying universalisability and recognising the legitimacy of *individual* moral requirements: what some philosophers have called 'moral necessity'. To many, I dare say most, philosophers the rejection of universalisability is beyond the pale. This is how deep the difference in the two conceptions of thought can go. I discuss universalisability in Chapter 4.

Another unfamiliar and controversial feature of the account I develop in this book is that in an important sense unbelievers need not deny the reality of God. What is essential to unbelief – certainly to unbelief on account of evil – is the rejection of an *allegiance* to God, of an obeisance towards him, a rejection in the name of an alternative loyalty to the victims of evil, to those whom Irving Greenberg has called the burning children. But that stand does not necessarily mean that unbelievers cannot consciously acknowledge the reality of God. A believer and an unbeliever can each acknowledge the reality of God and the reality of the burning children: the crux of their difference (in the face of evil) is over their loyalties. This is so even on my favoured understanding of God as love itself. But in any event it is certainly not a crucial difference between them that one affirms and the other denies (if they do; they need not) the existence of an entity (usually a kind of hyper-intelligent, immaterial Cartesian mind) satisfying a causal, cosmological hypothesis about the origin of the world. That is a mistaken understanding of God, one that reduces the Creator of Heaven and Earth to a creature, albeit a special one. In Chapters 4, 5 and 6 I develop the reconfigured, existential account of the problem of evil. In Chapter 6, as an essential part of that reconfiguration, I argue that God's reality is not of a kind understood in the impersonal, objectifying mode of thought, as in the cosmological hypothesis. Rather his reality is of a sort I call 'existential' – and he is no less real for that. There is no single, univocal concept of reality. The assumption that there is amounts *de facto* to setting up an invidious impersonal, physical-object model of reality as the criterion for reality *simpliciter,* a situation familiar from debates over moral reality. I argue that my position does not have the disastrous relativistic consequences many philosophers fear.

The vast bulk of the literature on the problem of evil (not all, of course) takes the impersonal conception for granted. By clinging to the narrow range of impersonal critical concepts philosophers' thought about the problem of evil has impoverished our sense of the possibilities, of the variety of defensible responses to the reality of evil which human life actually contains. It renders the voice of someone like Ivan

Karamazov unable to be heard, for to hear it you need to recognise that thought is answerable to more than logic, fact and so on. And you are precisely not recognising that if you begin from the assumption – almost universal in discussion of the problem of evil – that there is an *intellectual* problem of evil, the proper concern of the philosopher, sharply distinct from, and quite treatable without regard to, the *existential* or *personal* problem, the concern of ministers, therapists, friends, novelists and so on. That assumption makes it hard to hear Ivan in the sense of taking him seriously. And, of course, the same goes for the voices of the victims of suffering itself, which too often receive short shrift in the problem of evil literature (see the next chapter). But abandon the assumption and these voices become relevant. One of the central claims of the book is that the distinction between an intellectual problem of evil and a personal one is spurious, at least in the form in which it is typically drawn. The intellectual problem is inescapably personal (i.e. existential) and *vice versa*. The truth is that by ignoring Karamazov's challenge, by repudiating the existential generally, the debate over God and evil is being truncated at the point where it is really only beginning. As a person I admit to being in Ivan's camp when it comes to rejecting theodicy. As a philosopher the point I want to press is that the debate over the problem of evil, whether on the atheological or the theodical side, is fatally flawed by its rejection of the existential.

The impersonal mode of thought *dissociates* philosophy from life, which, really, is to dissociate it from its subject matter. If we reassociate them, the problem of evil becomes in a way much less tractable, more elusive. In that way, it is a lot harder. Once it is realised that *my* thought about the subject must be sensitive to things that are distinctive of me, and your thought must be sensitive to things that are distinctive of you – to the point perhaps of being 'claimed' by radically different 'moral necessities': I cannot see the world, and a God if it has one, as other than terrible; you cannot see them as other than good – then we will realise that if we confine our thinking to the rational faculty which supposedly unites us across our differences of individual character and sensibility, our thinking will not touch on those differences, which is to say it will pass over our most serious disagreements and difficulties, the real source of the problem. It oversimplifies the real depth of our conflict, its true sources and the way (if at all) that one or both of us can change or reach agreement – and whether indeed agreement is an important goal – and whether if we persist in disagreeing we *must* regard the other as making a mistake or being in the wrong.

## 6. Morality, love and God

Even readers sympathetic to the case against theodicy might neverthe-less feel that something important is missing. If good does not out-weigh evil in the world, then why do we go on? M. B. Ahern (1971, p. 51) has argued that if Ivan Karamazov is right to condemn God for creating a world (this one) in which babies are tortured, then it is an obligation on all of us to cease having children; otherwise we perpetu-ate the evil. That, he implies, is a *reductio ad absurdum*. He is right. There is an absurdity in the idea that, in the name of morality, we would put an end to the human race, even a wholly voluntary end. He is also right to imply that it is similarly absurd to suggest, on the basis of an analogy between God and human parents, that God should not have created the world.

But if I endorse the idea that parents – normal loving parents, not caught in a dilemma, not seeking to prevent the violation of some value dear to them and their sense of life's importance, and not subject to the sway of some unruly passion – would in fact, and do in fact, have children despite the high probability of their being subject to evil, do I not go back on my emphatic claim from Section 2 that such parents would find the very idea of that unthinkable, however great the ulti-mate good for their children or anyone else? And isn't it a clear and conclusive refutation of that claim that such parents do bring children into the world with a nearly certain risk of serious evil: witness the fact that until recent times most human children died in infancy of cruel diseases (and surely at least some of their parents were of the sort I describe)? My answer to both questions is no. Why? Because I have not claimed, and I do not believe, that such parents find it unthinkable to bring children into a world where there is a considerable likelihood of such evils. What I have claimed is that such parents would find it unthinkable to *agree* to their children being subject to such evils (and perhaps especially to agree to it as part of a *deal*, however good-promoting by the standards of the ideal observer). At first blush this might look like a distinction without a difference. By bringing children into the world in the relevant circumstances, have not the parents in effect consented to the evils being inflicted? A moral case can be made that these parents have compromised their right to resist the evils, or certainly to complain about them. But the parents do not mean that practical consent in their hearts. In what morality may well see as an audacious attempt to have it both ways, they want to consent to having the children but *not* to consent to the evils that in many cases this will entail. Hence the fact that such parents do everything in their power (once the children are in the world) to prevent and minimise the evil and, when they cannot affect it, to protest about it to humanity and God and anyone else who might listen. 'If they did not want their children subject to such evils they should not have brought them into a world where they are so likely.' Thus speaks the voice of morality. And it need not be just the morality of the ideal observer; Ivan Karamazov's morality of compassionate indignation on behalf of the children, if applied to human parents, might say something similar. But is morality the last word on the matter? Many philosophers believe it has to be, but they are not obviously right. The loving parents I imagine are under a powerful human impulse of love to create and nurture new life, to bring it into the world even in the face of terrible threats. But that very same passion as loving parents means they cannot really consent to the evils inflicted on their children. They must protest. They must resist. They can do no other. From morality's point of view that may indeed compromise their right subsequently to complain about the evil. But from the parents' point of view the issue is not about, or not just about, morality. They do not see themselves as doing a deal to improve the world when they have children, and they do not accept that their actions are to be judged by the criteria that apply to deals. Their relationship to their children is not that of consenting agents reaching an agreement. They are acting from love. We may or may not morally approve of such parents' actions in these circumstances, but there is no good reason in many cases to doubt the genuineness of their love, as their grief may prove. Love of this sort will take even quite high risks of serious evil – for some evils, even a certainty – in a way morality will not.

On this line of thought such parents do not (or if they were lucid would not) believe their original act of bearing the children, or their subsequent complaints about evil, to be morally justified. But nor do they think it is morally *un*justified. They believe (or so it can be said in their defence) that something more than morality is at stake here. There is also the love that impels them to create new life, and that is a rival value to morality, with the power to check its authority. In the light of that love, morality, by presuming to judge them, reaches beyond its jurisdiction. This is a consequence, or an aspect, of the fact that the parents do not bear children for the sake of any good beyond the children's existence, not any collective good or the children's eternal beatitude, if they believe in such a thing. They are borne along by the passion of love, a sort of personal necessity akin to what philosophers have called 'moral necessity'. The same may be true for God's creation of the world.

The upshot is that theodicy will not find any rescue in Ahern's point about the absurdity of parents ceasing to have children, or of God not creating the world. Far from it. It remains the case (i) that human parents – and so God if he is loving in the way human parents are, as Christianity says – find unthinkable the idea that they should consent to their children being subject to serious evil for the sake of a greater good, as theodicy requires of them,[19] and (ii) that they and God nevertheless are driven to create. The source of both these necessities is love, perhaps a paradoxical love. Atheologists attack God in the name of morality. Theodicists choose to fight on the atheologists' own battlefield: the tribunal of morality. I have argued that they lose. But the upshot of the atheologists' win – that, basically, the world should not be here – is absurd. There is something too purist, something inhuman, about the whole idea. Evil or not, we are glad God made the world (or that it is here) and we want it to go on! But it is precisely *morality* that is the source of this purism and that produces the absurdity. Morality – and thus theodicy – cannot do justice to the absurdity, as proven by the fact that the atheologists win. So rather than conclude that theodicy might be right after all, what we should do is question the assumption that the atheologists must be met on their own territory, the assumption that the problem of evil is a matter of determining God's guilt or innocence before the moral tribunal. Perhaps this is an over-moralisation of the issue. Morality is not the only voice which speaks for humans, including the innocent victims of evil. There is also love.

Once the impersonal conception of thought, to which the sort of moral discussion we find in the literature on the problem of evil belongs, is abandoned, an appeal to love, an appeal that belongs to the existential domain of thought, becomes possible. There is a tradition in western thought which has denied that morality has a monopoly on important and serious value, and that it always trumps any other such value. It does not always have the last word. In particular, to take the Christian version of the thought, it can be opposed, and have a limit set to its authority, by love. Love can establish a domain of value independent of morality, and resistant to its demands. In religious language we call this domain the *sacred*. We see it in the unconditional love parents have for their children, and that of saints for those depraved beyond what good-will can withstand or morality tolerate. Sometimes what an impersonal morality, or a morality of compassion, will condemn, love will sanction and even demand. For example, parents who conceive and bear a child they know will be handicapped may stand condemned by morality. But morality may thus show itself to be sometimes an insular thing. The parents know something greater: the insatiable love which drives them to create. Just like such human parents, God may create the world, a world he knows must contain terrible evil, in an act of reckless love. Again, like Ivan's contrary response in the name of compassion, this is deeply individual in the sense I have tried to elucidate. Some look at the world's horrors and find the very idea of a good and loving God absurd and intolerable. Others – and in the light of the world's evil we may either wonder at this as a miracle or find it utterly repellent – accept the world as the gift of a creative love, to be responded to with love. But in neither case is there an impersonal system of reasoning that compels the answer. There is nothing mandatory – by the light of the impersonal conception of thought, as opposed to an individual moral necessity – about preferring love over morality in such cases, or *vice versa*. Morality has a claim on us as well as love, and many people will find God's action (and that of the human parents I have imagined) inexcusable, and they will find they cannot set aside that verdict in the name of love. Nothing in the argument of this book shows they are wrong.

While this line of thought is powerful, it does not succeed so long as the analogy between God and human parents – and human beings in general – is taken too anthropomorphically. So long as God is conceived as a very big version of an immaterial agent so that his acts are distinct from his nature – an agent performing loving acts as you and I might, only perfectly so – then we face the convincing objection that though love may indeed sometimes over-rule the claims of universal morality, it cannot do so without any limit: morality at some point draws a line in the sand, reasserts its authority over individual values. That is, there is surely a moral limit on the evil parents may, in the name of love, effectively inflict on their children just by conceiving or creating them. Under the analogy, God seems to have trespassed over that limit.

The parental analogy line of thought can get around this objection once we recognise that God is not a person or agent in the anthropomorphic sense of a being who performs loving acts. Rather God *is* love itself – as he is goodness itself and truth itself – and his 'acts' under the analogy are the manifestations, the instantiations, of love in the world. The most fundamental of these is the good of the world's very existence: that manifestation of love itself is what we call *creation*. It is not a causal process: that belongs to the impersonal kind of reality, and God's reality is existential. This is not to abandon the analogy between God and human parents. The love which God *is* can be seen imperfectly (in the form of agency) in the unconditional love of parents for their children; indeed, that is one of the principal manifestations of love itself. (If it has ever been perfectly manifested in human agency, as Christians believe, that has happened only once.) But once we see that the analogy does not extend to regarding God as a special case of an agent like you or me, then while the instantiation of good in the world can be seen as a manifestation of him – in that sense, attributed to him, telling us (non-inferentially) about his nature – *evil cannot be*. God is not responsible for evil causally because he is not a causal moral agent of any sort. And *trivially* evil is not a manifestation of him because he is love, goodness itself. So no adverse conclusions about God can be drawn from the existence of evil.

This position is not invented by believers *ad hoc* to get out of the problem of evil: it has always been central to the Judeo-Christian conception of God, quite apart from the problem of evil, that God is to be loved and praised *unconditionally* – that is, *worshipped* – rather than praised proportionally to his merits like a moral agent. This picture of God is one I shall develop in the last two chapters and I shall argue it is not irrationalist, idealist or perniciously relativist. But it is true that believers do not reach the position via an impersonal metaphysical argument about the nature of God. It is an existential matter of being able to see love itself clearly, unclouded by the reality of evil (by the pain that causes in our lives), and that is a matter of being able, existentially, to give one's loyalty to God. Perhaps it is even to see that ultimately this does not conflict with a loyalty to the burning children. There is an argument lurking here to the effect that unbelievers must ultimately be mistaken in construing their loyalty to the burning children as in conflict with a loyalty to God, that in the end evil has so sullied their perception of the world that, in their need to lash out, to find someone to blame, they cannot see love and goodness clearly, and fall into the mistake of bringing them, God, under moral judgement, as if they were causal forces responsible for evil. The argument would turn on the thought that, far from being in conflict with compassion for the burning children, we can see the burning children properly only in the light of love itself, so must acknowledge it as a first loyalty if we are to be loyal to the children at all. But I am not confident of this. At any rate, in this book, I allow the rational and moral possibility of people, however rare in practice, who lucidly see love itself, but in the name of the burning children do not acknowledge it as their highest loyalty. Perhaps Ivan Karamazov, despite saying he does not reject God, does approach such a case.

I begin investigating the parental analogy in Chapter 3, arguing, against mainstream authors such as Richard Swinburne, that, in contrast to human parents, God is not even *prima facie* answerable for the blemishes and inconveniences (like slight toothaches and twisted ankles) suffered by his children that he could correct. That is, he has no need to justify them *at all*, by reference to greater goods or anything else. It is serious evils (such as disease, death, war and disaster) that raise the real – the existential – problem of evil, rather than the artificial intellectual problem of academic philosophy. The development of the analogy continues in Chapter 4, where I explain the appeal to parental love as a counter to the demands of morality, and put the appeal in the wider context of the refigured, existential problem of evil. Then in Chapter 5 I develop the understanding, just described, of faith as the capacity to remain loyal to God despite evil – that is, to see goodness itself clearly, without confusing it with causal power. Finally, in Chapter 6 I defend an existential understanding of God's reality, drawing heavily on the Platonic conception of the good.

For believers who can understand the world as the creation (instantiation) of love, God is not an agent who has earned an acquittal before the tribunal of morality. Nor has a guilty verdict simply been ignored. Rather the authority of that tribunal to be the only or the last word over the case has been denied on the authority of love: the very love that God is and that moves believers to respond to that love and to accept the world and its Creator not according to merits but unconditionally. This need not mean that believers – even ones unable to feel any doubt of God's love – do not feel powerfully the reality of evil, and the case that makes for the prosecution. They could, if of generous sympathies, well understand why some others cannot believe, even while finding they themselves must believe; indeed – as I argue in denying universalisability – they need not judge the others to be at fault, though they may well seek to change their perspective. But morality – both the greater good soil and the morality of compassion – is transcended in the sense that the tribunal has lost the power to dictate the rejection of God, because *for them* its authority is met and overcome by love. As I shall argue in Chapter 4 this position does not mean that God's love or the existence of human beings is being treated as a greater good that justifies creation. The believers need not take their stand on any such moral judgement. It can rest *entirely on God's love* (i.e. the love that God is). Much less, as I contend in Chapter 3, is that love (or normal human love) itself simply a calculating beneficence, though theodicists often confuse the two. In contrast to the ambition of greater good morality to constitute a neutral vantage point from which the confrontation between belief and unbelief can be 'rationally' resolved, on my account they confront one another as rival, incommensurable gestalts on the world as a whole. The matter is not resolvable by consideration of this or that particular circumstance, good or evil, for each party will see the significance of that circumstance for the reality of God through the lens of their own gestalt (Chapter 5). But this does not mean that they cannot understand one another or that intelligent discussion cannot go on between them, only that it will not take the impersonal form aspired to in so much philosophy.

I have pointed out that love can conflict not only with an impersonal morality of the cost/benefit, greater good sort, but also with Ivan Karamazov's instinctive morality of compassion. Perhaps this may partly explain one of the more puzzling things he says. He makes it clear that his repugnance at the world is not the result of totting up the evils and the goods and seeing which prevails. He is even explicit in believing that the good, in one sense, prevails:

> ...I accept God and am glad to, and what's more I accept His wisdom, His purpose – which are utterly beyond our ken; I believe in the underlying order and the meaning of life; I believe in the eternal harmony in which they say we shall one day be blended. I believe in the Word to Which the universe is striving, and Which Itself was 'with God', and Which Itself is God and so on, and so on, to infinity. ... Yet would you believe it, in the final result, I don't accept this world of God's, and, although I know it exists, I don't accept it at all. It's not that I don't accept God, you must understand, it's the world created by Him I don't and cannot accept. Let me make it plain. I believe like a child that suffering will be healed and made up for, that all the humiliating absurdity of human contradictions will vanish like a pitiful mirage, ... that in the world's finale, at the moment of eternal harmony, something so precious will come to pass that it will suffice for all hearts, for the comforting of all resentments, for the atonement of all the crimes of humanity, of all the blood they've shed; that it will make it not only possible to forgive but to justify all that has happened with men – but though all that may come to pass, I don't accept it. I won't accept it. (Dostoevsky 1912, pp. 240–1)

'It's not that I don't accept God, you must understand, it's the world created by Him I don't and cannot accept.' In those words Ivan sums up the problem of evil for believers. Believers want God, but cannot accept the world we know, the world of the suffering children. The perpetual temptation of theodicy is to try to ease the severity of this conflict by making the world a better place than it seems to be, trying to make it more palatable to us in order to make God acceptable. Ivan's words are a howl of protest against this attempt to justify the unjustifiable. He makes it clear that no matter how good the world is, so long as it contains even one suffering child, that goodness is poisoned beyond redemption by any 'greater good'. The atonement and eternal harmony he acknowledges – and even more so, one can imagine, the cool calculations of the theodicists – are too other-worldly and inhuman, too inured to the suffering of the children, for him to accept them. If we are to hold to God in face of that evil we must do so without succumbing to the fantasy which seeks to dilute or even exorcise the evil in happy endings. We owe its victims no less than that. Only love can accomplish this. Believers will point to the Cross as the supreme example, where, they believe, the whole world has been redeemed by a love that palliated nothing and bore everything.

# 2
# The Intellectual and the Existential

## 1. Theodicy and the burning children

William Hasker's book on the problem of evil begins with this quotation from *The Brothers Karamazov*:

> Imagine that you are creating a fabric of human destiny with the object of making men happy in the end, giving them peace and rest at last, but that it was essential and inevitable to torture to death only one tiny creature – that little child beating its breast with its fist, for instance – and to found that edifice on its unavenged tears, would you consent to be the architect under those conditions? (Quoted in Hasker 2008, p. 15)

By quoting this passage, Hasker implies that discussions of the problem of evil should be answerable to examples of this sort. Unfortunately his own discussion misconceives what such answerability consists in, and so falls short of doing the example – and thus, ultimately, the problem of evil – justice.

The misconception is evident from the beginning in the very different *tone* of Hasker's discussion, a tone for the most part remote and academic in comparison with Dostoevsky's. Hasker's tone is markedly aloof from the personal urgency that evil has for people's lives. The defining feature of this dissociation of thought from life is the assumption that the 'problem of evil' is essentially a *theoretical* and *technical* problem in a sense akin to problems in science or mathematics. I do not mean by this that he thinks of the problem as predominantly empirical, or as substantially tractable to formal methods or definitive proof. I mean that he treats it as essentially a conceptual conundrum about how to reconcile (logically or probabilistically) the existence of an omnipotent, omniscient, perfectly good Creator with the existence of evil, a problem largely tractable to the intellectual resources of relevant factual information, instrumental rationality, logic and greater good morality. This is the sort of problem of which it is appropriate to ask, as Hasker does in the title of his first chapter, 'What Is the State of Play?', an inquiry made in the same spirit as one would ask for a progress report on a scientific or technical investigation. His treatment also makes the problem a matter of expertise. It is the sort of problem which it makes sense for the layperson to hand over to experts – in this case, people trained in the discipline of rational thinking – who will solve the problem for them. For if what matters in finding the solution is the cultivation of factually informed, rational and logical thought, supplemented with a greater good morality, thought of the sort where we can expect *in advance* of investigation that ideal thinkers will converge on a universally valid resolution,[1] then it is of no importance *who* does the thinking so long as their mind is trained in the appropriate way. Thought here is anonymous. The fact that *I* am thinking about God and evil, as opposed to *you* or *him* or *her*, should make no difference to *what* I think (so long as we are all thinking ideally, without errors of fact, logic, rationality etc.). If we think ideally, we all think alike, and *necessarily* there cannot (under ideal conditions) be one answer permissible or mandatory for me that is not permissible or mandatory for you.[2] This is in contrast with the existential understanding of the problem, mentioned in the previous chapter (and to be described in detail in the next), where the existence of a *universally* valid resolution is not guaranteed in advance. The existential approach leaves it open that a resolution might be binding on me, or possible for me, that is not binding on, or possible for, you.

The irony of approaching in this impersonal manner a topic of aching importance to nearly any non-philosophical interest in it is a subterranean discomfort running below the texts of most academic discussion on the problem of evil. The discomfort surfaces in the felt need, very common in the literature, to distance the *intellectual* problem – whether 'the evil in the world provides rationally compelling reasons to disbelieve in the God of theism' – from the *existential* problem, the problem of the significance that evil has for the faith of believers 'on a personal and emotional level'. Hasker fully endorses the position that these are 'very different concerns' and that 'conflating the two is a source of trouble' (Hasker 2008, p. 21). This severance then bears fruit in Hasker distancing himself, as someone addressing the intellectual problem, from the sort of eminently personal demand to be answerable to examples of the Dostoevskian sort. Thus he gives short shrift to Irving Greenberg's remark that 'No statement, theological or otherwise, should be made that would not be credible in the presence of the burning children' (quoted in Hasker 2008, p. 22), pointing to the platitude that '*any* theoretical discussion' (his emphasis) would be callously out of place if conducted *literally* (his own word again) in front of burning children. But this literal reading misses what (regardless of his intentions) is surely the force of Greenberg's words: that no theodicy is worth the paper it is written on *unless it makes sense in the light of the sort of experiences the burning children have undergone.* And 'makes sense' here means that it is something we are still able to judge to be true even when we have fully appreciated the worst cases of evil. That we imagine ourselves having to say it to the victims of evil – or indeed that we actually say it to them (not, of course, while they are literally burning to death: that is a furphy) – is one form of attending soberly to the nature of evil. Thus, reflection on cases such as the experience of the burning children is essential to thinking about God and evil, in which case listening to the victims' own accounts, including their own reactions to what philosophers say, surely must carry substantial weight in that thinking. To require this is to require no more than that we be answerable to the very phenomena our theories purport to explain. The issue is whether there is (in this context) a credible notion of truth, and of judging truth, that is not answerable to the seriousness of the evil it is supposed to account for, and then whether there is any reckoning with that seriousness which does not take account of the bearing it has on the lives of those who have suffered such evils. To what notion of truth do we think we are answerable if we deny we are answerable to examples like the burning children? Hasker accuses people who have used Greenberg's words of intimidation and of trying to shut down debate. But ironically it is Hasker's accusation which threatens to shut down debate, over the answerability to examples like Greenberg's. Not to admit such accountability is effectively to say one does not have to meet Karamazov's challenge. But not to discuss that challenge is to dodge the problem of evil.

Answerability to victims of evil (especially real ones, but also those of soberly imagined fiction) is part of what gives substance to the idea of thought being existential, personal and individual, as opposed to impersonal, technical and theoretical. The burning children interrogate *us*, every bit as much as we interrogate them. The confrontation with *them*, real or sensitively imagined, is crucial to the seriousness and genuineness of what we judge, believe and say – and its truth. It is in the attention to such suffering – and to the detail of human life more generally – that our theodical ideas, and our personal responses to evil, are appraised as decent or indecent, courageous or cowardly, compassionate or hardhearted, serious or frivolous, and so on. The conduct of such appraisal depends not just on the rational faculties that define standard academic practice (the skills necessary *and sufficient* for success in academic life) and which define a certain conception of a person or rational agent that pervades analytic philosophy at large, but on existential capacities of judgement that are not guaranteed to yield a single, unique, correct perspective, the same for every person. The problem of evil is not one that I can hand over to experts to take an answer on trust from, because it is crucially a matter of whether I can respond, or find myself required to respond, to the world with a grateful love despite the evil it contains, or whether that evil makes this a moral impossibility for me. And just like whether or not I can or must love another human being, this is a question I must (after all the advice I might receive) answer *for myself,* must *own* the answer for and must be *answerable* for the consequences of. So thinking on this topic goes deep into our personal lives in ways that simply being able to appropriate facts and arrange arguments, however dextrously, does not. Our thought needs not only those latter skills, but also to be informed by compassion, justice, courage, wisdom and other qualities. These are not, and plausibly should not be, necessary attributes of academic preferment. Nor are they likely to be found in academic practice – as distinct from the private lives of academics – if the attitude is adopted that they are irrelevant to such practice. That attitude is the intellectual/existential distinction.[3]

## 2. Argument and example

To Hasker's credit a sense of the need for the sort of accountability in question does appear at several places in his book. Thus on pages 23–4 he writes that various 'theistic perspective[s] on suffering' can comfort the afflicted and even says that 'success in addressing this problem' (the problem of comforting the afflicted) is 'an important part of the basis for evaluating theological views'. But if Hasker believes this is true, why is he so dismissive of Greenberg's remark about the burning children? The greater part of his book comports with that dismissal, which is in line with the separation of the intellectual and the existential he endorses in chapter 1 as a central plank of his methodology.

That separation sometimes betrays Hasker into a failure to hold theodicies accountable to the real moral world. Thus he defends Stephen

Davis against criticism by D. Z. Phillips over Davis's defence of the (standard) theodical view that all evils – and that means even the worst, such as the Holocaust – will be outweighed by sufficiently great goods, and in particular the good of the heavenly beatific vision. In the course of making this argument, Davis illustrates the principle of good overcoming evil with an autobiographical example of being forced to wear an embarrassing pair of short trousers to junior high school, something that was traumatic at the time but which now, as an adult, he can recall without pain.[4] Phillips had objected that this example could not sustain a general principle that would cover serious evils. Hasker retorts that Davis was not comparing his trousers' case to the Holocaust, but presenting an example 'in which we can readily see how pain and suffering can be overcome so that it is no longer troubling – something we admittedly cannot now see in the case of horrendous evils' (Hasker 2008, p. 45, n. 45).[5] But this misses Phillips's point, which is that the example is relevant only if it sustains the principle of good overcoming evil with a generality that will include cases such as the Holocaust. And it simply does not do that, as Hasker comes close to admitting in writing that we 'cannot now see' how the pain and suffering of horrendous evils will become un-troubling. And it does not do it because of the vast difference in the seriousness of the cases, which makes it completely impossible to treat them as two instances of the same phenomenon in any relevant sense. But if we cannot do that, if we cannot move from the one case to the other, the example is pointless.

When Hasker says that we cannot now see what future good would render the Holocaust no longer troubling he implies that the problem is one of a contingent limit to our imaginations. It might indeed be that if the issue were purely a *psychological* one, a question of the psychic pain being healed. The psychic pain of terrible evils can indeed be healed (and it is not at all clear that theodicy, or even religion, is necessary for that in every case). But the issue is not just psychological; it is also *moral*. Psychologically, the distress felt by school-children teased for wearing daggy clothes may indeed start out as (moderately) significant and move over time to insignificant. But *morally* it is insignificant right from the beginning, and the important change in the young person is the moral one by which they learn to recognise that insignificance. That is why we regard it as a character-building experience and why parents are justified in doing what Davis's parents did to him. But the Holocaust was not a character-building experience, even if in some cases it had that effect. Morally the Holocaust was significant from the beginning and remains every bit as significant even if everyone, including its victims, forgets about it. It cannot become insignificant and we are not morally at liberty to regard it as such. The problem of evil is hardly touched by supposing that one day it will all be un-troubling to us psychologically. That doesn't change the fact that very significant, indeed horrendous, evil once existed and the problem is how to reconcile *that* with a good and loving God. If Davis's argument is to address the real problem of evil it has to equivocate between these psychological and moral senses of suffering and evil ceasing to be significant and to mean the conclusion in precisely the moral sense that Phillips objects to.[6]

The problem with Davis's thinking here is that, in this context, treating the matter as merely psychological, he thinks the difference in moral seriousness is irrelevant, that it is no impediment to the good-overcomes-evil principle stretching to cover both cases. Davis makes this mistake, which *as a human being* he no doubt does not make, because *as a philosopher* he subscribes to the intellectual/existential divorce, which the philosopher/human divorce parallels. It is an implication of that divorce that examples don't matter much (so the simpler, more familiar and less 'emotional', the better) since beneath any changes in the seriousness of cases, the underlying intellectual problem remains the same. The seriousness is treated as *external* to the nature of the problem. Theodicy's determination to make the problem of evil an impersonal, rationally tractable, 'intellectual' one encourages philosophers to ignore the *content* of examples and to look only at their *formal* structure: in this case, good outweighing evil.

The same resistance to taking examples seriously is evident in the way Hasker again backs Davis in a dispute with John Roth. Like Phillips, Roth is highly critical of the whole idea of theodicy, stressing the unaccountable 'waste' of human pain and suffering in creation. Hasker endorses this quotation from Davis:

> Sadly, Roth and I are at an impasse here. I argue that in the light of the eschaton a perfectly good God morally can allow the waste that we see in human history. To counter this, Roth keeps pointing to how terrible and massive the waste is. And I keep looking for an argument why this admitted amount of waste – whatever amount it is – could not have been allowed by God. He thinks I am looking at the evidence blindly; I think he is not producing an argument. (Quoted in Hasker 2008, p. 37)[7]

It is true that Roth has an unfortunate tendency to frame part of his argument in cost/benefit terms. If the issue is thus viewed quantitatively,

Davis may have a point: *whatever* (his word) the quantity of evil, God can simply ramp up the good of the afterlife until it outweighs the evil. (But notice the consequence: there is nothing this strategy cannot justify God enabling or permitting.) But Roth's argument is not entirely in these quantitative terms. He also provides examples, one of which Hasker also quotes just three pages before the quotation from Davis. It concerns the Holocaust survivor Jankiel Wiernik, a carpenter by trade who apparently was forced to help construct the machinery of killing, and who confessed:

> My life is embittered. Phantoms of death haunt me, specters of children, little children, nothing but children. I sacrificed all those nearest and dearest to me. I myself took them to the execution site. I built their death chambers for them. (Quoted in Hasker 2008, p. 34)[8]

Hasker then quotes Roth's telling comment:

> The suggestion ... that the torment of burning children and their parents is 'not worth comparing to the glory about to be revealed to us' [a quotation from Davis quoting St Paul] may get high marks as religious hyperbole, but it scarcely seems like solidarity with the victims. (Quoted in Hasker 2008, p. 34; ellipsis added)[9]

Davis demands 'argument' from Roth. Hasker endorses this demand, repeating it two hundred pages later (p. 215). What Roth gives is an *example*, the one of Jankiel Wiernik just quoted, and on the basis of it makes the point that any satisfactory theodicy must have 'solidarity' with the victims, which in the context I take to mean that the theodicy should take serious account of the suffering of these victims and of their own perspective on that suffering. Hasker does not find any compelling argument in Roth, and reports that Davis thinks Roth has not advanced *any* argument *at all* (Hasker 2008, p. 215). By what standard of reasoning does Roth's appeal to Wiernik not count as an argument? Or if appealing to the force of examples is stipulated not to count as 'argument', then why should the only legitimate reasons be argumentative? Hasker acknowledges Roth's appeal to examples, but immediately belittles this as 'intuition' (p. 215), effectively treating Wiernik's powerful personal testimony as equivalent to the armchair speculations of philosophers. In analytic philosophy the word 'intuition' commonly denotes untutored 'folk' opinions that form part of the data for the important work of argumentative theory-construction, opinions which, on most accounts, are vulnerable to revision or over-throw if they do not fit a good theory – such as theodicy. That attitude is natural if one thinks that thought about this topic must be *intellectual* in a way that contrasts with the sort of deeply personal and existential testimony Wiernik is giving. Such testimony can fit the 'intellectual' mould only by being seriously distorted – or ignored, as in Davis's attitude to Wiernik. This is part and parcel of keeping the existential out of the intellectual. The assimilation of examples to the economic notion of waste (which Roth unfortunately is complicit in with his language) performs the same dissociative function: any given evil appears merely as a datum, an increment in a calculation, and the principal dimension by which the matter is judged is quantitative (so that we might as well be counting apples and pears as good and evil). The sort of seriousness in an evil that would provoke Ivan Karamazov's thought that it contaminates any good, however great, of which it is the inescapable cost is covertly ruled out from the beginning. But the force of examples, and especially the testimony of sober and serious witnesses to, and perpetrators and victims of, evil (and Wiernik was all these), can count as heavily as any argument; indeed, more heavily, since any theodical argument is only as good as its inescapable – albeit often hidden – moral premises. And there is no serious discussion of these premises that is not existential, that will not, say, demand that we listen to the voices of Wiernik and of the burning children. Why else did Hasker quote Dostoevsky? But why then embrace an approach which, by dissociating one's philosophising from life, guarantees that one will not pay the necessary attention to those who have actual experience of the relevant subject matter? In what other field would one do that? To appreciate the force of examples you have to be open to them, and you are not likely to be open if you come to them convinced of the idea that the problem you want to address is 'intellectual' and that the views raising existential issues are just 'intuitions', whose value and fate largely depend on one's favoured theory – in this case a greater good theodicy which has by and large already conceptualised evils as economic commodities which can be outweighed by greater goods. Again, to what is theodicy answerable if not the moral reality of Wiernik and the burning children? To say it is answerable to 'argument' is to invoke a phantom. Indeed, when philosophers demand 'argument', too often what they are really demanding is the treatment of a topic, and certainly of the problem of evil, confined to the inadequate resources of factual information, instrumental rationality, logical reasoning and their ilk.

## 3. Adams's organic theodicy

While they do have a special claim on our attention, I am not suggesting that the voices of Jankiel Wiernik and the other victims of evil, and of those who have seriously reflected on such evil, are beyond criticism, that they are a trump card which silences debate. For one thing, they do not speak in unison. The testimony of those who have suffered includes that of people whose faith in God has survived or been strengthened, or even created, by suffering, as much as that of those whose faith has been destroyed, or their unbelief confirmed. But these former voices too are absent from most analytic discussions of the problem of evil (a point I take up in the next section).

No doubt, as (I would say) Hasker alleges, examples can be used to bully people, as can the demand for 'argument'. To repeat: no one enjoys *a priori* exemption from criticism. The issue is what the *terms* of criticism are. The cost/benefit form of thinking, at least in any ordinary form such as we find in theodicy – entirely appropriate for building a bridge or devising a road safety or public health programme – is out of place in discussion of the problem of evil. The problem is not the familiar one of how to compare incommensurable goods and evils (unless 'incommensurable' includes a good not being commensurable with an evil because the evil contaminates the good). It is more radical than that. It is a matter of one's heart and mind being open to being moved by the qualities displayed in an example, by, say, the courage, patience and compassion a person brings to their suffering and their testimony. Or better perhaps, as Raimond Gaita (2000a) has stressed in a different context, being moved not by the person, but by how the world and human life appear in the light of that person's response to it: as a gift to be accepted with gratitude and humility, or a curse to be borne and ameliorated in mutual sorrow and kindness, and so on.

The greater good theory is not the only approach to the problem of evil which separates the existential from the intellectual and in effect puts the variety of human responses to the problem beyond our hearing. Another is the theory that the various goods and evils combine with one another to form a quasi-aesthetic organic whole or unity. The champion of the 'organic unity' theory is Marilyn McCord Adams. She is a philosopher who seems, on the face of it, to attend to the individual 'participants' in evil, both victims and perpetrators. She believes that to deal adequately with the problem of evil philosophers must address not only how God will create a good world (nature, life, human beings, free will, moral virtue) but also how he will 'defeat' evil and bring goodness into the lives of individual human beings, especially those whose lives have been broken by what she calls 'horrendous' evils. She writes:

> My notion is that reason to doubt [whether the lives of people who have participated in horrendous evils can be worth living] can be outweighed, if the evil *e* can be defeated. The evil *e* can be defeated if it can be included in some good-enough whole to which it bears a relation of organic (rather than merely additive) unity; *e* is defeated within the context of the individual's life if the individual's life is a good whole to which *e* bears the relevant organic unity. If the evil *e* is defeated within the context of an individual *x*'s life, the judgment 'the life of *x* cannot be worthwhile given that it includes *e*' would be defeated... (Adams 1999, pp. 28–9)

This passage contains many of her key ideas: the focus on actual horrendous evils, on individual lives rather than the cosmos, the concept of organic unity and the concept of *defeat* (acquired from Roderick Chisholm). Defeat is closely related to organic unity. But what is organic unity? It is not enough (to distinguish it from the additive, greater good, method) that 'a significantly smaller, negatively (or positively) valued part can contribute to a greater overall positive (or negative) value in the whole' (Adams 1999, p. 21), for there is a clear sense in which mainstream theodicists will say this about (for example) a world in which physical pain is outweighed by the goods of patience and fortitude it instrumentally occasions. The pain contributes in the sense that it is logically necessary and causally sufficient for the goods. Perhaps the idea is that evils are defeated as part of an organic unity (as opposed merely to being outweighed) if they contribute to a whole (are 'organically integrated' into that whole) to make it into something good, yet that good whole is not the product of weighing (greater good style) any good parts the whole may happen to contain against that evil part. The whole is in some way a result of the parts, but the result is not achieved by pitting parts against one another in a calculative, or what Adams calls 'additive', mode. Their interaction to create the whole cannot be captured in that simple way. Perhaps the crux is that in greater good calculations the values of parts are uninfluenced by their relations to other parts and by their place in the whole: their values are self-contained. But in organic relations the values of some parts can be altered by the parts' relations to other parts, that is by their context, up to and including the totality. This is how Adams sees that working in the case of a human life:

...I do claim that because our eventual post-mortem beatific inti-macy with God is an incommensurate good for human persons, Divine identification with human participation in horrors [the incarnation and crucifixion] confers a positive aspect on such expe-riences by integrating them into the participant's relationship with God. ... Retrospectively, I believe, from the vantage point of heavenly beatitude, human victims of horrors will recognise those experiences as points of identification with the crucified God, and not wish them away from their life histories. (Adams 1999, pp. 166–7)[10]

Thus the value of one part of a person's life is importantly altered for that person by their seeing it in the light of the rest of their life. The evils retain their horrendous aspect but their integration into the indi-vidual's life with God partly transforms them, to the extent that they acquire a 'positive aspect' – so much so that victims will not wish they had never suffered them.

I have two criticisms of Adams's position.[11]

### First criticism: Karamazov's challenge

Adams (1999, ch. 1) is aware that the moral assumptions of traditional theodicy are vulnerable to challenge. She has trenchantly criticised the view that makes evils instrumental means to good (e.g. in Adams 2008). Her desire to remedy the defects of mainstream theodicy by attention to healing the lives of those who have suffered horrendous evils is admirable. But does it meet Karamazov's challenge? Her claim is that the logical problem of evil is solved in the light of this logically possi-ble scenario: every victim of evil comes to see a 'positive aspect' in the evils they have suffered, so much so that they do not wish that suffer-ing out of their life history. I shall call this giving 'Adams-consent', or 'A-consent', to those evils. If there is a possible world where universal A-consent is rightly granted, then, she claims, there is no inconsistency between God and evil. The 'rightly' is an addition of my own, indicat-ing that the victim's A-consent is, say, not sentimental or wish-fulfilling or in some other way a flawed judgement. I assume that Adams does not want to include mistaken A-consent in her account.

I certainly do not want to deny that a victim of horrendous evil *can* rightly accept their life was (or is) worth living despite the evils it con-tained. With considerable trepidation and doubts I will also allow that even in the worst cases (for who am I to set a limit?) A-consent can rightly be granted.[12] But only in a *non-universalising* sense. That is, while I am willing to allow – at least for the purpose of not disputing a matter incidental to my main argument – that even in the worst cases a person can rightly find that being true to themselves they can or must give A-consent, I also allow that a person rightly might find they *cannot* give such consent. Adam assumes that a world in which every victim grants A-consent is logically possible. I shall not dispute this.

So does this solution work? Is the logical possibility of universal A-consent enough to exonerate God?[13] Remember that that question is being addressed here to Ivan Karamazov and those who share his outlook. As we saw in Chapter 1, Ivan has already rejected the idea that the bestowal of great post-mortem blessings on the victims of evils makes the creation of a world with those evils acceptable. And in any event, the idea of such blessings as essential and crucial for an adequate solution to the problem of evil is hardly a new idea of Adams's. Many years before her work it was central to the theodicy of John Hick, among others. What is distinctive of her work is the idea of A-consent – of an incommensurate good whose nature involves a divine intimacy with victims' suffering such that the suffering takes on a 'positive aspect' and victims will no longer wish it out of their life histories. The idea is important because it seems to take seriously the life and perspective *of the victims themselves* – their own attitude to their suffering – rather than merely theorising about the problem without reference to their outlook and responses. So the question becomes this: should universal A-consent, if it existed – added to the more general idea of a post-mortem beatitude – change Ivan's mind? Would not Ivan be the one ignoring the wishes and perspectives of those victims themselves if he held out against their A-consent, continuing to reproach God for his creation of the world? He cannot foist upon Adams the suggestion that this A-consent *must* be due to brainwashing, or *must* be just a kind of bribery: not if he follows me in admitting (with serious reservations, and for the sake of the argument) that A-consent can rightly be granted even in the worst cases. Adams does not need to universalise: she does not need to say the conditions of ideal judgement *require* A-consent of any victims of relevantly similar evils (a highly dubious claim). She can allow that worlds with victims of evil for whom it is *not* morally possible to grant A-consent rightly are logically possible. All she needs for her resolution of the logical problem of evil is that a world in which every victim *does* rightly grant A-consent is also logically possible. And that I grant her.

But still her argument does not succeed. I have already argued in Chapter 1 that a child's retrospective consent to their suffering does not save theodicy from Karamazov's challenge. The Christian God is a God of love in a sense akin to that of the love human parents have for their children. But no human parents would even *consider* sending their children to Auschwitz *simply* for the sake of a good that makes an already good or not-bad world better – no matter how lavish the good and no matter that the children share in it, and no matter if they give consent, prospectively or retrospectively. The parents might of course consider it, and even do it, if their love is overwhelmed or subverted by some corrupt human passion. They might do so if faced with a dilemma, that is to avoid a disaster, or if not doing so would mean the violation of some profoundly important value that constitutes the central significance of their lives. But not *just* for the sake of a greater good. For love, such an act is unthinkable. But if God's love for his children is like theirs, then the act is unthinkable for him too. If he does not create at all, or creates only a world of insentient vegetation, then he has worlds that are good or at least not bad. So creating our world, with all its suffering, is not something he would do to avoid disaster, but in order to make a good or not-bad state of affairs better (as theodicy sees it). And to suppose that he would do that is to suppose that he would do to his children what no decent human parent would even consider doing to theirs. It makes no difference that the retrospective consent is not merely consent to the evil occurring, but an embrace of it as something not to be wished out of your life. Appeal to the consent of an ideal observer will not help Adams's argument here (not that she wants to make that appeal). If the ideal observer is possessed of the kind of love we see in human parents and attribute to God, then he cannot create a world in which children go to Auschwitz and salve his conscience on account of the eternal felicity with A-consent they enjoy afterwards. If he is not, and he can do such things, then, as I argued in the first chapter, he is irrelevant.

As I also pointed out in the first chapter we cannot translate claims about the beneficial nature or effects of suffering – claims that, properly qualified, certainly contain truth – into *justifications* for the infliction of that suffering by God in creating the world. That barrier cannot be passed through. While people may legitimately embrace their life and the world, including a post-mortem beatitude if it exists, and (arguably) do so even to the point of not wishing out of their lives horrendous evils they have suffered, it doesn't follow, and it isn't true, that the goods of the world, even the incommensurate post-mortem beatitude with universal A-consent, justify God creating a world with such evils. A person who grants A-consent does not thereby grant moral exoneration for the infliction of their sufferings upon them. Someone may, eventually, come to accept being confined to a wheelchair as in some way a deep good, as well as an evil, in their life – and so much of a good that, as Adams puts it, they no longer wish this evil out of their life history. They may also forgive and even love the person who attacked them and put them in the wheelchair. But it is a *very* different matter from either of these things to grant that their attacker acted rightly, did nothing wrong. In the example that is just a falsehood, and any argument which requires me to grant it is a corrupting argument and therefore an unsound one. This is why evil-doers cannot cease wishing they had never done their evil-doing in the way their victims may (consistently) cease wishing they had never suffered it.

The argument is not improved if we emphasise, as Adams does, the importance of the incarnation and crucifixion. These are of the highest significance to the problem of evil, but not if they are understood merely as cases of spectacularly impressive moral effort (by a moral agent). To take the wheelchair case again, suppose the attacker, to show solidarity with his victim (and no doubt remorse for his own wrongdoing), made himself wheelchair-bound. Suppose further that he undertook to pay all debts and living expenses for the rest of the victim's life and even to suffer vicariously any punishments the victim might incur in the course of their life. All this is enormously significant, but does it make the slightest alteration to the morality of the original act? The question answers itself: no.

### Second criticism: the conflict of levels

It is true that Adams's argument, if it succeeded, would show *now* that an argument against God in the form of the logical problem of evil fails: we would not have to wait (on our own and others' responses in the afterlife to our sufferings in this life) to have *that* problem solved. The solution does not depend on the logically possible world of universal A-consent being *this* world. We have seen that her argument does not succeed, but, even if it did, a victory over the logical problem of evil is hollow indeed if the logically possible scenario it relies on is not one likely to be true in the real world. This latter question is usually called the evidential problem of evil and is typically given the usual theoretical construal: for example, the merit of the inference from our not knowing of a morally sufficient reason for (perhaps some specific) evil to the likelihood of there being one. In Adams's case this would amount to the serious problem of how the theoretician could know, or reasonably believe, that everyone in the universe will grant A-consent. But for her the problem also takes what might seem to be a drastically personal form, or at least it will sometime in the (post-mortem) future.

The theoreticians, the philosophers, who ponder these intellectual problems are also of course human beings, themselves victims of horrendous evil perhaps, who (according to Adams's post-mortem story) at some time will themselves have to make decisions about their own A-consent. Now I have just argued in the previous section that universal A-consent does not make God's creation of this world any more compatible with his being a God of love, and that an individual's giving A-consent to their suffering is far removed from their approving of God creating a world with that suffering. But if A-consent is to be taken to bear on the problem of evil, one must assume otherwise. It is necessary that the people who give it not only cease to wish they had never suffered the horrendous evils they did, but also see that cessation as involving a seal of moral approval on God's creating the world: it would be odd indeed if theoreticians declared the problem of evil solved by appeal to the actual or possible attitude to their sufferings of people who did not agree about that. So, on this approach, in actually deciding whether to give A-consent or not one is effectively casting a vote in favour of the view that God acted rightly in creating the world. But by Adams's own theoretical criteria for that view being right (now applied to the actual world) the matter is resolved in God's favour *only if everyone, including the theoreticians themselves*, grants A-consent and thereby casts a vote for God having acted rightly in creating the world. But that means that if their decision is to be a justified one (the decision cannot be an arbitrary one), the theoreticians (and, for that matter, anyone) must know, or at least have a reasonable belief to the effect, that *everyone else* is going to A-consent. But how does one know that? Do I have to *wait* until *everyone* else has A-consented before I do so? It would seem to mean that we would all be looking at one another to see what the others were going to do before we could finalise our own decision, and so a sort of decision-making paralysis would set it. We would also need to know that everybody's decision met the conditions of ideal judgement; that it was right, or at least right for them. But how on earth could we know *that* for literally millions of people? Can Adams just *stipulate* that each person is supposed to decide their A-consent considering everything *except* what others do? But if A-consenting already amounts, in effect, to exonerating God, then surely agents (certainly those who are philosophers) – if their decision is to be correct or at least acceptable – must meet all criteria for ideal judgement on this matter, which, if Adams's theory is correct, include knowing, or reasonably believing, there will be *universal* A-consent. So agents' judgement is, on Adams's own showing, flawed if they do not take into account what others, *all* others in fact, do. And even if all the non-philosophers were held to a lower standard than the philosophers, that would still leave the philosophers with the paralysing paradox of needing to know what others will do to decide what they should do. But if we relieve the philosophers of answerability to that standard – the standard Adams has herself set, of requiring universal A-consent for God's exoneration – then we are abandoning that standard, and so abandoning Adams's theory. The philosophers who are also victims of horrendous evil cannot be accountable to *two* standards for answering the problem of evil, one for them *qua* victims of evil – that is, *qua* human beings (do *I* A-consent to the evils I have suffered and thus exonerate God?) – and the other for them *qua* philosophers (does *everyone* A-consent to their sufferings and thus exonerate God?). It seems they cannot settle the matter as human beings first, since the correctness of any such decision (whether God is *really* exonerated) is hostage to the second decision. On the other hand, they cannot decide the matter as philosophers first, because of that very paralysing philosophical requirement that they must decide as human beings first in order to fulfil the philosophical condition (on a solution to the problem of evil) of universal A-consent. Effectively, they are trapped in a circle: they cannot decide the matter as human beings without deciding it as philosophers first, and they cannot decide it as philosophers first without deciding it as human beings. The whole thing can appear to be feasible only because the philosophers are treated as if they were *not human beings*, not among the possible victims of evil, as if they were merely spectators to events and not people who themselves had to make a decision *for their own lives* about God and evil.[14]

The basic problem is that Adams is working with two levels of accountability. There is an apparently practical and personal level, where individuals must decide their own attitude as human beings, and a theoretical and impersonal level, where philosophers deal with the intellectual problem of evil, as opposed to the existential one, as if they were *not* human beings, not *participants* in the drama. But the force of her apparently radical appeal to the first level is effectively negated by making it hostage to the theoretical one by requiring that the personal decisions be, in effect, subject to philosophical imprimatur for their legitimacy. In the end Adams's appeal to the personal is very different from the sort of appeal to the existential (as I prefer to call it) that I am making in this book. For her the personal in effect functions as a condition for solving the theoretical problem. My appeal to the personal is intended to undermine the need for a distinct theoretical problem. At its most benign the latter merely recapitulates the personal problem and indeed collapses into it. But if this collapse is resisted, it becomes a source of serious confusion. My advice to Adams is: let the theoretical level go.

## 4. Different worlds

The intellectual ideal of theodicy – like the intellectual ideal of philosophical theory-construction in general – is that of rational beings deciding their beliefs (and thus their actions) on the basis of evidence. Its characteristic intellectual virtues are factual information, rationality, logic and their ilk. In the end, Adams's theodicy conforms to type. As in other sophisticated philosophical theories, one's own personal responses are put at a theoretical distance to be treated as *data* for theory-construction. Thus Adams treats the personal, *existential* resolution ('defeat') of the problem of evil in everyone's lives as *another datum* (albeit one of crucial importance) in the attempt to find an *intellectual* solution to the problem of evil. But the intellectual problem is a problem for mere rational agents, for uninvolved spectators who might as well be from Mars. As we have seen, by forcing her discussion into that impersonal mode the existential significance is wrung out of her account.

There is a deep problem at the heart of the attempt to turn an existential problem into a purely intellectual one. The ideal of rationally apportioning belief to evidence is in radical tension with the sort of certainty most people actually have in these matters (when they are not either perplexed or uninterested). So long as the meaningfulness of one's life is at the mercy of evidence, of conflicting reasons, one can never – if one is true to the implied ideal of rationality – have peaceful confidence in that meaning. The nagging doubt will always be there that new evidence will turn up which will alter the balance of probabilities. The point is not confined to the greater good approach. The same doubt will pervade any account in which a judgement is made as the result of reasons interacting with one another, whether in self-contained 'additive' mode or in an 'organic' one (that is, it will pervade theodicy). Yet people *do* have such confidence, despite the most unspeakable evils. Are they just irrational? Or are philosophers over-intellectualising human life?

The point is dramatically illustrated by the appeal to eschatology which a great deal of theodicy, including of course Adams's, crucially relies on. We ought to twig to something being wrong with putting so much weight on eschatology from the fact that its speculations are, in many cases, as far as the existential problem of evil is concerned, *unnecessary*. Time and again people's attitudes to the problem of evil – both belief and unbelief – are fixed in this life, well before any experience of the hereafter. And often, on the believing side at least, their faith seems on the face of it to run *against* the evidence. There are those whose faith has survived overwhelming personal experience of evil: from the standpoint of the intellectual problem it has survived a mass of apparent counter-evidence. More than that, there are people whose faith has been created by such evils. The faith they find may or may not heal them, but that is not necessarily the test of it. Some must praise God – well, *because they must*, healed or not, and they are not necessarily failing to grasp the seriousness of the evils. For them, God is more like the *solution* to the problem of evil than one half of the source of it. These are people whose sense of the goodness of the world, and their gratitude for it, seems to *fly in the face* of the evidence, rather than to be *based upon it*. There are more religious perspectives than most philosophical discussion of God and evil recognises.

So is the faith of such people an unjustified brute consequence of the sheer disabling effect of horrendous evil? Or do they perhaps have a rough theodicy in practice, relying on the hope of a beatific future life, itself based on credible evidence that outweighs the evidence of this life alone? The real problem with this is not epistemic, about what the believer can rationally justify on the basis of the evidence (the evidence for the beatitude *versus* the evidence of the evil experienced so far). The real problem is that there do not exist any such impersonal 'rational' grounds for deciding the matter. The clash between the believer and the unbeliever is much more radical than that. Consider again Ivan Karamazov's morally compelling insistence that the lives of children are not for sale. In that marketplace the offer of an 'incommensurate' goodness is a trump bid, and when Adams writes that the moral trivialisation charge 'seems to me to reflect an insufficient appreciation of what "incommensurate" means' (1999, p. 189) she is making an essentially quantitative appeal: *'nothing* can outweigh *that'* is the implied thought. But for Ivan it is not a matter of weighing (or defeating, or in any way comparing) things at all, for human suffering is not up for sale in the first place. In an important sense theodicists' heaven is Ivan's hell, because it is bought at the price of a child's suffering. Ivan and the theodicists are not in an epistemic dispute – according to a shared set of evidential and moral criteria – but a much deeper moral dispute. They see the 'good' of the eschaton in a wholly different light. Calling it 'incommensurate' cuts no ice.[15]

We should repudiate the assumption that belief (and unbelief) is legitimate only when it is defensible in the narrow terms of factual information, rationality and logic. A wider view includes the existential criteria of judgement mentioned in the first chapter and made use of at places in this one, which create a much richer dimension for thought about this sort of issue. People whose faith survives, or is even created in, horrendous evil sustain their sense of the goodness of the world and of God, without underestimating the evils the world contains, in a very different way from that presented in theodicy. On this alternative, it is not a matter of weighing parts of the world against one another, *or* of relating them in a quasi-aesthetic organic unity. Both approaches (the latter at least in Adams's hands, as I read her) assume a model whereby a conclusion about a whole is drawn from consideration of parts. It doesn't matter if that consideration is merely additive, or if some parts may influence the nature or valency of others. Either way, the parts are comprehended separately from the conclusion (the conclusion is analysable into the parts) and debate focuses on whether one has identified the number and nature of the parts correctly, or on the correctness of the inference to one's preferred conclusion. The alternative is to deny that the whole is understandable in terms of the parts in this way, to deny there is any shared level of description between the disputants which will, by the force of logic alone, compel, or make highly probable, a universally correct answer. It is not a matter of relating parts to one another to create an understanding of the whole, *at all*. It is a matter of *how one sees the world*, whether it be part of the world or the whole of it. It is a matter not of relating goods and evils in a moral accountant's ledger, or in an organon, but of a transformed perception of the whole shebang, of having an altogether different *gestalt* upon it. Our *existential gestalt* towards the world of which our convictions are a discursive abridgement *cannot* be a function of comparing the parts – such as the good parts and the evil parts – that compose the world, because any principle that we employ to conduct the comparison will itself already reflect a fundamental gestalt towards the world, and will read those parts in such a way as to preserve or confirm the attitude. For example, that no amount or type of good can rehabilitate a world with certain evils or, alternatively, that no amount or type of evil can – as the religious person would put it – separate us from the love of God. It is the gestalt which is fundamental. It determines how we see the parts, not *vice versa*. The conflict between those who can believe in God given evil and those who can't is not a conflict between two views with shared criteria of rational judgement. It is a conflict between two views whose decisive criteria are very different. Between, for example, those for whom an indignant thirst for justice on behalf of the burning children is most important and those for whom love defeats this. Unless we are all going to be simply brainwashed into one way of thinking, there is no reason to believe the same differences between people would not exist in any future life: perhaps this has some significance for the distinction between heaven and hell. As Wittgenstein said, the happy and the unhappy live in different worlds.

The person who can see the world as something to celebrate in awe and gratitude, as an act of creative love (and who is not deceived or corrupted in various possible ways), does so despite a firm sense (perhaps personally experienced) that the world contains profound evil, just as a parent may see their child as irreplaceably precious despite grotesque physical or mental deformity or moral depravity. Indeed it is less a matter of the world's being *good* at all than of it being something like *sacred* (or good *in the sense of* sacred). Raimond Gaita (2000a) has written of how people can be revealed as precious or sacred in the light of others' love for them, especially the love of parents for their children. This love can stretch to include those who are otherwise beyond our reach. Those for whom morality can find nothing good to say, for whom justice demands only severity and compassion, only a merciful despatch from the world, love reclaims. We say in jest that 'only his mother can love him', but we thus speak an important truth: that there are some realities only love can see. Paradoxically, we speak the same truth when we say that 'love is blind', for to see the reality of the sacred it must be blind to what we all too normally give great weight to. So it is not surprising that religious imagery is so often that of a loving parent: only love of that sort can see as sacred a world with so much evil in it. It is just one of the irresolvable conflicts of human life, one of the joints at which life is carved, that some people respond to this by despising it, and others by respectfully dissenting from its full implications. The latter at least are not *obviously* wrong. To think they are is precisely to undersell the *radical-ness* of the Christian Gospel.

# 3
# The Problem of Evil and the Problem of the Slightest Toothache

## 1. Blemishes and serious evils

In the Introduction to his *Providence and the Problem of Evil* Richard Swinburne writes:

> If the only good things in the world were thrills of pleasure and the only bad things stabs of pain, then it would be easy for God to make a good world with nothing bad in it. And if there was any pain at all – if just one human felt the slightest toothache – that would be conclusive evidence against the existence of God. (Swinburne 1998, p. xii)[1]

But why think that *the slightest toothache* is evidence against God *at all*, even *prima facie* evidence needing to be accounted for, let alone (in the circumstances Swinburne envisages) conclusive evidence? Swinburne's point, in the passage this quotation comes from, is that, of course, the real world contains a web of much richer goods and evils than the world he imagines, and that the evil of a slight toothache is readily outweighed by the goods, so that it is very far from being conclusive evidence against God. But this entails that a slight toothache in *some* degree counts against God, and this is what I find problematic. When people, both religious people and non-religious people, are deeply disturbed at the facts of suffering and evil – when they sense them to be undermining their very apprehension of the world as a place they can welcome and celebrate, a reaction which in the case of the religious person they are likely to express as a loss of their faith in God – the slightest toothache is *not* the sort of case they are, or *could be*, encountering or contemplating. We cannot imagine Dostoevsky's Ivan Karamazov 'returning the ticket' to this world because just one child suffers the slightest toothache. Not because it is so readily outweighed by other goods, but because it is *not even relevant*.

Swinburne may acknowledge this much about people's reactions. But he will likely appeal to a distinction introduced in the previous chapter and say that I am confusing the *intellectual* problem of evil with some form or other of the *existential* problem – perhaps with the personal problem of how to maintain faith when evil touches our lives, or the pastoral problem of how to minister to people facing the personal problem.[2] He may well say that we should not expect an answer to the intellectual, the philosophical, problem to relieve the distress and restore the faith of those whose encounter with, or contemplation of, evil has cast them into a crisis. Indeed, there is no reason to expect that even the issues addressed by the intellectual problem will all be ones that concern believers at an existential level. In the case at hand, there is no reason to expect that people will be existentially disturbed by a slight toothache. But, he might say, that does not mean that the toothache is not a legitimate part of the intellectual problem. That the answer to the intellectual problem does not map onto an answer to the existential problem does not mean that the answer is not *true*. Personal or pastoral value is one thing; philosophical truth is another – so the thought would go.

As I wrote in Chapter 1, a distinction of this sort between the intellectual and the existential pervades the literature on the problem of evil. One symptom of it, expressed to a nicety by Swinburne in the above quotation, is that the problem of evil – the intellectual problem – arises without consideration of serious evil at all: it arises from mere blemishes such as the slightest toothache. Even if that were the only 'evil' in the world, we would have the gist of the problem of evil, the very same problem in principle, though not of course in degree, as is raised by disease, earthquakes and genocide. Swinburne is not alone in this view: to name just some others, Nelson Pike offers a 'a spoonful of bitter medicine' as counting against God, Peter van Inwagen mentions twisted ankles, and Herbert McCabe cites the damage dinosaurs did to plants by eating them.[3] I believe these philosophers' outlook is (in this respect) reasonably representative of the literature on the problem of evil by analytic philosophers. I am not suggesting that these writers equate blemishes with serious evils in degree of seriousness, or denying that they discuss the latter. Much less am I suggesting that philosophers in general do these things; many ethical theories imply, or at least can accommodate, the distinction between blemishes and serious evils. My point is that by and large the literature on the problem of evil assumes that the *logical core* of the problem is essentially the same across the whole range of severity, whether one is talking about twisted ankles or talking about genocide. God is *perfectly* good, so even the tiniest spot of evil is relevant.[4]

But Swinburne *et al.* will say, I predict, that once the intellectual problem is distinguished from the existential one, we can see that my criticism misses the mark. The absence of an existential problem – the absence of crises in people's lives – does not imply the absence of an intellectual problem, and it is the latter which the philosophers are concerned with. The intellectual problem is about the consistency of a set of propositions (or the probability of one proposition given others) and that has nothing to do with psychology. Thus it is a problem that holds regardless of the severity of the evil in question. People's existential indifference towards toothaches does not show that toothaches have no bearing at all on the existence of God. The upshot of this line of argument is that philosophical thought about God and evil can proceed independently of people's *actual reactions* to evil. And that includes philosophers' *own* reactions, their reactions *as human beings*. And, very largely, philosophical discussion of evil *does* proceed like that – with the sort of dissociation between philosophers' intellectual judgements and their personal responses that makes possible passages such as that from Swinburne. We may lose sleep from the slightest toothache, but not from contemplating its implications for the goodness of the universe and its Creator. We do not need to remind ourselves of the various greater goods which the slightest toothache would make possible and which would outweigh its badness in order to convince ourselves – perhaps just intellectually – that God remains good despite the slightest of discomforts. Such meagre discomfort simply does not constitute a threat to God's goodness in the first place. Indeed it scarcely deserves to be counted *suffering* at all, with all that term's 'existential' implications of fear, terror and dread, which, as Hick (1978, pp. 292–7) points out, are normally associated with significant pain.

To create the impression that such blemishes threaten the goodness of God philosophers assume the existence of necessary truths that connect the goodness of God to the absence from his creation of any blemish, or, more precisely, of any *gratuitous* blemish, that is one for which there is no justifying greater good. These truths supposedly arise from the very concepts of *good* and *evil*, and hold regardless of people's actual responses to serious goods and evils as opposed to trivial benefits and blemishes. They may defend Swinburne by endorsing something like John Mackie's principle that – again, unless greater goods stand to be gained – 'a good thing always eliminates evil as far as it can', which he seems to regard as, at least arguably, integral to the very ideas of good and evil (he calls it a 'quasi-logical rule' concerning the terms; 1990, p. 26). Since God is a perfectly good being his creation will contain no evils unwarranted by greater goods; hence, there will be no gratuitous slight toothaches. But even if we accept Mackie's principle, what application does it have to the slightest toothache? In any ordinary sense of the word, such a toothache – indeed nearly any toothache – does not (in normal circumstances) count as *evil*. 'Evil' is a term that in *serious* usage – I mean usage that (in the sort of context we are dealing with here) is sensitive to the moral demands of such a word, to the moral realities it has been used to try to capture – is reserved for cases of a vastly graver kind than this, the sort of cases Ivan Karamazov raises, cases which shake our confidence in the goodness of creation and Creator.[5] Yet philosophers such as Mackie – in a good example of what Wittgenstein called language going on holiday – have dissociated 'evil' (and 'good') from its serious contexts of use and fashioned it as a term of art in which it comprehends every kind of discomfort or imperfection, however slight. No doubt they are lured into this by the physical continuity from tiny injuries and pains at one pole to murder, torture and dreadful affliction at the other. But in doing so they illicitly extend the usual existential associations of 'evil' to include cases of trivial injury to which it normally has no application, and thus produce the illusion that those trivialities threaten the goodness of God. This is what Swinburne would be doing if he appealed to Mackie's principle.[6] On this approach a slight toothache and the Holocaust are both evil in the way that a garden shed and the Sydney Opera House are both rain shelters. One is a bigger $X$ than the other, but both are $X$s, and whatever applies to $X$s in virtue of being $X$s applies to both of these: in the case of evil, it is not being permitted by goodness powerful enough to prevent it (unless there is a greater good). So in a world created by a perfectly good and omnipotent person we should no more expect gratuitous slight toothaches than gratuitous holocausts. But, as I say, this in effect equivocates between the serious moral use of *evil* – the sense in which Stalin and Pol Pot, or childhood cancer and great natural disasters, get called *evil*, the sort of evil that disturbs us existentially – and the jargonised use of it to embrace the smallest blemish, treating our vastly different reactions as irrelevant. When believers – outside the academic seminar room – talk of the goodness of God, they are opposing that goodness to the serious existential evils, to Evils with a capital E we might say, not to the small-e evils of slight toothaches.

Peter van Inwagen is another philosopher who insists on a sharp separation of the intellectual and existential problems. He is up-front in declaring that the problem of evil is really 'the problem that the real existence of bad things raises for theists' (2006, p. 12), where 'bad things' (which he equates with what he calls 'ordinary evil') include the previously mentioned twisted ankles (pp. 12–14). But it would be no good for Swinburne to appeal to some amended version of Mackie's principle such as 'a good thing always eliminates *bad* as far as it can'. A linguistic move like that misses the point. Whatever we call it, a slight toothache can threaten the goodness of God only insofar as it disturbs our spiritual sense of being at peace in the universe, and that degree of disturbance is, surely, zero.

## 2. The religious problem of evil and the academic problem

But *why* should God's goodness be opposed to serious evil but not to blemishes? After all, there is a physical continuity, as I have admitted. And it is not as if opposing *good* to *bad* is eccentric usage. *Why* should existential reactions be relevant?

We speak of good and bad cars, sewing machines, football teams and so on. We can speak of these as good and bad relative to their functions or purposes. Sometimes we may call them good and bad according to their impacts on human pleasures or health (good foods and bad ones). Sometimes – usually in the philosophy seminar room – we may speak of good and evil in the same common-or-garden way. But if we speak of Good and Evil *per se* – almost as if personifying them – something more radical, drastic or primal is involved. Certainly we would not be tempted (as we surely are, even if we are sceptical about the temptation) to use the word 'Evil' in such a way as to identify the world's *horrors*, as opposed to its discomforts and inconveniences, unless the horrors affect us in ways the discomforts and inconveniences do not. I have briefly alluded to that effect by talking of its power to undermine our sense of the world as something to welcome and celebrate. One may also speak of its power to fuel resentment at the world and God, and to erode our will to live. This existential sense of Good and Evil informs the serious moral use of these words, and consequently I shall call evils that can affect our lives in this way 'serious' evils, in contrast to mere blemishes and inconveniences.

What I am suggesting is that the serious use of Good and Evil is distinctive of serious religious faith. I am deliberately contrasting serious religious faith here with merely academic speculation. I do not of course deny that there is an intellectual problem of evil about slight toothaches in the sense that one can stipulate a set of propositions that creates just such a problem (that is exactly what Mackie does). The question is: what is the relationship of that problem to actual religious life and faith? Swinburne, Mackie and many others take the answer to that question to be obvious: the intellectual problem accurately represents the heart of the believer's religious problem. They think this because they believe the problem arises from the meaning of terms such as 'good' and 'evil', where that meaning is somehow formed independently of people's actual human responses in religious contexts, and requires a sort of quasi-hygienic perfectionism. In contrast, I believe that the problem they treat is far removed from the problem believers confront in their lives. Faith in God as Creator and Redeemer of the world is born and sustained in precisely the violence of existential feeling that mainstream thinking treats as strictly irrelevant to 'the' (academic, intellectual) problem. The dread of serious evil is one of those responses; loving gratitude for the gift of life, and the oppressive sense of sin, are two others, and there are more. Religious feelings are existential feelings, virtually by definition. It is in these responses – not in any cool calculation of damage ranging from the largest to the tiniest case – that the need for God (or for rejecting him) is made in our souls.

I am not denying that one can come to believe in God (in *a* god) merely through intellectual and academic speculation, about the causal origin of the world say. What I am denying is the claim that the problem of blemishes is in essence *the same* problem as the problem of serious evils, and so blemishes – however more readily accounted for by greater goods theodicy – are in principle, intellectually, just as much in need of that theodicy. One might even say that the small-g god of the philosophy seminar room, the god of deistic speculation, is not the big-G God of living faith. The God of religion, I submit, is not affected by the existence of blemishes. If there were slight toothaches which we knew for a certainty to have no redeeming greater good, or any other theodical justification, this would not cause believers even to hesitate in their faith.

It is no good, in this context, to plead that this point is 'just psychology'. There are some 'psychological' facts about human beings – those concerning various kinds of unthinking reactions of a very basic sort, in this case religious reactions (awe, dread etc.) – which describe

the shape of human nature, and of certain important human practices, and go to *form* our concepts. One way in which we can identify
those concept-forming reactions is by being alert to how the attempt
to ignore them, to divorce concepts – in this case *evil* and *God* – from
the relevant contexts of human response that condition the sense of
those concepts, produces parody. A religious faith which agonised existentially over slight toothaches, the bitter taste of cough medicine and
so on, in the way people do agonise over serious evils, is just such a
parody. To lose a more than nominal faith in God is to have one's
world rocked – but blemishes do not rock one's world. Job, from the
heart of his pain, cries out:

> From out of the city the dying groan,
>> and the soul of the wounded cries
>>> for help;
>> yet God pays no attention to their
>>> prayer.
>
> Job 24: 12 (RSV)

Would the 'cognitive content' of that lament remain the same if Job had
said the following instead?

> From out of the city they groan from the slightest toothache,
>> and the soul of those tasting the bitter cough medicine cries
>>> for help;
>> yet God pays no attention to their
>>> prayer.

The question answers itself. The result is pure parody. That does not
merely tell us about some contingent idiosyncrasy of Job. It tells us that
the idea of God being subject to reproach *makes sense* only in the context of serious evil. If one attempted to take the parody seriously one
would *cheapen* Job's crisis and the whole topic. And that cheapening
would not be some existential or moral consequence, externally and
incidentally related to the 'cognitive', 'intellectual' core of the problem.
For in showing that reproach makes sense only in the context of serious
evil, the parody also shows that the seriousness of the evil is *internal* to
the problem – and that philosophers too readily separate the intellectual from the existential.

But could not the believer have *both* problems, separate as they
may be? I have admitted that of course anyone will have a problem of

evil who accepts the stipulations about 'God', 'good' and 'evil' made by Mackie, or something similar to that, and no doubt some believers would do so. But the believer has to have these commitments *qua* believer, in virtue of the nature of his religious faith. Swinburne and Mackie think their academic problem of evil is important *because* they think it is something believers have on their plate in virtue of what they believe. They take themselves to be defending or attacking the faith of the believer. And that is what I am denying. On my account, if the believer accepts Mackie's tenets and recognises the intellectual problem they create, that *is* merely a matter of individual psychology. In contrast, the serious problem of evil is indeed the conceptual product of the believer's faith. I hope it is starting to be clear why I think that is not something to be *contrasted* with the believer's existential responses to the world and serious evil, for these in large measure determine the nature of those beliefs.

The existential impact of evil – its power to undermine our very apprehension of the world as a place we can welcome and celebrate, to make us curse the day we were born – is, as I said at the beginning, something common to both believers and unbelievers. This implies that the believer's problem of evil depends upon a prior problem of evil that is *shared* by theists and non-theists. Van Inwagen thinks the very idea of this is silly. As we have seen he defines the problem of evil as actually 'the problem that the real existence of bad things raises for theists', where 'bad things', or in his oxymoronic phrase 'ordinary evil', includes everything from twisted ankles to the 1755 Lisbon earthquake which destroyed the city and took thousands of lives. In line with this he brusquely dismisses the idea that believers and unbelievers share the problem of evil, or that it depends on a related problem that they share. The most he will concede is that theists and atheists *may* (he's not sure) share a common problem of how to explain the existence of what he calls 'radical' evil, which he glosses as 'the extreme reaches of moral depravity' (2006, p. 13) and which he counter-poses to the 'ordinary' evil. He pours scorn on the claim that the traditional problem of evil has anything much to do with an idea of Susan Neiman's (2003) which he expresses thus:

> Evil threatens meaning. Evil threatens our ability to regard the world in which we find ourselves as comprehensible. The Lisbon earthquake presented late eighteenth-century Christians with an intractable problem regarding the meaning of existence, and the death camps have had a comparable or analogous effect on post-religious

thinkers. The problem of evil is the problem of how to find meaning in a world in which everything is touched by evil. (van Inwagen 2006, pp. 15–16)

Van Inwagen does not deny there is such a problem, or that theists and atheists share it. But he denies that it has anything to do with the theistic problem of evil as traditionally understood, and which he identifies with the problem of bad things (which includes the problem of slight toothaches) on what he takes to be the obvious ground that acknowledging the existence of bad things is an intellectual problem for theism because it is *prima facie* inconsistent with the theist's defining belief in a perfectly good, omnipotent, omniscient God, whereas there is no such *prima facie* inconsistency with the defining tenets of atheism (or agnosticism, one can add).

I certainly agree that the intellectual problem for theists *as van Inwagen understands it* – the problem which includes slight toothaches, bitter cough medicine and twisted ankles – is radically distinct from any problem believers and unbelievers may share. But my argument has been that, precisely because it makes God's existence depend on trivialities, it is not a problem believers actually face. The problem they actually face is the problem of serious evils (such as the Lisbon earthquake). I accept that of course this problem has a dimension to it – the compatibility of such evil with the existence of God – that is not there for the unbeliever. But that dimension depends upon an underlying problem of evil shared by believer and unbeliever, and it is *exactly* the problem Neiman identifies: the problem of how to find meaning in a world in which everything is touched by (serious) evil.

The theist's 'intellectual' problem *depends* on the shared 'emotional' or 'existential' problem. The latter is necessary not only to respond to the former problem, but even to pose it. *In the context of a genuine religious life* what could it mean, what sort of point would there be, to judge the world, or its Creator, *good* if the world were not, at least in some circumstances, able ('normally', i.e. absent a special explanation) to inspire hope, courage and faith, or at least to raise the promise of such inspiration? And what could it mean to judge something evil – or, if you prefer, a bad thing threatening the goodness of the world and its Creator – if the thing did not normally disturb one's wider happiness in the world, one's being at peace in it? The believer and the unbeliever will both speak of good and evil. As Neiman says, for both of them the problem is how to find meaning in the face of the reality of evil. And chief among the various ways in which this 'meaning' may be elucidated is, as I have said, whether they can respond to the world with love and gratitude. The religious person makes this explicit as the question of whether they can believe in – believe, that is, in their heart, with their own response of love – the love of God. The existence of gratuitous twisted ankles and slight toothaches does not constitute a problem for either the believer or the unbeliever, because in both cases these phenomena do not upset our capacity to respond to the world with love and gratitude. And if we think something can upset belief in God without having the capacity to disturb us in this way, then, as I keep saying, we produce an intellectualist parody of religious faith.

## 3. Existential trauma

Someone may object to my argument so far like this: 'The Job parody is unfair, a cheap shot. Swinburne and the others are not committed to it. They can acknowledge that blemishes do not cause existential trauma in themselves. But they can acknowledge that *and* satisfy the requirement that for believers' faith to be vulnerable to something that something must bring existential trauma in its train. They can satisfy those two apparently conflicting desiderata by pointing out that, although slight toothaches and so on are non-traumatising in themselves (and thus Job rewritten for slight toothaches is a parody), *the loss of faith they entail* does traumatise believers *qua* believers: they suffer the trauma of discovering God does not exist, with all the reorganisation of their emotional and practical life this entails. An intellectual realisation, non-existential in itself, entails existential consequences.'

My reply is that the existential trauma following on the intellectual discovery has to be of *a distinctively religious sort*, or else the person's belief was not a serious religious belief in the first place. It would be no good if it were just injured intellectual or professional pride, for example. The belief and the loss of it have to be *qua* serious believer, and even *qua* religious believer in the right sense (for example, an effect on someone's career in the Church, which might have consequences that are existentially traumatic, might be called trauma *qua* religious believer, but it is not so in the right sense). That is, there has to be a distinctive existential significance to the belief and a distinctively existential crisis or trauma at losing the belief (at least in normal cases). But what is that distinctive existential significance? The existential significance of religious faith is that it sustains meaning in the face of the Big Facts of human life: our mortality, our strange combination of nobility and wretchedness, our vulnerability to suffering at the hands of both external forces and our own passions, and so on. Since most of these things are (rightly) counted evil in theodicy, Neiman is right to say that the existential significance of faith is that it gives meaning to a world in which everything is touched by evil. In that case the trauma that follows upon the loss of faith must be the trauma of losing that meaning. (This is not to say that the crisis cannot be overcome and meaning eventually found in some other way – but this normally takes time.) That brings me to the nub: the person who has lost their faith as the result of an encounter with evil feels existentially vulnerable in the face of that evil (unless and until meaning is restored in some other way). But once again, the 'evil' in question cannot be mere blemishes: blemishes are called 'blemishes' precisely because they *lack* that existential potency (again, the Job parody). The trauma in question will follow only if the evil in question is serious. But in that case the belief in God that was held, and then, courtesy of the gratuitous blemish, lost, was never a belief held *qua* religious believer in the right way – and couldn't be, on pain of parody. The moral is that a belief in God vulnerable to blemishes is a pale shadow of real religious faith: it mimics its outlines, but with no real substance. And just because of that, just because it lacks gravity, it is a conceptual truth (a 'grammatical' remark about the nature of religious faith) that it is not a belief the serious believer *can* hold *qua* serious believer (while the attempt to make it serious is sheer parody). Its triviality makes it actively antipathetic to serious belief, so it is not an option that the serious believer, as a serious believer, holds this belief in addition to the serious one, and has the problem of blemishes in addition to the problem of serious evils. The two faiths, the two problems, are in conflict with one another: a faith that can be knocked out by a blemish is something very different from, and incompatible with, one that can't be.

A different objection might ask how it is, if I am right, that believers-in-the-street so readily cotton on to the standard problem and take it seriously, at least intellectually. Think of how quickly first-year students, including religious students, grasp the problem as conventionally posed, and certainly don't object to the terms in which it is posed. They do not argue as I have argued here. My reply is that it is not condescending, but just a pedestrian observation, to point out that philosophy is hard and that people with little experience of it are at least as liable to be confused as those who have studied it for years. Moreover, no special authority, no immunity to confusion or error, is bestowed by the fact that one is a religious believer and the topic religious belief. The questions being asked are not about straightforward matters of fact. They require interpretation, appraisal and discernment. The significance and implications of one's own beliefs and practices, of things that in one way are very familiar, can often be opaque to oneself. The believer (or the atheist convinced by the argument from evil) is as liable to go wrong in a philosophical account of their faith (or anti-faith) as a morally decent person is liable to go wrong in a philosophical account of morality. This is why, as D. Z. Phillips once remarked, we cannot do philosophy by opinion poll. As a result, what someone says in class may not faithfully represent what they believe, or what problems they confront, *qua* religious believer, rather than *qua* philosopher of religion. Moreover, students are liable to defer to their teachers, and to form their philosophical minds in the dominant mould. The mould in this case has as one of its defining features the separation of the intellectual and the existential. For all I have said and will say against it in this book, I do not belittle that outlook. It is a powerful, austere and in some ways sublime and even noble conception of thought: certainly it exercises a deep appeal over the human mind. But that doesn't make it right. Perhaps if students were presented with the sort of contrary argument I have given here, they might agree.

On another matter, it is important to explain briefly that even if I am wrong in my claim that the believer does not face 'the problem of blemishes' at all, my separate claim that this is nevertheless an importantly distinct problem from the 'problem of serious evils' – even, if you like, that the gods facing these problems are not the same gods, one being the god of philosophers' constructions, the other the God of living faith – remains, of itself, of great importance. The implicit claims of Swinburne and others that they are *the same* problem – that 'the' believers' problem of evil is raised by blemishes alone, and would exist in a world with nothing worse in it, and that the logic of the solution (greater goods) is essentially the same in both cases, albeit accounting for trivialities more easily – are mistaken. Whether or not the believer (qua believer) does have to explain trivialities, as I have said above, the problem of explaining them is a very different fish from the problem of explaining serious evil. It actively distorts the serious problem by regarding the existential distress that characterises it as external to it (an important problem for pastors and psychotherapists, but incidental to the intellectual problem that concerns philosophers) and therefore fails to see the distinct intellectual problem that the distress creates. It fails to see (as I have been trying to explain) that the key terms of the serious intellectual problem – 'good', 'evil' and so on – are conditioned

by the existential responses, that those responses are not epiphenom-
enal to intellectual problems but constitutive of them.

Those points are a good part of the gravamen of this book. On my
account, the real problem of evil, far from beginning with the mer-
est blemish and continuing to the worst of horrors, all susceptible in
principle to the theodical greater goods solution, actually does not even
get under way until the point where theodicy (if it were relevant at all)
starts to fail: with serious evils and Karamazov's challenge. There is a
real (as opposed to academic and imaginary) problem of evil for many
people precisely because they find that greater goods, even if they exist,
*cannot* justify the serious evils they are supposed to. But by assuming
that they do (or would if they existed) theodicy is effectively complicit
in hiding the real problem of evil from philosophical study. That pretence rests on the separation of the intellectual and the existential, the
dissociation of philosophy from life.

## 4. God the loving father

Yet another objection to my argument might go like this: 'Just as there
is a physical continuity between a slight toothache at one pole and, say,
the unbearable pain of a fatal illness or injury at the other, so too we
should expect an existential continuity. Slight toothaches cause vastly
less existential distress than torture, but they cause *some* – very little,
certainly, but some nevertheless. That modicum is why slight toothaches count in correspondingly minute degree – but nevertheless in
some degree – against the existence of God. Of course substituting
slight toothaches for serious evils in Job produces parody, but only
because the existential disturbance from slight toothaches is so *little*,
not because they have absolutely no inherent existential impact *at all*.'

My reply is that it is sheer dogma to insist that there *must* be existential impact in slight toothaches and the like when people do not evince
the slightest sign of it. They do, of course, complain about discomfort
and inconvenience, but that is a different matter. Indeed we call such
things 'discomforts' and 'inconveniences' precisely to mark them off
from the domain of the existential, the domain of that which threatens
our capacity to find meaning in the world, to respond to it as something
to be welcomed and celebrated with gratitude and love and so on. The
danger here of committing a sorites fallacy in insisting that there *has*
to be existential continuity is obvious. As with so many other things,
a certain critical mass will produce a new phenomenon: in this case,
existential significance. A little bit of evil, a little bit of belief, a little bit

of meaning, a little bit of trauma: this will not do. A threshold must be passed, and blemishes are one name for things that don't pass it. And passing that threshold is the criterion for counting against God.

Still, perhaps this objection can be improved by appealing to a central image of God: God as loving father. The improved version would go like this. Surely slight toothaches and their ilk *do* count against the goodness (and so the existence) of God when we remember that he is, or is analogous to, a loving human parent. If my child had a slight toothache, or uncomfortable stones in their shoes, or some other minor irritation, and yet having the power to repair this, and there being no greater good realised by permitting the irritation to continue, I did nothing to repair it, then surely I would be open to criticism in having failed to be a properly loving parent: not very much, perhaps, but *some* at least. Of course, as a human being, I may have excuses. My attention might be distracted, or perhaps my child's ill-behaviour provokes a momentary irritation in me, and I do not hasten to their aid. Or perhaps I just have better things to do, not better for the universe as a whole necessarily, but better for me at the moment, and the minor irritation can wait. But God has no such excuses. He, after all, suffers no defects of memory or attention, and no limitations on his knowledge or power. Being omnipotent he can do any number of things at once, and always without cost (the economics of opportunity cost do not apply to God). For God, there is no excuse. If this is right, then it is an irrelevant truth of psychology that slight toothaches do not awaken our sense of evil, or do not lead believers to doubt God's love. That merely shows the limits of human attention or rationality. But, morally, God is on the hook. However slightly he misses the mark, he nonetheless cannot be the *perfectly* loving father he is supposed to be.[7]

At one level, my response to this is to rely on what I have already argued. People's faith in God as loving father simply is not affected by blemishes: in contrast to a human father, they do not hold such blemishes against the loving fatherhood of God. 'That just shows they are irrational, ignoring inconsistency in their belief system.' But it is not just that they *do not* hold such blemishes against God: they *cannot*, on pain of producing a parody of serious faith. That is very different from the situation where the failure to hold something against God is the product of individual psychology, a case where the charge of irrationality might have real force. In this case, the *conceptual* nature of not holding blemishes against God – the religious impossibility of doing so, one might say – indicates that the concept of God as loving parent may be different in this respect from the concept of Joseph and Mary as loving parents. My imaginary critic wants to say: 'God and Joseph are both loving fathers in the same sense (they instantiate *the same*, univocal concept, fatherhood); *therefore* if blemishes count against Joseph they count against God, and *therefore* believers are irrational if they don't treat them the same in this respect.' I endorse something close to the reverse of that reasoning. I argue: 'Since believers cannot (on pain of parody) treat God and Joseph alike in this respect, *therefore* there is no irrationality in counting blemishes against Joseph but not against God, and *therefore* the concept of father is not exactly the same in both cases.' Both arguments are valid, but mine has a stronger claim to being sound, for its first premise is far more plausible than the first premise of the corresponding argument, being supported by all the reasoning of this chapter. In contrast, the premise of my critic's argument is distinctly dubious. We really should not be surprised at the idea that God's father-hood and human fatherhood differ in this respect. After all, it *is* only an analogy or metaphor. God is *like* a loving father (or *vice versa*) – in certain respects. But not in others: he does not produce his children bio-logically, he has no sex, he does not (literally) cradle them in his arms or walk them to school or bind their wounds, and so on. This is simply another respect in which the analogy is not to be taken too strictly.

## 5. Loving father or cosmic social planner?

The analogy between God and human parents is of great importance. Historically, the Christian understanding of God is pervaded with images of parental and familial love. But far from supporting Swinburne's posi-tion, that imagery tells powerfully against it.

Swinburne's imaginary world – in which only pleasures and pains exist – is not one in which human beings – by which I mean, *inter alia*, creatures capable of love, conscience, fidelity and courage, rather than merely particularly intelligent primates – could exist. So let's abandon Swinburne's restriction of goods and evils to pleasures and pains and allow the whole gamut, including human existence in my sense, but suppose that every *creatable* world with good and evil is one in which *the quantity of good needed to justify the evil in the world falls short by the measure of the slightest toothache*.[8] If we knew our world was one of these worlds, then we would have Swinburne's 'conclusive evidence' that God does not exist. This scenario I have imagined puts sharply in focus the central question: can something so momentous as God's existence turn on something so trivial? Would God create a world with good and evil *at all* if the world had to be as I stipulate? Since creating

a world without any good and evil (or not creating anything) constitutes an improvement over any world he might create with good and
evil by the margin of the slightest toothache, Swinburne must answer
*no*: his greater good theodicy demands that answer. But if God refrains
from creating a world with good and evil, then he refrains from creating a world with human beings in it: all on account of an amount of
evil equivalent to the slightest toothache. Why on earth should such a
power of veto over creation be granted to something as insignificant as
a slight toothache? Such a veto is inconsistent with the central point of
understanding God's relationship to us on the analogy of human parents and their children.

Here we have a more acute variant of Ahern's absurdity, discussed
in Chapter 1, of putting an end to our world because of the evil in it.
Far from being admirable on account of their parental love, a human
couple who would refrain from conceiving a child because its life would
inescapably contain more evil than good by the margin of a slight
toothache – parents who *would* conceive the child *but* for the toothache – would scarcely be *intelligible* to us. What sort of desire for a child
is it that can be deterred by such a trifling thing? It can hardly be called
anything we would recognise as love. The point here is *conceptual*. I am
not making any moral criticism of this couple. Such criticism would
be misplaced, for the real issue is recognising their stance as a *normal
human* one – hence as an intelligible object of praise or criticism – in
the first place. It follows that slight toothaches do not have the power
to disprove the existence of God. (To be absolutely clear: I am supposing it is *the toothache* that makes the difference to these parents, not any
serious evil the child would suffer. *Ex hypothesi*, that serious evil does
not deter them (because it is balanced out by greater good) but the addition to that balance of an (unbalanced-out) slight toothache does. I am
of course assuming that the parents do not have the option of creating
their child without the toothache or something worse.)

What sense can we make of a love that would refrain from conception – from creation – on the basis of a slight toothache? More than
that, what sense can we make of a love that would even *hesitate* in the
face of that toothache, or regret having borne a child on account of it?
In which case, once again, we can make no sense of blemishes even
*counting* against the act of creation. There is a vast difference between a
parental love intimidated from conceiving or creating by slight toothaches and a love which unjustifiably ignores such toothaches (but not
serious evils) when it can do something about them short of refraining
from creation. The latter may tarnish someone's love to the point of

callousness, but so long as the imminent threat of serious evil would reawaken this parent's love, and an awareness of its responsibilities, this is not inconsistent with that love existing. But to postulate a parental love that shrinks from conception in the face of slight toothaches strangles the very idea of such a love at its root.

Thus, *pace* Swinburne and others, unredeemed trivialities such as slight toothaches do not raise an intellectual threat to the goodness of God construed as the goodness of a loving parent. A God who would refrain from creating on the basis that he cannot avoid evil winning over good by one slight toothache would be a strangely schizoid being. On the one hand he will create a world with appalling evils for his children if only they are balanced by greater goods, but on the other hand he will refrain from creating if, overall, there is a surplus of evil by so little as the slightest toothache. The result is a God *incapable of love*. Considered from the point of view of his paralysis in the face of toothaches he would not be a *good* parent so much as a nervous, mollycoddling one. Or he might be a father interested in spotless 'trophy' children to gratify his own ego, or someone with a strange fetish for eliminating discomfort. Considered from the conflicting perspective of his readiness to tolerate all manner of evils if only they secure greater goods, God would, at best, be someone with the sort of cool beneficence prized in consequentialism's ideally sympathetic observer, as if he were, as I said in the first chapter, a sort of cosmic civil engineer or social planner, crunching the numbers of cost/benefit analysis, seeking to achieve a goal with maximum efficiency. All of this is far removed from a God of love in the sense that really matters to all our lives, and which is central to Christianity, the love of a God who became a man and suffered and died on the Cross to defeat suffering, death and evil.

# 4
# The God of Love

## 1. Creative love, human and divine

The previous chapter argued that drawing an analogy between God and human parents actively undermined the claims of Swinburne and others about the in-principle relevance to God's existence of blemishes in the world such as the slightest toothache. It also argued that if God created the world from a love akin to human parental love, then he cannot be a God of the sort we find in theodicy, who would not refrain from creating the world with horrors (at least) as terrible as those of the actual world so long as they are outweighed by greater goods, but who would resile from creation on account of evil outweighing good by the margin of the slightest toothache. In this chapter I argue that the parental love image of God points us towards still more radical ideas. If the argument of Chapter 1 were the last word on the topic of God and evil, God might very well be dead. In this chapter I argue that the parental love image of God offers the believer a possible response both to standard atheology and to Karamazov's challenge: a response in the form of an appeal to love. The response does not ultimately succeed so long as we retain an anthropomorphic conception of God as an immaterial agent, a being who performs loving acts. It does succeed once we amend the analogy between God and human parents to acknowledge that while human parental love is indeed akin to divine love, this is not because both are instances of an agent performing loving acts. Rather in God there is no distinction between his nature and his action. He *is* love itself, and particular human parental loves (and others) are (imperfect) instantiations of that love. But I shall leave this development of the argument until the next chapter. In this chapter, working for the present within an anthropomorphic understanding of the analogy, I shall explore how the appeal to love can open up a rival route out of the problem of evil to that offered by theodicy. The appeal concedes that Karamazov's challenge is fatal to the moral arguments of theodicy. It recognises that just as Ivan's compassionate indignation is an attack on God that breaks radically from the terms of that tradition, so a defence of God must also make that radical break. The debate between greater good atheology and greater good theodicy is reconfigured as a debate between morality and love, between an approach to the problem which brings God under moral judgement and an approach which (for the believer) does not. This in turn is a central plank in a wider reconfiguration of the problem of evil as what I shall call an *existential* problem, rather than an *impersonal* problem. This reconfigured debate is a conflict of two incommensurable worldviews.

This section of the chapter sets out the basics of the appeal to love making use of the analogy between God and human parents. Love is contrasted with morality in general, and in particular the greater good morality of atheology and theodicy and Ivan Karamazov's morality of compassionate indignation. In Section 2 I clarify the radical difference between the old and the new forms of the debate over the problem of evil. There are two dimensions to this. The first is that in the old debate the believer submits God to moral judgement and judges him acquitted, but in the new debate the believer, in the name of love, exempts God from moral judgement. The second dimension, a consequence of this appeal to love, is the distinction between the old form of the debate as a technical and impersonal one and the new form as an existential one. This distinction is elucidated in terms of three concepts: *objectification*, *expertise* and *authenticity*. The final, third section introduces another, fourth crucial concept for the impersonal/existential distinction – the failure of what moral philosophers call the *universalisability* of moral judgements – and raises the suggestion that there is no single correct conclusion to the reconfigured problem of evil, a conclusion the same for everyone, but that belief may be the required position for some people and disbelief the required position for others, even though neither is at intellectual or moral fault. I also elucidate here the basic sense in which I contrast *love* with *morality*. Morality – as understood by most moral philosophers, and certainly by atheologists and theodicists – is committed to universalisability. So too is Ivan Karamazov's morality of compassionate indignation, albeit (as I shall explain) in an importantly different sense. Love in contrast – the kind of love I have in mind, and in the context of the problem of evil – is free of universalisable commitments.

The image of God as a loving father, akin to a human parent, can perhaps explain why the believer does not *have* to yield their faith in the face of serious evil on pain of violating what I shall call *the conditions of ideal judgement*. Since this notion is important to the argument in the rest of the book, I shall briefly describe it here. The conditions of ideal judgement are those under which a human judgement is as good as any human judgement can be. They are conditions that any human agent should, to the limits of their ability and opportunity, try to fulfil (though not all of them are relevant to every judgement). The conditions are divided into three categories. In the first category, agents should try to ensure they have all the correct (relevant) factual information, that they are rational and that they reason logically. A lot of things go into this category, including scientific knowledge and expertise as well as other forms of relevant information, such as history and law and various kinds of lay information and testimony, mathematics and scientific method (including criteria for theoretical merit), probabilistic and abductive reasoning as well as deductive reasoning, clarity and precision, and things of a similar ilk. The second category concerns morality and its relation to other values. This includes straightforwardly moral failings: we cannot endorse the morally unconscionable (this is the criterion on which Karamazov's challenge faults theodicy). Equally our judgement cannot, in the name of morality, make demands of everyone regardless of the importance they place on other values in their lives, such as friends, family, personal projects and so on. It cannot, for instance, demand of everyone in the same situation, and regardless of their personal values, that they give away the very shirt off their backs for the sake of the poor.[1] The third category concerns matters that can be called 'existential' in that they require agents to scrutinise their lives and thought for various kinds of subtle human failings of attitude and tone – what we might call a person's spiritual demeanour. Thus, to repeat some examples from the first chapter and add some new ones, we must ask ourselves whether our thought is marred by sentimentality or cynicism, whether it is refreshing as opposed to world-weary, passionate rather than jaded, lucid rather than self-deceived, or serious *versus* flippant. We must learn to distinguish genuine responses from their false simulacrums: love from infatuation, grief from self-pity, courage from bravado, humility from self-abasement. And so I might go on indefinitely, listing 'the concepts by which we appraise people, their lives and their moral stances when we are not philosophising in the professional sense', as I put it in Chapter 1. The terms of appraisal in this category are fundamentally conditioned by what we might call the

'Big Facts' of human life: among others, that we are mortal, that we love and hate, that the world is beautiful yet perishable, and that its existence is a brute, un-rationalisable and unearned contingency. These are truths about the world, but not truths subsumable under the first two categories of judgement and understanding. In short, the conditions of ideal judgement are (i) factual information, rationality and logic; (ii) the avoidance of the morally unconscionable and of unacceptable demands (in the sense defined) made in morality's name at the expense of other values; and (iii) the affective-cum-moral or 'existential' criteria just mentioned. I shall argue that faith in God, in the face of the reality of even the worst evil, can meet all these criteria (so far as the nature of the case allows) as well as the rejection of faith can – and *vice versa*. And moreover – this is the denial of universalisability – that there can be *individual* moral requirements upon people, so that A might be bound in conscience to believe and B to disbelieve. In the present chapter I want, specifically, to present the idea that an unconditional love, of a sort akin to the ideal of human parental love, is great enough to confront and *for some of us* overcome the powerful moral case against God's creation of the world. Perhaps love *can* make a claim on us competitive with, and maybe superior to, both standard moralistic atheology and Ivan Karamazov's compassionate indignation.

Consider parents who face the question of whether they should conceive a child who they know will be handicapped, or who will live, or rather die, probably in infancy, in grim circumstances of poverty and disease: the foreseeable fate of most human children until recent times. They may or may not decide to conceive the child. If they freely and willingly choose to conceive, this need not be because they have done any finer scrutiny of the circumstances and have backed themselves in, against the odds, to make the good outweigh the bad in the child's life; nor need it be that they have deceived themselves that it will. They may proceed in the clear-eyed recognition that any ordinary reckoning would deem the child's life more pain than happiness, and conclude that, impersonally viewed, the child's life will make the world as a whole worse rather than better. There are many reasons why parents have proceeded despite this, but the relevant case is that where the motive is love, a love of the sort that by its nature seeks to create and protect life, and in particular seeks to create life that is itself capable of the same love. (A love that, by the way, would refuse to say of any child's life, however terrible, that it had made the world worse.) The claim of this line of thought is that the parents need not be condemned in such a case, for their love is something serious and weighty enough to set a limit to the authority of the competing moral considerations to determine what we must do, to its power to condemn them. Something similar may go for God. If we are impressed by Ivan Karamazov's critique of theodicy, yet like him are unwilling to give up a faith in God, then in confronting the problem of evil perhaps love can show us that Ivan's compassionate indignation does not finally decide the issue. A moral appraisal unchecked by love might well condemn the actions of the parents, human or divine.[2] Love offers an escape from that condemnation.

Both love and morality – having in mind as morality both greater good atheology and Ivan Karamazov's compassionate indignation – have important claims on us. That is why there is a *problem* of (serious) evil. Morality is, so to speak, the *advocatus diaboli*, putting the case against the parents and against God, and if they are to exonerate themselves, then as far as morality is concerned it must be on morality's terms. But, the present line of thought goes, in the light of love we may acknowledge the force of the case against the parents and against God and, *without* claiming any kind of rationale other than love itself, withhold the condemnation, on the ground that, terrible as the consequences of the parents' action might be, they acted from a love the claim of which on the human heart we cannot deny or disparage. Anyone who takes this stance must (unless 'good' is taken in a very narrow sense) reject Mackie's principle that a good thing always eliminates evil as far as it can. These human parents have not eliminated certain evils, very serious ones, which they could have eliminated by simply choosing not to conceive (create), and nothing that would move us in the name of morality – greater goods, or anything else – is being appealed to in order to justify this. Yet, the thought goes, we need not condemn them or their act as evil; instead, we may see such a judgement as operating beyond morality's reach. And the parents need not be deficient in love: quite the contrary, they may have an excess of love. Ivan's protest on behalf of the burning children need not be enough for us to condemn God if we find ourselves moved to recognise the authority of his love, something we may be unable to deny without denying love's claim on ourselves. The case *against* the parents – human and divine – appeals to our compassion for the suffering children, while that *for* the parents appeals to our sympathy for the impulse of creative love, and if we *are* the children, to the impulse of a similar love, a love that embraces life, seeking to preserve and renew it, even in terrible circumstances.

Christian believers characteristically picture God as analogous to the human parents in my example. God's nature as love essentially involves creation, and especially creation of beings who are intelligent, morally accountable and themselves capable of love: beings like us. God created the world in an act of love, of which the human act is, at the level of created beings, an echo. In both cases – the human creation of a new child, God's creation of the world – Ivan's compassionate indignation, or the cool moral appraisal of the greater good model, if it is allowed to monopolise the discussion, hides from view the importance of love. Love is a force of nature (in this case a divine force of nature, if that is not a contradiction in terms) so important to us that sometimes it can challenge and over-rule the authority of these other compelling demands.

But isn't the analogy fatally flawed? For if God loves us as my imaginary parents love their child, then surely he will do everything in his power to eliminate the serious evils we suffer, just as human parents characteristically do for their child.[3] The difference is that the human parents are limited in how much evil they can banish, whereas God, being omnipotent, is not. Could God not have created a world with creatures like us, but without evil? I do not believe so. It is one thing for human parents to find a cure for their child's fatal illness. That merely delays the eventual evils, in one form or another, of suffering and death. It is quite another to abolish evil from the world entirely. The latter alters the circumstances of human existence in a fundamental way. My view is that a world with beings capable of love, but containing no serious evil, is not a logical possibility (a much stronger claim than Plantinga's view that it may not be creatable). Vulnerability to evil, serious evil of the sort that can break a person, both physically and morally, is an essential condition for the existence of creatures capable of love. The reader will recall that this was an assumption in my first chapter argument that the God of theodicy is really an impious creature. Unfortunately I do not have space to substantiate such a large claim in this book. As far as the present argument goes, however, I do not need to, since in the next chapter I shall develop a very different argument, denying the anthropomorphic conception of God as a supremely powerful, immaterial agent, to deal with this objection in another way.

## 2. A reconfigured debate: from the impersonal to the existential

It is important to emphasise how sharply this position differs from the orthodox greater good defence of God. The standard position is that in creating a world with human beings God creates something of such value (at least if a post-mortem beatitude is included as individual compensation) that it outweighs the evils involved (or that, if it does not, then the risk God runs of this not being so – due to human free will, say – does not exceed some moral limit). We have seen that Karamazov's challenge undermines this position. The argument I am exploring here is that there might be an alternative to both this approach *and* Ivan Karamazov's compassionate indignation. The alternative is to see God as creating the world from love.

Ivan's refusal to consider putting any price on the lives of children clearly repudiates the cost/benefit methodology of the mainstream debate. Likewise love is not some *additional factor* to be thrown onto one side of the scales, another greater good that tips the balance in favour of conceiving a child or creating the world. The claim is that love can transcend that mode of thought, that it can make a claim on us quite independently of it. It has the power to set aside that sort of justification and to lead us to act regardless of it and even in the face of it. We are of course still acting for the sake of the good of giving life to the beloved, but that does not mean we have to regard that life as a 'greater good' in the sense of something that morally justifies the act of creation. Just as Ivan's appeal to compassion does not depend on an absence of greater goods, as if their presence would satisfy the demands of compassion (as we saw in Chapter 1, Ivan makes it clear that even the existence of a massively outweighing eternal beatitude would not placate him), so too the appeal to love is not an appeal to the existence of such goods: their existence is neither necessary nor sufficient for the force of that appeal.

But it is not just greater good morality that I want to contrast love with. As we have seen, love may also defeat moral appeals to compassionate indignation such as Ivan's refusal to countenance the exchange of the lives of children for greater goods. It can also overcome Kantian or other deontological attempts to mandate Ivan's stand. Equally it can overcome virtue-ethical demands to act in a way that instantiates compassion or beneficence or realises human flourishing. Of course, one can always speak about love as itself a kind of morality. Such speech tends to assimilate love to impersonal beneficence. But even if it did not, in the present context the move is a verbal one that hides from view the important truth that love rivals and perhaps sometimes defeats the forms of justification most commonly recognised by philosophers as *moral*.

There are many kinds of love. My emphasis is on the kind of which the love of human parents for their children is a prime example. This includes their passion to create, protect and enjoy new life, often even in, and in defiance of, terrible circumstances; the ideal of an unconditional love for their child that is (tenuously) normative in many human cultures, and certainly those influenced by Christianity; the bounty they gratuitously lavish on their child if they can; and the grief and sorrow they suffer if the child is harmed or lost. Of course (*ceteris paribus*) this love includes beneficence towards the child, and would be unrecognisable as love without that. But even though we sometimes speak of beneficence as a kind of love, it does not require love in the parental sense and that leaves room for a contrast between love and beneficence. Equally compassion can exist without love in my sense and that leaves room for a contrast between love and Ivan's compassion for the burning children. Some readers may still find my distinction between love and morality to be artificial and aver that a common form of justification underlies both. I shall elucidate properly the point of these contrasts, and of the contrast with morality generally, in the last section of this chapter.

For the remainder of this section I want to show how the introduction of love into the debate on God's side transforms it. In what ways? The first dimension is that in the transformed debate believers do not bring God under moral judgement as in the traditional debate (acquitting him, while unbelievers condemn him). Instead, for them, the importance of love puts God's action in creating the world beyond the jurisdiction of morality. The gist of the second dimension is that the traditional debate between atheologists and theodicists embodies an *impersonal* approach to the problem of evil, an approach encapsulated in the distinction between the intellectual problem of evil and the existential problem, and the disowning of the latter by philosophers which we noted in Chapter 2. The contrasting understanding of the problem as a decision between compassion and love is distinguished by construing the decision as an *existential* one, in opposition to the impersonal understanding.

The impersonal and existential conceptions are distinguished by their opposing stances on three issues, which I call, respectively *objectification*, *expertise* and *authenticity*. The impersonal conception embraces objectification and expertise and denies the need for authenticity. The existential conception takes the opposing attitudes in ways I shall explain. The mainstream analytical literature on the problem of evil would be unrecognisable without its *de facto* commitment to the three defining stances of impersonality. I shall expound them in order.

## Objectification embraced

The mainstream literature seeks, in principle, a universally correct conclusion to the problem of evil, a conclusion all properly informed and
rational agents would agree on, at least under ideal conditions or at the
limit of inquiry. As I noted in Chapter 1, the correct conclusion may
of course be a suspension of judgement, or a judgement of probability, or the acknowledgement that each of a range of conclusions, even
ones inconsistent with one another, is permissible. Thus, strictly speak-
ing, the correct conclusion is not necessarily a *solution*, so I shall write
of a single, correct *resolution* or *conclusion*. But whatever conclusion is
reached, it is *mandatory* on *all* ideally rational and properly informed
beings; it is just the conclusion such ideal thinkers would converge on.

The literature embodies a *thin* conception of the resources a being
needs to reach this correct judgement on the problem of evil. It assumes
that the conditions of ideal judgement sufficient for a thinker (with
enough ability and time etc.) to solve the problem consist, for the most
part, in those belonging to my first category of such conditions: being
(relevantly) factually informed, being rational and being sufficiently
proficient in the techniques of logical reasoning – the sort of reasoning
exemplified in journals of analytic philosophy. There is also a moral
requirement, but of a strikingly minimal sort. Bruce Langtry, in a recent
state-of-the-art book on the problem of evil written from the mainstream perspective, presents a similar picture:

> Contemporary philosophical work on the problem of evil aims to
> refute certain objections to the existence of God based on evil, and
> to explain why God allows, or might allow, so much evil to exist.
> Theodicy and attacks on specific attempts in theodicy are largely
> carried out employing methods used in other areas of philosophy
> in the broad analytical tradition: fairly sophisticated resources from
> metaphysics, epistemology, and logic, along with fairly elementary
> moral philosophy. (Langtry 2008, pp. 5–6)

The tendency in practice is to assume a *de facto* greater good ethic, qualified by a concern for justice in the form of post-mortem compensation
for individual victims of evil. The compensation generally appears as a
caveat ('*if* you create, then you must compensate any victims') and the
greater good element is the consequentialist core of the theory, providing the central rationale for creation in the first place (this distinction
is explicit in Plantinga 2004). This consequentialist rationale is rarely
defended, a *de facto* assumption of the debate. Philosophical discussion

of the problem of evil focuses overwhelmingly on logical technique, the skill most prized in academic philosophy generally, and morally it is premised on a greater good consequentialism that is for the most part simply taken for granted.

That discussion is a *technical* practice, one in which it is possible to participate seriously only if one is trained in its specialised methods. Even the consequentialism preferred in the literature is the moral philosophy most amenable to an impersonal treatment. That fact, together with the largely unargued assumption of it, is one reason why there is no contradiction between saying that the traditional debate puts God under moral judgement *and* that it is an impersonal and technical debate. There are impersonal ways of treating morality, and central to them is the doctrine of universalisability, which I come to in the next section.

That the word 'technical' is appropriate for the thin intellectual resources of factual information, rationality and logical reasoning (as I expanded on these in Section 1) is supported by the fact that they are precisely the resources deployed in fields that are indisputably technical: science, law (or at least black-letter law), medicine, engineering, mathematics and so on. I call them 'thin' by dint of what they do *not* include: the moral and, more importantly, the existential conditions of ideal judgement. If the relevant specialist prescribes a medicine, drafts a contract or designs a bridge, it does not make sense to ask whether their thought, work and product are sentimental or cynical, or jaded or self-aggrandising, or anything like that.[4] When they propose resolutions to problems in the course of their professional work – what are the effects of a drug, whether a contract is valid, what types of materials and design are needed for a bridge to carry certain weights – they do not need to ask themselves whether the answer is one that could be endorsed by someone who was frivolous or living a lie, or whether it is the answer a serious person, living truthfully, could give. A frivolous lawyer or doctor or engineer should give the same answer to these problems as a serious one, if they are as competent. They do not need to scrutinise their answers to be sure they have not confused love with infatuation, or grief with self-pity, and so on. Or, more exactly, these sorts of criteria do not enter into the *content* of their thinking and their work, *qua* doctor, lawyer or engineer. One does not appraise their work, or the thinking that has gone into it, by these criteria. True, one may, for example, praise or criticise them for conscientiousness or laziness in the execution of their briefs, or they may examine themselves to see whether they are living by the ideals of their profession or are merely careerists. But these virtues and vices have only an external, *causal* effect on the resulting drug, contract or bridge, or on the thought and work that produce them. They are not qualities of that thought, work or final product themselves, not *criteria in terms of which the thought, work or product is appraised*. One can appraise these things without knowing anything about the people concerned. A good bridge is a good bridge even if designed by a machine.[5]

What goes for these uncontroversially technical specialisms goes for any other knowledge-claiming intellectual activity that aspires to limit itself to the intellectual resources of factual information, rationality, logical reasoning, scientific method, causal explanation and their ilk. The affective-cum-moral or 'existential' criteria I have been mentioning, the ones belonging to the last category of ideal judgement, are, by and large, not relevant, except perhaps causally in some cases, to the resolution of these problems. They are not among the criteria by which we appraise proposed resolutions, criteria that must be satisfied for a proposed resolution to be correct. In contrast, compare appraising poetry, music or a human life. These are the contexts in which these criteria have their home. The problem of evil is one of these contexts. I appealed to these criteria implicitly in the previous chapter, for example in the Job parody.[6]

Technical truth and technical judgement can be called *objectifying* in that the ideal of truth and judgement they embody is one that aspires to an Archimedean point, a point external to human reactions and practices. This is a perspective from which are irrelevant not merely the concerns of particular individuals, but distinctively human concerns in general, thus rendering the existential criteria by which human lives are appraised irrelevant too. The ideal is austere, but its severity is in some degree warmed by the understandable hope – a deep yearning of the mind, or at least for a certain cast of mind that appeals to nearly everyone in some mood – for a *neutral* ground or method in the light of which our disagreements can be 'rationally' resolved. In our age science is the epitome of this objectifying ideal of knowledge. It is characteristic of the elevation of the objectifying ideal to cast suspicion on claims to truth which rely on wider resources, wider criteria of appraisal, than factual information, rationality and logical reasoning (these last taken to be minimal enough to escape the human-centeredness which holds us back from achieving the Archimedean view). Whether that means the latter claims are at best inferior forms of truth, or not forms of it at all, or whether they are merely *different* forms – not objectifying ones – becomes a much-debated issue. (We might ask: is the claim that objectifying truth is truth *simpliciter* more than a rhetorical dressing up of the tautology that objectifying truth is *objectifying* truth? See Chapter 6.) Certainly other truth claims proceed differently from objectifying ones. They include forms of non-argumentative persuasion – for example, appeals to conscience or compassion, perhaps enabled by readings of literature or poetry – which from a rigorously objectifying perspective might look like propaganda or mere emoting, but which, their champions contend, contain their own rich and subtle forms of understanding.

Anyhow, however this may be, the present point is that mainstream analytic discussion of the problem of evil is objectifying in the sense outlined.

### Expertise embraced

In the proper exercise of a technical skill – that of medicine, law or engineering, say – it does not matter *who* the practitioner is, so long as they are properly trained. So far as determining the truth of the matter goes in such fields *it does not matter who it is that makes the judgement*, for all properly trained judges will think alike and (under ideal conditions) will reach the same conclusion. Thus any properly trained practitioner is substitutable for another. This is clearly an important sense in which the nature of thought in objectifying, technical practice is impersonal. The sorts of skills and resources that I have said are widely taken to be sufficient by philosophers to resolve the problem of evil – factual information, rationality and logical reasoning (plus the consequentialist rationale with a compensation caveat) – are impersonal in this sense. To appraise the arguments of the journals it does not matter who I am, only that I possess the relevant skills.

So there is no room in objectifying matters for the influence of any perception or choice that is distinctive of me (or you, or whomever), no room for giving a crucial role in thought to anything that might be called an *individual* sensibility or responsiveness, a *personal* judgement in the sense of one that is binding on me but not on others confronted with the same problem.[7] This is assumed (in practice) to be as true for judging the problem of evil as for prescribing medicine, drawing up a contract or designing a bridge. But if any properly trained practitioner is substitutable for another in these objectifying matters, then those lacking the requisite skill and unable or lacking the opportunity to acquire it are permitted to rely on those who do have the skill: the *layperson* relies on the *expert*. Thus it is that we rely on doctors, lawyers and engineers. The rationale for such reliance is that the layperson cannot reasonably be expected to possess or acquire the relevant skill or knowledge. (For just that reason there may even be an obligation of such reliance.) The relevant experts for the problem of evil are of course academic philosophers of religion. And if getting at the truth of the problem of evil really requires the level of technical expertise displayed in the professional literature, then the case for laypeople relying on philosophical experts is overwhelming – most volumes of law are more readily comprehensible by the layperson than, say, the arguments of Alvin Plantinga.

Lay reliance on expertise normally confers on the layperson a sort of insurance against responsibility for acting on mistaken expert advice. To say laypeople cannot reasonably be expected to possess or acquire the relevant skill or knowledge is to say, among other things, that they cannot reasonably be *blamed* for relying on expert advice even if that advice is mistaken and leads to disastrous consequences. The laity are, in general, deemed to have acquitted their responsibilities on technical matters (matters they have a lay status in) if they have taken appropriate care to ensure the expert they rely on is appropriately trained and conscientious. The layperson is entitled to say: 'I am immune from responsibility: I have passed it to the expert.' They can legitimately say, when things go wrong: 'I consulted the best expert advice. I could do no more, for the matters were technical ones beyond my knowledge. I am not to blame.' If the problem of evil is a matter of objectifying technical expertise, as many philosophers assume, then that expertise looks as though it will confer insurance on the laity who rely on advice from the experts.

But in the case of the problem of evil there is perhaps reason to doubt that the (supposed) objectifying nature of the problem entails lay insurance. Discussion of the problem, however technical, unavoidably includes some moral assumption. Mainstream philosophers of religion could argue that on account of this moral assumption they are not committed to lay insurance regarding the problem of evil. Typically, lay insurance does *not* apply to moral matters. If I make a moral mistake, I cannot escape blame or punishment by saying that I relied on the advice of the foremost moral philosophers, or religious gurus or respected sages and elders. I can, and perhaps should, listen to their advice, but I follow it or not with a decision I am answerable for. I cannot pass responsibility to them. That is, our extant practice *assumes there is no insurance on moral issues*. But then, since any stance on the problem of evil includes a moral assumption, it follows that lay insurance through reliance on experts does not apply to the problem of evil, or at least that we have reason to resist applying it.

On the other side, though, there is pressure to apply it. If the answer to the problem, whether it involves moral assumptions or not, requires only impersonal thinking as I have defined it, and such thinking entails lay insurance in wholly non-moral matters, then why should it not entail lay insurance even in matters that *do* involve moral assumptions? (My implicit agenda here is, of course, that the objectifying conception of thought about the problem of evil is in conflict with our extant practice of moral responsibility and that this gives us reason to doubt that conception of the problem. Objectifying thought licenses moral insurance for reliance on expertise; morality does not admit moral insurance for reliance on expertise; therefore objectifying accounts of moral thought are mistaken.) Joe Mintoff has pointed out to me that the inference from objectification to lay insurance is not straightforward. I cannot assume that the only reason we have for our institution of individual-moral-responsibility-without-lay-insurance is the absence of moral expertise due to the non-objectifying nature of moral thought. It may be that in moral matters, their going deep into our lives in a way technical matters do not, we just do expect people to accept responsibility even when they have relied on advice from someone else – and that this is a value we cleave to *regardless* of whether moral thought is objectifying. Moral responsibility might be a technical matter that we expect *everyone* to become expert in, so to speak. But what does this moral responsibility consist in? Central to any account of it that is not gratuitously placed on a Procrustean bed to fit an objectifying perspective are things such as that I am not *blindly* following a rule or principle, of beneficence or honesty or courage or whatever, but that I do so from some understanding of these values and from the right motives. Thus it is important that I am *genuinely* charitable to strangers, or loyal to my friends, or courageous in the face of my hardships and not merely producing an outward imitation of these qualities. But this requires scrutinising my life in the 'existential' way that I described in Section 1 (the last category of ideal judgement). Am I truly charitable, loyal, courageous and so on? And answering those questions requires distinguishing charity from condescension, loyalty from fear of offending others, courage from braggadocio, and so on for all the virtues and related, value-ridden concepts (such as friend, spouse, father, mother, child). But these existential questions are of course just the ones *excluded*, by definition, from objectifying thought, thought which requires only the thin resources of facts, rationality, logical reasoning and so on. However, in that case our institution of moral-responsibility-without-lay-insurance is not correctly understood in objectifying terms. So it cannot be that moral responsibility is an objectifying practice that we expect everyone to become expert in. The appeal to moral responsibility as an explanation for why we do not have lay insurance in moral matters just returns us to the non-objectifying nature of moral matters, the very rival explanation the appeal was meant to dislodge. In the absence of some third suggestion, I am entitled to move from objectification to lay insurance for reliance on experts, specifically from the assumption that the problem of evil is an objectifying matter to the conclusion that it licenses lay insurance through reliance on philosophers of religion, the relevant experts.

The stance of the impersonal conception on the third topic, authenticity, is more conveniently explained after expounding the existential conception of thought in terms of objectification and expertise, so I shall postpone it until then. In the meantime we can sum progress so far by saying that thought about the problem of evil in the traditional mode of atheology *versus* theodicy, in virtue of supposedly being a technical problem, is *impersonal* in the sense of being objectifying and a matter of expertise (including lay insurance). The claim of philosophers to objectifying expertise concerning the problem of evil is not only evident in practice, but sanctioned and rationalised by the doctrine that the problem of evil they examine is a *cognitive* or *intellectual* problem, to which expertise is essential and sufficient for any progress that can be made, and not an *existential* problem, to which expertise (at least of this sort) is not (or not very) relevant and certainly not sufficient. As I explained in Chapter 2, that doctrine is ubiquitous in the literature.

As I have said the chief intellectual resources brought to bear on the problem of evil by mainstream analytical philosophy are the technical ones of factual information, rationality and logical reasoning, requiring specialised training to a high degree of expertise. Thus viewed, the problem of evil is an impersonal one. In contrast consider again my scenario, from Section 1 of this chapter, where, by analogy with the case of human parents and children, a person must choose between the case against God's creating a human world, a case most forcefully expressed in Ivan Karamazov's compassionate indignation, and the love implicit in that creative act. Love, I have said, can defeat that case. However, my focus at the moment is not on that, but on the nature of the choice. That choice defies both the elements which defined impersonality. Again, consider them in order.

### Objectification repudiated

A judgement is objectifying, recall, if the criteria for its appraisal are the thin ones of factual information, rationality and logic, ones that aspire to the impersonal Archimedean point and so do not include the existential criteria which belong to the final category of ideal judgement, and with which (among others) we typically evaluate human lives and the arts. Judgement on the problem of evil is taken to be largely objectifying in the literature on that problem. But when judgement on the problem of evil is seen as addressing the competing claims of compassion and love, it is freed from the objectifying constraint by acknowledging (i) the relevance of moral appraisal that goes beyond the automatic adoption of the greater good model, and (ii) the relevance of what I have called 'existential' criteria. I shall concentrate on the latter.

Consider yet again the human parent whose children might, given the conditions of their existence, plausibly protest to the parent for having brought them into the world, assuming circumstances in which the parent could have spared the children only by not conceiving them at all. As I observed in Section 1, even today in many parts of the world children have grounds (poverty, disease) on which they might plausibly reproach their parents just for having conceived and borne them. I say 'might' because it rarely happens. Why not? It is not enough of an explanation that the child would supposedly be in a hypocritical position if they made the complaint but did not commit suicide, nor that their conditions perhaps do not seem as bad to them as they do to people in more fortunate circumstances (what about children born in zones of regular famine and war?). The real explanation is that the children naturally love their human parents, and understand and sympathise with the parents' motive, a motive which, as I put it above, the children cannot disparage without disparaging something important inside themselves. Rarely then do they feel indignation against their parents just on account of having been conceived and borne. Rather, if there is indignation, it is directed at God. For people concerned about God at all, and deeply affected by evil whether as victim or witness or both, a real struggle between love and indignation (sometimes resentful, sometimes compassionate, sometimes just terrified, or all of these) can and often does exist. The issue for someone facing doubt about faith in God on account of evil is whether they can, consistently with the conditions of ideal judgement, be released from the indignation they feel; whether they can, consistently with the conditions of ideal judgement, accept the love on offer to them and love in return; or whether, instead, that love must be repudiated in the name of the suffering children, in the manner of Ivan Karamazov. But there is no adequate answer to this to which the following sorts of questions are not relevant. Can one accept this love without being unfaithful to the suffering children? Is a compassionate concern for them which requires repudiating that love inescapably a sort of histrionic self-dramatisation – so that these existential criteria also apply to Ivan's compassionate indignation? Is talk of love in this context inescapably maudlin or sentimental? And so on. That is, an agent in this situation must, in order to resolve the problem, ask questions whose answers are appraised by criteria that include the sort of existential concepts that the treatment of the problem of evil as an objectifying problem – an intellectual one, not a personal or existential one – is designed to exclude.

In short, on the existential conception, the problem of evil, understood as a decision between compassion and love, is not characterised by the first element of impersonal thought, objectification. Or, put positively, it sees thought about the problem as needing to be existential in the sense of requiring appraisal by the sort of existential concepts I have given examples of, those from the final category of ideal judgement, concepts essential to the evaluation of human lives rather than impersonal, technical problems.

### Expertise repudiated

Objectifying problems are matters of expertise because the thin resources sufficient to deal with them do not admit of individuals being bound to different judgements. Proper thinkers will think alike and reach the same, universally valid conclusion, so that in principle I can hand a technical problem I have over to someone else to solve for me. And if I lack the relevant technical skill, if I am a layperson in some technical matter, then I am not only permitted but arguably obligated to hand the problem over to someone who has mastered that skill: the expert. In return I enjoy insurance against moral accountability for acting on the expert's advice. The mainstream literature on the problem of evil treats that problem as if it were a technical problem and a matter of expertise.

But this is not true of the problem once it is seen as a clash between compassion and love. The decision a person must make between love on the one hand and Ivan Karamazov's compassionate indignation on the other is not a technical decision in the sense defined earlier. What are crucial are the existential criteria by which someone must assess the seriousness and truthfulness of possible responses to evil. Consequently, there is no moral insurance for anyone who relies on the expertise philosophers have in technical forms of thought. If my response to evil is insular and flippant, it is no defence to say that I relied on the advice of the most distinguished philosophers of religion.

But must one not also address the complex technical arguments of the philosophical atheologists, those of Mackie and Rowe, for example? No. If their conclusions do not follow from their premises, then it will not matter if their arguments are ignored by everyone. On the other hand, if they do, it will not matter either, *provided* that the appeal to love really does transform the debate in the way I have claimed. My claim is simply that the evils which, as such atheological arguments show, would count fatally against God in the absence of an appeal to love no longer need do so once love is appealed to. The layperson has a general reason for thinking that those evils, even if predominant or gratuitous, are not necessarily the last word on the matter, a general reason for rejecting both the greater good approach of the academic atheological literature and the compassionate indignation of Ivan Karamazov.[8]

Now I come to the third factor separating the personal and impersonal conceptions.

## Authenticity

The existential (as opposed to objectifying) view of thought about the problem of evil does not mean that a person can see the truth of the problem only if they manage to overcome the various struggles with evil in their own life – only, for example, if they can find peace and love God without reservation. Bringing an existential understanding to a problem, even a successful (truth-finding) understanding, does not translate seamlessly into practical results in one's own life. That is a germ of truth in the intellectual/existential distinction. But the existential nature of the problem as I have elucidated it does mean that one cannot possess the truth of the problem, really understand that truth and *own* it as a truth one stands by, unless one has in a sense tested that truth in one's own life. The point is not just that one cannot really understand a problem and the answer to it unless one has thought it through for oneself (as opposed to taking the answer on trust from an expert); that is equally true for technical problems. The point is that understanding and owning the truth of the problem of evil requires some attempt to live out in your own life what the truth involves. This is not true for technical problems. I can understand how a drug works by testing it on others as well as by testing it on myself. Cutting a suit is a technical problem but it is only the contingent fact that I do not have a conveniently available identical twin which requires the suit be fitted on *me*. I can of course be told the truth by someone, or read it in a book. I can parrot 'love defeats resentment', but without some testing of it in my life that enables me to say it wholeheartedly, to say it *authentically* as something I seriously mean and will risk something on, then my understanding is feeble and my 'belief' merely nominal (the word 'faith', more appropriate here perhaps, already connotes such willingness to risk in a way that the more anodyne 'belief' does not). I have been told that R. M. Hare once remarked that having been a prisoner of war of the Japanese did not give him the right to talk nonsense about ethics. That is true. No one is exempted from any of the criteria of ideal judgement. But that does not mean that life experience is irrelevant or unnecessary (or only causally and contingently so). And I mean *one's own* life experience. Of course we must learn from the experience of others, and from vividly imagined fiction. But, no matter how inspiring, insightful or true the testimony of others, it is hard to see how what someone takes from it avoids remaining second-hand – in the extreme case, merely parroting or plagiarism, the antithesis of serious thought and understanding – unless it is in some degree (and obviously this *is* a matter of degree) and in some way tested in the person's own life. An authentic belief is one that I find 'works' for me, is what I am able to live with truthfully in the whole of my life, not just something I might assert in a seminar room or in a paper and then forget about. In the context of the reconfigured problem of evil this is as true for judging that compassionate indignation for the burning children defeats love as it is for judging the reverse.

The forms this self-examination might take don't admit of any simple summary. But examples might be such things as whether one can continue to pray without a sense of emptiness and mere routine, or whether one could speak of God's love to those victims of evil, the burning children, without finding one's words crumbling into mere cliché under the weight of a sense of hypocrisy or fatuousness. This does not mean that I *will* do these things or even that I *can* – life may defeat me in all sorts of ways: fear, inertia and many others – but, in the absence of that, I do need at least to imagine myself seriously able to do these things for me to find out that *this* is, so to speak, who *I* am: someone who is under a requirement to live like this, even if I do not. What would distinguish that imagining from mere reverie or wish-fulfilment might be a sense of sorrow or shame at my failure to put my belief into action in my life, these responses in turn needing to be examined for their genuineness: that they are not really self-pity or histrionics or something else. (This is all a way of illustrating the thought: genuine belief here requires being lived out unless there is a special explanation otherwise.) Thus, authenticity is not just psychological. It is sensitive to the existential criteria of evaluation, and a person can be quite mistaken about their own authenticity. Authenticity expresses the truth that there is no applying those criteria that is not applying them *in* one's life, finding what is genuine love or courage or patience, and what merely imitates them, by finding what one is willing to risk one's life on regarding as love or courage and so on. Authenticity does not of course guarantee that one is right about one's own moral and existential situation and condition, if only because one may err in some factual matter or in one's reasoning. Authenticity is not sufficient for truth then, but it is necessary in that (outside objectifying and technical matters) a view which *no one* could authentically live by, which no one could (without existential fault) take seriously, cannot be true. What is existentially true for us cannot transcend the possibilities of human life. We cannot coherently say: 'That is a fine ideal of human life, but no one could take it seriously.' And none of us individually can coherently say: 'That is a fine ideal of human life, but (putting aside mere psychological and circumstantial limitations) *I* cannot take it seriously.'[9]

It is also important to this form of learning, however much influenced by the example and testimony of others, that one learns from the adventures and bruises of one's own life, however relatively suburban these may be. One's understanding of love, for example, is different and deeper at 40 than at 20 and different again at 60. But understanding love is not like understanding electronics, even though understanding of electronics can deepen over time too. The difference between a merely nominal or narrowly intellectual understanding and an understanding that reaches far into a person's life is fundamental to love, but admits of only trivial examples (such as plagiarism) in the case of technical matters. It is the difference voiced when we hear a person say: 'I used to talk about love and goodness, but didn't really understand what I was saying. I was just using words for their effect, to sound grand. But now I really see what those words can mean.' And that sort of realisation cannot come without pain in a person's own life. Young people who have confused love with infatuation or with sex, and treated others shabbily on account of it, cannot truly be said to have seen through their mistakes (at least in the absence of some special explanation) unless they are ashamed of or at least embarrassed by their past behaviour. Without this, or something else of the same sort, we rightly say: 'It's just words; they doesn't mean it' or 'They don't know what they are saying.'

The upshot of this discussion of authenticity is that the existential conception of the problem of evil requires that views on the problem be authentic in the sense described, and that the impersonal conception does not. That now puts me in a position to summarise the differences between the two conceptions. Karamazov's challenge and the appeal to love in response to it transform the problem of evil from an impersonal one into an existential one between the rival claims of compassion and love. This section has been concerned with elucidating and contrasting the differences between these two understandings. Much of the reason why this different understanding of the debate is not simply a matter of loading compassion and love onto the scales, a procedure that aspires to be thoroughly objectifying and subject to expertise, should now be clear ('much' because the most important point comes in the next section). The former debate is technical and impersonal in that it is objectifying, a matter of expertise, and does not require authenticity. The latter debate is existential, in that it takes thought about the problem to be existential rather than objectifying, in that it denies expertise and in that it requires authenticity.

The hero of the impersonal conception of thought is the ideally rational agent, who taken to the ideal is released from those human bodily limitations which restrict our knowledge to what our senses can detect, what our brain-confined intellects can figure out, what exists in our local region of space and time, and so on. Morally this hero is a perfectly beneficent and impartial ideal observer, familiar from Chapter 1. But what sort of guide does this ideal give us to morality? Does the ideal observer sympathise equally (and, as it were, at the same time) with everyone's suffering (and feel equally indignant at every act of wrongdoing) regardless of whether they lived a thousand years ago or will live a thousand years hence? If a human being claims to sympathise equally with *all* of humanity and even all of life – with sea slugs and prehistoric animals, and Roman legions and medieval peasants, and people a thousand years hence, as much as with their friends and family – we rightly suspect them of *sentimentality* and even empty posturing. If we attempt to do something like that, the result is not an intensified moral awareness but a flattening out of sympathy, a fanciful dilution of it.[10] Moreover what is relevant to evil for us is not only sympathy, but grief, anger, fear and horror. But if we suppose that we feel these equally for the suffering of everyone who has ever been or even will be, or even for a representative sample, the bogus-ness of it is even more apparent. 'Well, *we* would be sentimental and so on if we tried to be like it, but that is because of our contingent limitations. The ideal observer would not.' True, but that is not because the ideal observer would be lucid or sober. It is because the concepts of sentimentality – or of lucidity or sobriety – have no application to this being. The ideal observer does not exist in the existential domain. Its concepts do indeed apply only to beings 'limited' as we are. But unless we are prepared to dispense with them – with, for example, as I argued in Chapter 1, the sort of love for our children that cannot send them to Auschwitz for the sake of a greater good they will share post-Auschwitz – the fact that we have them and the ideal observer does not means that the ideal observer does not represent an ideal form of our moral capacities, but a stripping away of them. There is no reason a resolution to the problem of evil which satisfies *it* should satisfy *us*.

The existential conception of the problem of evil rejects this idealising away of the human-dependent nature of morality. It can be seen as inviting people to abandon an impersonal ideal of justifiable persuasion (the decisions of the ideal observer) that would, so to speak, box others, or themselves, into an intellectual corner by the sheer force of logic and some 'elementary' moral notions (Langtry, from the earlier quotation) without needing to address how others – or they themselves – respond existentially, with all their human 'limitations', to the situation. Without, say, trying to get someone to see their resentment, sorrow or indignation in a different light, to evoke or awake in them responses of a deeper love, and so on. But this is not something that can be demonstrated (purely) argumentatively from shared criteria, even shared existential criteria – let alone from the meagre resources of factual information, rationality and logic, essential as they are. As Peter Winch once observed, it is more like learning to hear the beauty in a piece of music or see it in a painting or a face: things the ideal observer cannot do because of their dependence on empirically conditioned human (or at least human-like) responses. It is a deep and common philosophical prejudice to think that these forms of understanding and persuasion are legitimate only if they can be provided with independent and impersonal argumentative sanction.

If we think in particular (and anthropomorphically of course) of God addressing his human children, it is a matter less of a debater's strategy than of a lover's overture. It is as if he were to begin a discussion by saying: 'I cannot justify my creating you in a world with such evil in terms of impersonal thought that compels you to accept my actions intellectually regardless of your personal, existential responses. It would be an insult to you even to try. I did it because I love you, and I can only ask you to love me in return.' And as if the child, the beloved, has granted the exoneration, in recognition of a primal force in human life that they cannot gainsay. Or else resists, on the ground of something like Ivan's compassionate indignation, a resistance requiring existential exploration just as much as the parents' appeal to love.

That exploration is not a concession to the emotional pragmatics of parent/child relations, or human limitations generally, the real 'intellectual' justification reserved for other occasions, such as the academic seminar room. The need to address the moral and existential categories of ideal judgement is essential to *any* serious examination of the problem (though no doubt the tone and manner in which one does so vary with the nature of the occasion). The unsettling moral questions (so dramatically raised by Ivan Karamazov) and the existential questions *must* be raised about any resolution to the problem of evil (indeed about any statement of it too). A greater good theodicy, Ivan's compassionate indignation, my appeal to love: all must face these questions. The move to the reconfigured understanding of the problem of evil *is not optional*: it is a necessity because the existential is a necessary part of the conditions of ideal judgement, conditions a judgement must fulfil to be true.

## 3. Universalisability

I said in the previous section that the mainstream literature on the problem of evil assumes, in principle, a universally correct resolution to that problem, a resolution binding on all properly informed and rational agents under ideal conditions or at the limit of inquiry. This is a fourth assumption of the traditional debate, the deep assumption on which the earlier three depend. In contrast again, the reconfigured debate is not committed to this assumption. The assumption is also the key to understanding the contrast I draw between love and morality.

The reconfigured view rejects a universally binding resolution to the problem of evil because it rejects the view that there are universally binding moral and existential requirements on all agents in the same circumstances. On this view, the problem of evil is a dilemma in that equally powerful cases can be made for God and against him, in the sense that the most that can be established as binding on everyone – as universalisable – is that they are permitted to go either way. But that in itself is not radical: the impersonal conception can allow it. What *is* radical is the idea that despite this failure of a single *universal* requirement, a person may be bound by a single *individual* requirement. A may be individually required to believe and B may be individually required to disbelieve. One provocative way to put this is to say that God can be consistent with evil for me because of a requirement that is *true of me*: despite evil, I *must* respond to the world with a loyalty to God's love. And he can be *in*consistent with evil for you because of a requirement that is *true of you*: given evil, you *cannot* morally reconcile yourself to responding to the world in that way. We might differ in what we find to be morally-cum-existentially possible for ourselves. (Notice that in saying it is true of A that they are required to believe and true of B that they are required to disbelieve I am not in any way qualifying the notion of truth. This is no different as far as the notion of truth goes than saying it is true of A that they have brown eyes and true of B that they have blue eyes. This is one reason it is better to say true *of* rather than true *for*.) This is how deep the difference between the two conceptions of thought can go, and it is not surprising that people on either side of this divide largely talk past one another, when they talk at all. To anyone wedded to the first conception, and especially the universalisability of morality, the alternative seems not merely wrong but obscurantist.

Most moral philosophers, and no doubt most philosophers of religion too, assume the universalisability of ethics. This principle says that if two agents are in the same morally relevant circumstances, then they are subject to the same permissions and requirements. As I assumed in the previous section, the resolutions to technical problems are also universalisable (albeit for different reasons perhaps): any given problem has a single resolution, the same for everyone (always allowing that that may be to identify a range of acceptable resolutions, and so on). The problem of evil is both a moral problem in reality and, as construed in analytic philosophy, a technical one (or something close to that), so it is perhaps over-determined that it should have a universalisable resolution. Certainly that is the *de facto* assumption of the mainstream literature. On this view there cannot be one answer to the problem of evil binding for me and another binding for you.

A small minority of philosophers have denied the universalisability of ethics, and I agree with them.[11] The core of this denial, to put the matter positively, is that there exists a species of moral requirement that can vary from person to person. Two people, in the same morally relevant circumstances, may each acquit all the conditions of ideal judgement (as far as the case allows) yet be subject to different moral requirements on the matter confronting them. Typically these are the cases where we use the modalities 'must' and 'cannot' – so-called *moral necessity* or *moral incapacity* – rather than the more intrusive and nagging 'ought' and 'should'. To take Sartre's case of the young Frenchman who must decide whether to fight against the Nazis or remain home to look after his ageing mother, I might feel that I *must* join the fight, while you might feel that you *must* look after your mother, and yet, even though our circumstances are relevantly the same, neither of us *has* to be guilty of infringing any of the conditions of ideal judgement (or doing so more than is necessary in a dilemma). If we are not, then it will be *true* that I must join the resistance and *true* that you must care for your mother. (Clearly there is no inconsistency here unless the principle of universalisability is granted. No one is saying of any person that they are required to φ and that they are not required to φ.) That 'must' is a moral one in that our self-respect, our ability to live with our consciences – perhaps our ability to be true to ourselves, to what we take to matter most, to what we have experienced or witnessed – turns on our living this way rather than that way. But the 'ways' may differ from person to person. There is no space here to defend moral necessity and the denial of universalisability. The gist to keep in mind is that what is at stake is a species of individual moral requirement such that it can be *true of me* that I am morally required to join the resistance and *true of you* that you are morally required to care for your mother. But then there is no course of action here that is a *universal* moral requirement, binding on people regardless of how they personally react to the situation.

At the hands of most philosophers the doctrine of universalisability is a formal or logical claim. That is, it is necessarily true (since it is definitive) of moral judgements that they are universalisable. That is a feature of the logic of moral discourse. So the *content* of a moral judgement is irrelevant to its universalisability. We know in advance of knowing its value that if p is a moral proposition, then p is universalisable. Those philosophers who deny universalisability are certainly denying this *formal* claim, so that there are at least possible cases where agents in the same situation are subject to different requirements. But that leaves it open that *some* judgements of *universal* moral requirements *are* warranted, depending on their *substantive* content. For example, I rightly judge that *anyone* in the same morally relevant circumstances as Charles Manson should not have done what he did. Call this *substantive* universalisability as opposed to *formal* universalisability. Notice that the impersonal conception of thought, because it covers only problems amenable to technical treatment, is committed to formal universalisability, and thus permits *only* universal moral requirements. In contrast the existential conception rejects formal universalisability but permits substantive universalisability. It allows *both* (substantively) universal moral requirements *and* individual requirements.

Thus the reconfigured debate on the problem of evil leaves open the possibility of substantive universalisation. That, I take it, is where Ivan Karamazov is standing. When he says that no greater good will justify what the children suffer in this world he is not only expressing an individual stand with no regard for how others should stand. He takes anyone who denies it to be mistaken. On that I agree with him. But the introduction of the appeal to love by those on God's side changes the picture. Although torn, on balance I am inclined to deny the existence of a substantive universal requirement pertaining to the (reconfigured) problem of evil. I want to allow, in the case of the problem of evil, that even ideally judging agents in the same relevant circumstances may be subject to different requirements. Unbelievers are people who, faced with the reality of evil, find they cannot but submit God to moral judgement and condemn him. They are people who, so to speak, find their loyalty is to the victims of evil, the burning children. Believers are people who, faced with the reality of evil, find they cannot condemn God. But this is not because, in the manner of theodicy, they have examined his conduct against moral standards and issued him a pass mark. It is because their love for him, and the importance they find they must put on his love for us in creating the world, set limits to the authority of morality to submit him to judgement (parallel to the human case). Believers are people who find their loyalty is with God. This is the first dimension of the difference between the old and new understandings of the problem of evil that I distinguished: the one under which the believer exempts God from moral judgement over evil.

That both belief and unbelief are acceptable does not mean that anything goes. All the conditions of ideal judgement have to be complied with as far as the nature of the case will allow. In the previous section I tried briefly to indicate that the existential conditions of judgement are as demanding in their own distinctive way as fact, rationality and logic. Whether someone can, in their heart (authentically), in the face of evils they have suffered or witnessed, still love the world – and so, if they are religious, its Creator – may be something that is not ruled out by ideal judgement, but which can come only from a gestalt shift that believers might call 'grace'. We have a clash of incommensurable worldviews, which is just to say that there is no neutral standpoint (within any of the categories of ideal judgement, moral and existential as much as fact, rationality and logic) from which the dispute might be argumentatively resolved. This is not to say that the two parties cannot understand and even appreciate one another's point of view. Nor, importantly, does it mean that there is nothing people can do or say to one another, or that what they can do or say is thereby irrational, or merely causal (propaganda, 'emoting'). For example, being inspired by an example of a certain pure love to see the world in a different way is not well understood under those sorts of descriptions.[12] What is true though is that neither position is universally binding: we are dealing here with individual requirements, personal necessities.

I am finally in a position (as promised) to complete my account of what I mean when I say that love opposes and can defeat morality. There are four distinct points here. First, the greater good morality we find in theodicy and atheology – as it is standardly understood in those contexts – assumes all three of the defining features of impersonal thought identified in the previous section. Atheologists and theodicists proceed as if their moral assumptions did not introduce any non-technical matters that required more than impersonal thought for dealing with the problem. But love is not committed to any of these defining features of impersonality. An appeal to love to explain my actions is not an appeal to anything objectifying – to factual information, rationality and logic. It does not appeal to an Archimedean point composed from these resources. It is subject to existential evaluation, it is not a matter of expertise and moral insurance, and it requires authenticity. Second, morality as usually understood in all its standard academic forms – including theodicy and atheology – is committed to formal universalisability. Love is not. To summarise these two points, love belongs to the existential domain of thought, not the impersonal. Third, there are moralities, or moral appeals, such as Ivan Karamazov's compassionate indignation, which are not committed to formal universalisability but which make a different kind of universal claim I call a *substantive* universal claim. Considered generally, love is consistent with substantive universal claims. But in the case of the problem of evil (I maintain) love imposes no substantive universal claim. The second point above was that it is not subject to formal universalisability. So now we can say that, as far as the problem of evil goes, *morality is universalisable and love is not*. These three points all belong to what I called the 'second dimension' of the difference between the traditional and reconfigured understandings of the problem of evil. The fourth and last point belongs to the first dimension, which concerned whether God is brought under moral judgement. Morality (unchecked by love) brings God under that judgement. But love, according to believers, protects God from moral accountability, and thus from condemnation, by exerting a claim upon us as authoritative as, or even more authoritative than, morality itself. In sum, these four elements give point to my distinguishing love from beneficence, from compassion and from morality at large. They are the substance to saying that the appeal to love is not just putting a new consideration on the scales. I emphasise that I am not talking about love quite generally, in any sense of the word in any context, but only about the sort of appeal to love over the problem of evil that I have described in this chapter.

Moral philosophers who deny universalisability have talked of individual *moral* necessities (or 'incapacities'). But because I want to contrast morality with love the adjective 'moral' is a misleading one for me to use to describe believers' individual requirement to exempt God from moral judgement in the name of love. So for the sake of clarity I shall hereafter speak of individual *existential* requirements or necessities in this context. Nothing more than clarity hangs on nomenclature though. As I said back in the previous section, call the appeal to love a moral one if you like, but it is a verbal move that does not undo the substantive contrasts I have just enumerated.

In line with the way some philosophers have denied the universalisability of morality, I have suggested in this section that there may not be a single final judgement on the problem of evil that is correct for everyone. On this view, the bond between human beings and God lies deeper than in anything we ordinarily call 'morality' in the sense of an impersonal and universalisable system of rights and duties. To say we are *morally obligated* to love God is deeply misleading if it implies that there is a moral relation to him deeper than the love and on which the love is founded. That is why, in the first chapter, I contended that the moralistic context of theodicy was not the right one to explicate the compelling thought that there is an absurdity in putting an end to human life (even painlessly and voluntarily) to spare us the suffering it involves. If our love for God were conditional on his behaving like a parent should, on his meeting certain standards of behaviour, then, as we have seen, Ivan Karamazov would have a compelling case that God had fallen well short of deserving our love. What, in the face of moral failure (on both sides), ties us nonetheless to God (and to human parents) is another human response, or set of responses, that it is not in the power of morality to rationalise. If anything, arguably, it is this inarticulate bond of love affirmed – or denied – that is the source of morality. The sense that other human beings and the world and God are something *momentous* – a sense displayed in love, but also in grief, remorse, sympathy and other responses – is a founding condition of moral ideas of rights, obligations and so on (see Gaita 2000a). If I say I am under a requirement to love my parents or God *unconditionally*, then it can only be the *individual* requirement of existential necessity. If I try to impose this on others as an impersonal obligation, then I undermine the essential personal response that is necessary for love. God the lover, in the erotic overture sketched in the previous section, would forgo any claim to *demand* of his beloved – *regardless of how they personally felt about it* – that the beloved accept what he had done in creating them and love him in return: would give up the right to tell the beloved, naggingly and moralistically, what they *should* do. The lover would be opening himself up to accepting rejection and condemnation without complaint. He would know love cannot be compelled, and he would run the risk of an injury – rejection – for which he could not console himself with the thought that the other party was *necessarily* in some way ungrateful, unjust, illogical or otherwise mistaken.

# 5
## Is God an Agent?

The previous chapter developed an analogy between divine and human parentage. It traced an argument to the effect that the passionate, creative love of human parents was a value that could check the authority of morality to condemn them for knowingly conceiving children whose lives would be judged (certainly by the sort of cost/benefit analysis found in theodicy) miserable, and that on the basis of the analogy God could be saved from moral condemnation in the same way. Love could confront and perhaps defeat the claims of morality – 'perhaps' because, on my account, some people might be bound by an existential necessity to judge this is so and others bound by an existential necessity to judge it is not so.

I wrote that the argument confronted the obvious objection that the analogy was flawed because God could create us without our being subject to evil, but we could not bear a child without it being subject to evil. I replied that the existence of creatures like ourselves necessarily involved evil, but admitted there was no room to argue that controversial point in this book. In addition to that problem, Joe Mintoff and Chris Walsh have convinced me that *in the human case* the argument will not bear the weight of its conclusion. The objection they raise is that there are surely limits to what love can do to protect a parent from an adverse moral verdict. There are forms of suffering, child suffering in particular, so horrendous that we simply cannot set the claim of compassionate indignation aside in the name of creative parental love. At any rate, I cannot: on this issue, I find I must substantively universalise.[1] So there are two serious problems for the appeal to love.

But the objections apply to God only so long as we take an overly strict view of the human–divine analogy. The analogy of God to loving human parents points to something of great importance, yet its limits must be acknowledged for that importance to be properly grasped. It turns out that what is not possible for human beings is possible for God. Love can indeed defeat the authority of morality, and that remains the existential crux of the argument, but it is not that love licenses God, a *personal and causal agent*, to proceed with a *causal process* called 'creating the world', which is a claim the argument of the previous chapter would be consistent with. The parental analogy misleads us if it suggests this anthropomorphic picture, and that is why the argument of the previous chapter is ultimately flawed. But a similar argument, preserving the appeal to love and the reconfigured nature of the problem of evil, and relying on an amended understanding of the analogy, can succeed. We have seen one limit to the analogy in Chapter 3: God is not answerable for blemishes such as slight toothaches. That limit prefigures on a modest scale the much larger difference I shall explain here. The gist is that (i) believers analogise God and human parents in respect of parents' love for their children being a form of (indeed a manifestation of) the love that is God's nature, but (ii) they *do not, in effect, regard God as a moral agent answerable for the consequences of his actions, or more generally as any sort of causal force producing effects in the way, for example, that among created forces an exploding volcano or a raging cyclone or a human being performing an action produces effects.*

Take clause (i) first. On the human side are (as I put it in the previous chapter) the passion of lovers to create, protect and enjoy new life, often even in, and in defiance of, terrible circumstances; the ideal of an unconditional love for their child that is (tenuously) normative in many human cultures, and certainly those influenced by Christianity; the bounty they gratuitously lavish on their child if they can; and the grief and sorrow they suffer if the child is harmed or lost. Beyond the specifically parental context, the love in question also displays mercy and compassion and joy, though these are typically felt with a special intensity towards children. God is likened to all these things, as we often say – though perhaps it might be better to say that *our* love is likened to *his*, being a reflection or (imperfect) manifestation of it. Thus believers speak of human beings as children of God to reveal them in a light of unconditional love as inviolable creatures; thus they praise and thank God for the good things of life, in saying grace, or in a service of thanksgiving after war or harvest; and thus, too, the crucial importance of the incarnation – *Jesus wept*. At the heart of this is a conception of God's love of the world and of us – normative as I say for a certain ideal of human parental love – that is not conditional upon the way the world is or the way we are. This love is not a function of weighing the good and bad things in the beloved. It loves the social outcasts, the sick and the lame, the wretched and the criminal – all those from whom we naturally resile – as much as the popular, the powerful, the healthy and the well-behaved. In its light every human life is momentous, or in religious language *sacred*.

Clause (ii) has two elements. The first is the denial that God is a special case of what we are, morally responsible agents who perform actions for which we receive credit and discredit (God being special partly because his actions are always good and thus he receives only credit). As classical Christian theology has it, God is not distinct from his actions as I am distinct from mine and you from yours. He is not subject to praise and blame, admiration and censure, according to how well his conduct abides by the standards applicable to moral agents in general, including human beings. He is not a greatly magnified human being occupying an unusually, even uniquely, exalted office and subject to the same norms of behaviour you and I are subject to, but applied to the peculiar powers and circumstances of that office (as with a prince, president or prime minister). To bring God under such moral judgement – as theodicy does – is to treat him as a creature not the Creator. Rather than being a special case of a loving agent – a being who performs acts motivated by love – God *is love itself*. He is also goodness itself, where goodness is centrally understood in terms of love. Equally he is not a special case of a moral agent – a being who performs acts motivated by a sense of duty, or a thirst for justice (or whatever) – but in this case it is not because he is morality itself. As love itself, rather than an agent motivated by this or by that, God does not act in the sense a human being does, and morality simply has no application to him. God is beyond mere morality, an institution peculiar to the human predicament.[2]

The other element of clause (ii) denies that God is a *non*-personal causal force like a volcano or a cyclone. God is not the *cause* of either the good or the evil in the world – or of the world – in the ordinary sense, the one philosophers call 'efficient causation', in which a potter produces a pot, a volcanic explosion a devastated city and so on. Rather, because he *is* love itself rather than a loving agent or an impersonal efficient causal force that can in some way be analogised to a loving agent, God is *present* in or *manifested* in whatever is good in something like the sense (though too pedestrian an account of this threatens to vulgarise it) that philosophers talk of properties being instantiated. 'Whatever is good' includes both the non-moral good that befalls us and the moral good we do as agents. Thus there is a sense in which when we encounter such good we encounter goodness, love, itself: we encounter God.

In contrast, though, evil is the very antithesis of love itself – that is, of God – so that with evil *in itself* (as opposed to its victims and how they may suffer it, or some of its effects) God is, trivially, not present or manifest.[3] The resulting picture is that when we encounter good and evil, we do not encounter two phenomena each of which is ultimately the effect of a single efficient cause, God, whether taken to be personal or impersonal. Equally we do not encounter the same thing, God, in the sense that he is present in both good and evil. On the contrary, God is present or manifested only in good, in love. It is in good and not in evil that we encounter God.[4] What we have is not a single moral agent or efficient causal power with different effects, but two different phenomena, good – that is, God, love and goodness themselves – and evil, each manifested separately in the sense that, however intertwined causally within creation, they remain as distinct as oil and water. Thus there is no question of determining God's nature partly by drawing inferences from the evil in the world (a self-contradictory enterprise) in the way that we estimate people or natural causes from what they *do*: that the person is a saint or a villain, or that a volcano or cyclone is destructive. Rather, as I say, we encounter God directly as goodness, as love itself. We see God in the goodness of good human acts but also in the goodness of the good blessings we enjoy – health and food and fellowship – and pre-eminently in the very fact that we and the universe exist at all. That something – anything, even the cyclone, even Hitler – exists at all is a manifestation of goodness, of love, though some of its conditions or actions (such as killing people) are manifestations of evil.

So a correct understanding of the parental analogy is more like this. God does not stand to human parents or human beings in general as one moral agent or causal force to others, as we or volcanoes and cyclones do. God stands to us as human parents stand to their children in that the human parents' love is a manifestation of the love that God *is*. But just what does this 'manifestation' come to? I have said it is like the instantiation of a property, though that can mislead. A specific example might help understanding. Consider a good human action, the Good Samaritan's for instance. There are two ways in which we might respond to the goodness of it. The first is to concentrate on the particular good act itself as, so to speak, an entry in the ledger of moral accountancy. It is one item to be placed on the credit side of a ledger that records merits and demerits for the purpose of an overall summing up of the Samaritan's moral condition over a life-time. (We might do something analogous with the good or bad effects of non-personal causal forces, though of course we would not be appraising their moral character. Bearing that in mind, I'll go on with the personal case.) More ambitiously the ledger may record not just the Samaritan's actions but those of all humans, or indeed all created agents, for the purpose of appraising the moral condition of creatures quite generally. (Despite the accounting imagery, the agents' actions do not have to be deemed good or evil according to a consequentialist morality.) The second way in which we might respond to the goodness of the Samaritan's action also goes beyond the particular action, but in a very different way. It pays no regard at all to any attempt to appraise the Samaritan's life as a whole, let alone the condition of all the creatures in the universe (and ditto *mutatis mutandis* for a non-personal causal force). It goes beyond the particular agent and their act in the sense that it perceives in this action a manifestation of goodness generally, in the form of compassion and more generally of love. In its biblical context we might see in it a manifestation of the love of God as the love of our neighbour. The first kind of response is practical and worldly. This is not to denigrate it. In the individual case at least it is an essential and important part of human life, the part we call 'morality'. But it is not the existential part, the religious part. The second kind, the religious or proto-religious response, is meditative and contemplative, in which one dwells on and is perhaps absorbed by the beauty, the awesome wonder, of the reality one has encountered, a reality of which any case is just one appearance. (This of course is not the only sort of religious response, but it is the central one to the present argument.) It is more like what Simone Weil (2002) calls *attention*. Iris Murdoch writes of a Platonic Goodness (she herself would not have identified it with love or God) such that we can 'look right away from self towards a distant transcendent perfection, a source of uncontaminated energy, a source of *new* and quite undreamt-of virtue' (1991, p. 101).[5] In the contemplation of good actions – actual ones and those represented in great art – we learn more about what goodness is. Over a life-time our understanding of it may deepen and become more lucid and precise. It is given to writers and artists, and perhaps a certain sort of philosopher, to put this understanding into words or images. We are acquiring a progressively richer picture of something which no individual instance of is ever wholly adequate to. (Notice how this puts together complexity, detail, precision and clarity with open-endedness and incompleteness and how different this is from ideals of necessary and sufficient conditions, prototypes and so on. Here there is always a remaining element of the ineffable, the incomplete, something always just beyond our grasp. Notice too that we both learn from particular instances and judge them in the light of the growing understanding.

Here there is a glimpse of how we might get beyond too simple a dichot-
omy of particular and universal.)

Whereas the Good Samaritan's act can be, and typically is, viewed
in both the practical and contemplative modes, in God's case, for the
believer *qua* believer, God is neither a moral agent nor a causal force –
these are categories *within* creation – and only the second kind of attitude is available towards him. So, when the believer says God is like a
human parent (or perhaps *vice versa* as I have said) the point of making
the analogy is (among other things) to draw our *contemplative* attention,
rather than the practical and moralising sort, to the love that God is.
Thus it is that our praise of God is praise of the love that he *is* (and that
our contemplative praise of the Samaritan's love is praise of the love
that he *manifests*) rather than praise of an agent accumulating merit, or
a causal force doing something analogous. And thus it is too that our
praise of God is of the *unconditional* sort that we call *worship*. This praise
of God is not meted out in accordance with the good or ill things that
befall us; it is not something he *earns*. God is outside that sort of moral
accountancy. Because we are praising *love itself*, and not how often it
occurs or prevails – how big a figure it cuts in the world – the propriety
of the praise is not under threat of falsification from the frequency and
distribution of evil; it is not hostage to the way the world goes on. This
is consistent with the fact that believers ask and praise and thank God
for specific good things – food on the table, health, a good harvest, the
coming of peace and so on – yet do not blame him for evil occurrences.
For what we ask and praise and are thankful for *qua* believers is the *love*
that is manifest in these goods. God is that love, that goodness, rather
than an agent performing either good or evil acts, or an efficient causal
force having good or evil effects, and thus there is no double-think in
the believer not cursing him for the evil. We recognise the good and
praise it as good just as we recognise the evil in condemning it as evil.
What matters to believers is love itself and not how often or how far it is
manifested. (I mean, as I have indicated, that it matters *qua* believer, in
virtue of a faith in God. I am not suggesting that believers are or should
be indifferent to the distribution of good and evil in *all* aspects of their
lives. Or that the religious thankfulness for God's love is not easily confused with normal human gratitude, or even animal relief, for a tangible benefit, or that these are not nevertheless importantly connected.)

Where a human being, if they knowingly created at least some human
lives subject to unrelieved suffering, would not escape condemnation,
God does because he is love itself and not a personal or non-personal
efficient causal force, and does not create in the sense involving efficient

causation. And that is the answer to the Mintoff–Walsh objection. If (absent some extenuating circumstance) human parents deliberately conceive a child who they know is certain to suffer a disease that means spending every moment of its life in unspeakable pain, there is a serious moral doubt about their conduct. Our ordinary understanding of human beings as morally responsible agents means that praise of them is conditional upon their conduct as judged by certain standards. The kind of praise involved, the sense that it has, in part depends on the fact that it is conditional upon compliance with norms, on the fact that it is the flipside of blame, censure and punishment. If someone is to be praised as a good mother or father, then they must behave as a mother or father should.[6] The same goes for being honoured as an upright citizen, leader, hero and so on, through all the contexts and accomplishments of moral effort. But the same does not go for God. In Christian life and thought God is *not* seen in the practical, this-worldly mode as a moral agent, or as a non-personal causal force. He is not an especially virtuous person, so virtuous as to contain no vice; he is not even *necessarily* a supremely virtuous person if this means that he is accredited this virtue on the basis of his necessarily meritorious acts. Insofar as God is regarded as a moral agent or as an efficient causal force Ivan Karamazov is right to think the problem of evil is fatal. But for believers the solution to the problem of evil ultimately involves the recognition, or the renewed recognition, that God is *not* a loving moral agent, or a non-personal causal force producing the effects a suitably empowered loving agent would, but instead is to be seen in the contemplative mode as love itself.

It might seem that on this argument God escapes condemnation in a way very different from that in which I wrote in the previous chapter of love or other non-moral values sometimes checking the authority of morality in human affairs. There I assumed, in my example, that certain profound interests human beings can have in their personal lives and projects (including having children from the urge of creative love) can set a limit to the claims of morality upon us: for example, that it cannot, in the name of the poor, demand the very shirt off our back. It might seem that the present argument in the case of God is very different. In one way this is very from the argument of the previous chapter. I am arguing now that God is not a moral agent or efficient causal force at all, rather than that he is a moral agent whose accountability in certain cases is limited by the demands of non-moral values, values which sanction his exercise of the causal power to create. That is a real difference. But it does not, despite appearances, rest upon a metaphysical thesis about the nature of God *established independently* of the places of love and morality in human affairs. Rather, just like the human case, it too rests upon the authority of love to check the authority of morality. I maintain that there is *no* justification for saying God is not (or is) a moral agent or causal force in the sense that most philosophers seek a justification, a justification that is *independent* of our personal and existential responses to God and evil, and seeking to *justify* those responses: usually a justification in the form of some sort of metaphysical argument. Believers do not somehow know (or reasonably believe) God is not a moral agent or causal force independently of their contemplative response to God as love and their refusal to hold him responsible for the evil in the world, with the knowledge justifying that response. Saying 'God is not a moral agent' is not an *argumentative response* to the Mintoff–Walsh point that is supposed to convince people they *should* see things the believer's way (by producing impersonal philosophical argument to justify the claim he is not a moral agent or causal force). It is a (generalising) *description* of the way believers *do* see them. Believers are people who can sustain faith in the face of evil. They are people who by dint of being able to worship love itself unconditionally despite evil are thereby *in effect* judging love itself to be of supreme importance and giving it their absolute loyalty and turning their worshipful praise onto it, and thus denying that God is a moral agent or causal force. The same goes for unbelievers, but in reverse. They cannot sustain such a faith in the face of evil; indeed they are people who find they *must* not, that the loyalty which defines their lives is to the burning children, that *that* reality is the most important, or at least important enough to deny anything else unqualified celebration or fealty. They are people for whom the reality of evil makes the world so dark that they cannot enjoy any unencumbered love. Believers and unbelievers have conflicting existential stands. It is a matter of which – the love of God, or compassion for the burning children – they judge more important, which of them secures a person's loyalty.[7] That is why believers' denial of God being a moral agent or efficient causal force does not rest upon a metaphysical thesis about the nature of God established independently of the demands of love and morality upon us. Rather, just as in the previous chapter, it rests upon the authority of love – of love itself – to check the authority of morality, just as in human matters love for friends and family may check the authority of morality to demand things from us in the name of others in need. Only here that love, love itself, *is* God.

   On my account, though, believers and unbelievers are not just mirror images of one another. Specifically, unbelievers are not necessarily people who deny that love itself is real. Empirically, believers are people who, despite the reality of evil, remain able to see love, goodness itself – God – clearly, their perception unclouded by the evil. In contrast, unbelievers (and there is at least a bit of an unbeliever, often more than a bit, in most of us, even those who count ourselves believers) are people whose perception of God is in some degree obscured by evil. Very often that obscuring is very serious, and in the need to lash out in response to evil they anthropomorphise God as the one who must take the blame.[8] But it need not be universally so. In principle, someone may, at least to a very great extent, recognise the reality and authority of love itself, but fall short of judging it of supreme importance, of giving it the deference, worship and love expressed in calling it 'God'. That is possible and, I expect, while rare, still more common than one might think. However that may be, the point is that the possibility of it means that the *conceptual* (as opposed to the empirical) difference between believers and unbelievers is not well captured as the difference between people who believe in the reality of love itself and people who do not. It is the difference between people who regard love itself as the most important thing and give it their first and absolute loyalty and people who do not. Unbelievers *need* not blame God for evil, and if they are lucid they will not. They *need* not fail to see the reality of love itself, and if they are lucid they will not. It is enough to make them unbelievers that given the reality of the burning children they cannot wholeheartedly love and celebrate love itself and its gift to us, because that would be a kind of insult to the victims of evil and the suffering they have endured.[9]

In the previous chapter I explained that there are two principal dimensions of difference between the conventional problem of evil debate and the reconfigured debate. The first was that on the conventional account both believers and unbelievers bring God under moral judgement (the former acquitting and the latter condemning) and under the reconfigured account believers do not put God under moral judgement. I have just qualified that to allow that unbelievers *need* not do so either, though typically they do. The second was that the conventional debate was impersonal and the reconfigured debate existential (see Section 2 of the previous chapter). This chapter's revised 'appeal to love' argument, according to which believers deny God is a moral agent or other kind of efficient causal force, enhances the first dimension by clarifying the sense in which God escapes moral judgement. He is not subject to morality at all: not a moral agent or even a causal force. And yet, as I have just explained, that view of God as not a moral agent or causal force also ultimately rests on the *existential* truth of people's capacity to see love clearly unencumbered by evil, a capacity central to believers and according to me even possible in principle for unbelievers. It does not rest on any sort of impersonal metaphysical argument. So my position in this chapter is a further step in the reconfiguration of the problem of evil as an *existential* problem. I am saying: 'Don't think of the debate as an objectifying, metaphysical one, going on independently of our personal, existential responses and with a view to justifying them. Rather the debate is an existential one of how we respond to the gift of life and its terrible reality of evil.'[10] (Here it is important to avoid the dispute becoming a merely verbal one. I am happy to let someone say God *is* a moral agent or causal force, so long as when they qualify this by saying that 'of course, he is not a *created* moral agent or causal force' they realise that this means he is, *in principle*, not to be held responsible for the evil in the world in the way you and I are for our actions (he has no need of morally sufficient reasons and so on) and that he is to be praised in a way that bears no relation to moral merit as we ordinarily understand this among human beings, or non-moral good or evil effects as we understand these for volcanoes and cyclones.)

If there is a justification believers or unbelievers have for their positions it consists just in whatever they can do and say to get the other side to see the world in a different light: to inspire them with the same spirit – the spirit of God, believers would say – that can respond to the world with unconditional gratitude for it, despite the evil in it. That may include criticisms of fact and logic, but it will be more about matters of morality, and especially of the sort I have called 'existential'. But there is no neutral ground from which an argument can be made to lever the other side into changing their stand. An argument designed to get someone to judge that God is not a moral agent (or that he is) – or one to determine where people's loyalties should go – independently of judging these existential questions would be an argument of that sort. There is no such argument.

Theodicists say we should not blame God for evil because, in the end, there is a morally sufficient reason why God permits evil. God is a perfectly good moral agent and is to be praised and not blamed because he has a perfect moral balance sheet, all credit and no debit. This is a truth we could see if we were, like God, able to see (as the saying goes) 'the whole picture', the distant future as well as the present. We cannot do that, at least not now, but we can accept the truth of it as a matter of faith or reasonable supposition. The position I am advocating is very different. When theodicists say we would understand if we could see the whole picture they assume that the understanding we would gain is an understanding *in human moral terms* (or at least what theodicists take those to be). That is, they treat God as a moral agent, in the sense that he is to be praised or blamed for his behaviour (as evidenced in the state of the world) according to the same standards human moral agents are judged by. That is why our current bafflement is blamed on the *circumstances* of our present dispensation, which do not provide us with enough information, and perhaps brain-power, to see the solution. In contrast I'm suggesting that the 'answer' to the problem of evil lies not in more information, or better logic, but in a *drastic reorientation* of our whole attitude, the achievement of a very different *way of seeing* the whole situation: specifically, that in our hearts the resentment that we naturally have at there being evil in God's world, and the indignant demand that someone be answerable for it ('God' is the name of that someone, the address to which we post our existential curses – and blessings), is overcome by love. What needs changing is not the amount of information we have to apply our standards to in judging God, but the idea that God must be judged at all, as opposed to loved and worshipped unconditionally. What is needed is not theodicy, not God's morally sufficient reasons for acting, but a revolution in the human heart. By submitting God to human judgement theodicy stands squarely in the way of that revolution. Theodicists of course can acknowledge the need for a practical response to evil as well as a theoretical one, and that the former requires a change of heart, but the problem is that that practical change is thwarted by the theory which puts God under our judgement, and makes our allegiance to him conditional on his good behaviour.

Three other miscellaneous matters. First, I take it that a moral agent must be a person, but that – in theology especially – there are senses of 'person' in which persons need not be moral agents or causal forces. Still, for my purposes, the distinction is of little moment. God is not like a person who performs loving actions: he *is* love itself. Consequently, I shall tend to equate 'moral agent' and 'person'. Second, and more importantly, when I deny that God is a person or moral agent, or a causal power, I do not mean to deny that he is these things incarnate as Jesus Christ. That he is them as Christ the Son but not as God the Father is part of the mystery of the incarnation, though maybe less of a mystery (in the bad sense of the word at least) when we cease to view the relation between the two as causal. Third, when I write of what 'believers' (and 'unbelievers') believe and do I am not making a purely sociological or historical claim, but neither am I simply prescribing what I think believers should believe and do. I am describing what I take to be the *central logic* of faith in Judeo-Christian religion, the general normative thrust of that faith. (A very rough analogy might be trying to arrive at the rules of cricket just by watching people play. You don't just list everything that happens as equally licit, or a part of cricket, but neither do you just impose your own notions.) Moreover I mean the central logic of that faith *in practice*: what believers do, how they live, rather than what they might *say* if asked to explain the nature of faith philosophically. It is a principal theme of the book that in these difficult matters it is very easy for practice and discursive understanding to be far apart. For this reason alone my account of belief carries no implication that theodicists *qua* people are not genuine believers. It is their theory I attack, not them. This theme returns in the last section of the next chapter.

From this point my position is best developed by responding to a series of objections.

> Objection 1. *The position is morally objectionable, making the Christian view of God Janus-faced. On the one hand God is treated as a moral agent in that he is analogised to a human parent who is moved by love to create, takes joy in his creation and is praised and thanked for, and petitioned for, the good things of life. But on the other hand he is, as a matter of principle, not blamed for any of the evil in the world and is hyperbolically praised without regard to whether he merits it. A being cannot be praised and thanked for the good they have done, but not blamed and censured for the evil they do, without blatant partisanship. Someone who expected such treatment would be an odious hypocrite and tyrant, while anyone who gave it would be a craven sycophant.*

But it is misleading to say that God is praised and thanked 'for the good [he has] done'. That way of putting it risks the suggestion that we are counting up God's good deeds and evaluating his character, as we can do with human beings. I am suggesting that what believers celebrate (*qua* believers) is the love itself that is present or manifested in the good things that befall us or the good deeds we perform. We are praising in the contemplative way some wondrous reality which has touched us in this way, but it is this reality, not the benefit to us – the iceberg beneath the sea, not merely the tip we can see and touch – that is the focus, the specifically *religious* focus. So in treating God asymmetrically in relation to the goods and evils of the world, we are not unjustly giving a worldly advantage to one agent over another. God is not an agent who, or non-personal causal force which, shares in worldly advantages and disadvantages. If someone objects that it is unfair that God is praised not only for the good things in the world, but also quite regardless of these good deeds, and even in the face of what would be counted bad deeds if perpetrated by a human being, they are forgetting that his love, and his goodness, are not a function of his 'acts': goodness and love are just what he *is*.

> Objection 2. *But doesn't the denial that God is a moral agent simply license evil-doing? Surely any religion which breaches basic human decency discredits itself.*

That is true, so long as we are talking about *human* behaviour, and supposed divine commands about human behaviour. Any religion that believes God has ordained child sacrifice, for example, discredits itself. Human sacrifice, the witch persecutions, the apparent genocides of the Old Testament: these perversions of human behaviour are the things we rightly fear in demanding that religion conform to human decency. But these things are not consequences of denying moral agency to God in the way that I am explaining. On my account when we love and thank God for good and when we loathe and fear evil, we are responding to different phenomena, not to a single agent, or causal force, acting well on this occasion and badly on that one. Thus we are in no way condoning evil-doing when we fail even to countenance holding God responsible for it. It has no bearing on holding human moral agents responsible.

Ironically it is precisely if we *do* treat God as a moral agent that we are more likely to fall into religious endorsement of human evil-doing. Or, more accurately, supposing divine sanction for human evil-doing is *one form of* treating God as a human-like moral agent or person. The image of God in the manner of a human lord, issuing commands and governing a territory, gets taken too literally if, as often has happened, God is dragged into being a kind of player in human affairs, a partisan for this side or that, able to be beseeched for ends deemed desirable: a recruitment of him only too likely when he is seen as giant efficient causal force, and a personal one to boot. Sometimes this takes the form of reducing him to the image of a limited human understanding of goodness. One example is supposing that if a human being enjoyed the infinite knowledge and power of God, they would be justified (as he is) in creating a world with terrible evils if they were outweighed by greater goods.

> Objection 3. *The denial of God's moral agency or efficient causal power is a gratuitous expedient devised* ad hoc *to dodge a problem. What reason – apart from dodging the problem of evil – do believers have for denying God is a moral agent?*

As I have said, the 'contemplative praise' of God as I have called it is necessarily *unconditional*: what is there not to praise about love itself? And as Simone Weil has suggested, that praise we give to God is the same unconditional love that God *is*, coming from him and through us returning to him as the praise. It is the love in the light of which each human life is sacred. It is no accident that an alternative formulation speaks of people as children of God. What is celebrated in the affirmation that human life is sacred is not any merit on our part. Indeed, the whole point of the affirmation is that it is *not* deserved in any way and thus reaches all of us regardless of our character, our station in life, our accomplishments or lack of them, and so on. What is celebrated is *the love manifested in the bare, gratuitous – unearned – fact, the glorious gift, that this person exists*. That is, what is celebrated is God, though it would be a mistake to see this as somehow at odds with celebrating the life of the human person concerned, as if they were alternatives with one precluding the other. Rather the *form* that celebrating God takes in this instance is celebrating the person whose reality (as opposed to behaviour) is a manifestation of love.

I am trying to bring out the importance and appeal of this ideal of an *unconditional* praise of God. *That* sort of praise is a form of love. If believers' love of God were conditional on his actions, if our love for him were rationed according to the good and evil in the world, then it seems plausible that believers' love of human beings would be rationed in the same way – as if it *were* moral appraisal – and the ideal of an unconditional love of other human beings, and a basic human equality before God, would be lost. But if this is so, then it is not true to say, as the objection does, that there is no independent reason to deny God is a moral agent, that this is just a move introduced *ad hoc* to get out of a problem. There is very compelling reason for it quite independently of that.

A similar objection might be advanced here to the effect that the position amounts to sealing religious faith off from criticism, turning it into a self-verifying, irrefutable position. This is a common objection to the sort of position I defend, but it is mistaken. That criticism of their religion is in the end mistaken is *of course* built into the religious person's viewpoint. But that, trivially, is built into any viewpoint. If one believes p, one believes criticisms of p are mistaken. That does not mean others cannot *say* anything to convince me of not-p: it does not mean there cannot *be* criticism. The problem of evil is one such criticism and it convinces many people. Of course, if p is true, there cannot be *correct* criticism of p. But again, that is true for *any* value of p. If p is false, though, then of course there are criticisms which *are* correct, even if available only to a mind of unlimited powers. Religious faith here is no different from atheism or from *any* other belief. The grain of truth in the objection is that on my account there is no *neutral* ground from which faith can be established or refuted argumentatively, from which to make the criticisms *binding* on *any* (ideally judging) party to the dispute. But again, this is not unique to religious belief. It is, symmetrically, equally true of unbelief, and moreover (if I am right) it is true of many more topics than religion: morality, for example. But this does not mean there cannot be intelligent debate, criticism and discussion, that exchanges on these topics are limited to propaganda, emoting and so on. That is an extraordinarily limited view of the forms of legitimate discussion and persuasion.

> Objection 4. *It is one thing to have a motive for believing God is not a moral agent or causal force, but what is required – for intellectual honesty – is a ground. You have given us a motive in the form of unconditional love, but what about a ground? We cannot simply assume that God is going to be what we would like him to be. But if our reason for believing God is not a moral agent or causal force is just that this satisfies our existential needs, then we are making just that assumption. Our attitudes and beliefs cannot make it true that God is not a moral agent or causal force. I cannot switch him from being a moral agent or causal force to not being one by changing my allegiance. To deny this is idealism or relativism. Whether God is a moral agent or causal force – just like whether you are – is an objective matter of fact.*

The crucial point to grasp here is that the word 'God' does not function purely as a name or label, or an abbreviated definite description, of an evaluatively neutral kind like (usually) 'bachelor' or 'president'. A crucial part of its use is to function as an honorific title. The bestowal of an honorific title both attributes a great importance to its object and declares an allegiance to it. That is so with calling someone a 'friend', 'leader', 'hero' or 'saint'. In the case of 'God' a supreme value is attributed and one's foremost allegiance declared. Now of course there is a descriptive element to these terms as well. In a case like 'mother' the descriptive (biological) element is so strong and stable that the word can be used without any honorific force (but it often does have such a normative force, perhaps most visible in its denial: 'She's no mother to me'). In other cases – such as 'friend', 'leader', 'hero' – the descriptive element is less stable. It can vary from person to person and can be controversial: whom I regard as a leader or hero you may not. I suggest that 'God' – God with a capital G – is like that. If this were not so, there would be no issue of *idolatry*, of worshipping *false* gods. It is true that in much academic philosophical discussion the descriptive element is taken for granted, for instance in the 'perfect being' tradition of thought that is so prevalent among contemporary analytic philosophers of religion: the tradition defining God as an omnipotent, omniscient, perfectly good immaterial person, where those terms attribute power, knowledge, goodness and so on in the same sense in which they are attributed to you and me, only in vastly greater degree. But, even apart from the fact that goodness can obviously prove controversial, that tradition is by no means the only one in Christian thought, or the one that best represents belief in its actual practice. It comes under challenge, for example, from the apophatic, Thomistic and Platonic traditions, which in various ways challenge its anthropomorphic outlook. In effect, their challenge raises the question of whether the God of that tradition – what John Bishop (1998) calls the 'omni-God' – might itself be an idol. And when we return from intellectual discussions to the world at large we find it aflame with charges of true and false worship, whether in the disputes between religions or in the worship of more quotidian idols, as by those for whom, as we say, pop stars or footballers are their God. The early Christians were famously accused of being atheists. I suggest that the problem of evil is essentially a question of the same nature, a question about idolatry: a question of what is of supreme importance and where our allegiance should lie.[11] Unbelievers (on account of evil) are people who cannot acknowledge *anything* as important enough to warrant a higher loyalty than the victims of evil, the burning children. But they need not thereby deny the *existence* of anything. For example, they need not deny the reality of the omni-God, just as the deists did not deny the existence of a creator, though they had little or no interest in it. More importantly, as I have already said, lucid unbelievers need not deny the reality of love itself. If they do not they will recognise its *great* significance (because that is essential, I would argue, to recognising its reality) but not its *supreme* significance. They will not bend the knee to it as God. That is not because it is responsible for evil, but because (as they see it) to give such wholehearted deference to anything in a world with the burning children in it is a disloyalty to them. In a sense it misrepresents the universe. A universe that includes the burning children is not a place to enjoy such an unconditional love.

On this account there is no idealism or relativism involved when it comes to the reality or unreality of anyone's God. The Hindu Gods, the omni-God, the deistic God, love itself: these exist or do not exist quite independently of anyone's beliefs, attitudes, existential states and so on (if you doubt this for love itself, I argue the case in the next chapter).

Consequently – to finally come to the question – neither do we determine with our mental states whether any of these entities are persons, moral agents or causal forces. If the omni-God exists it is a moral agent (at least if its supporters are right) and a causal force. If love itself exists it is neither. There is no idealism or relativism here.

Admittedly, my denial of universalisability for the problem of evil means that there is no *universal* truth about whether love itself is to be worshipped as the true God, or that worship withheld in the name of the burning children; no universal truth, that is, about which has the highest claim on us. Rather it is true of me that I have to acknowledge love itself as the highest claim on me and true of you that you have to acknowledge the burning children as the highest claim on you. But bear in mind how limited this is. It is not an 'anything goes' position. As I have already explained, it makes no difference to the reality of love itself, the omni-God, Thor or any other deity. And while believers being bound to acknowledge God as their highest loyalty is not something that is true independently of their individual natures, it is not the case that they make it true for themselves by merely wishing it, willing it or anything like that: they have to comply with all the conditions of ideal judgement, so far as the case allows. Moreover, it is not as if the world outside believers plays no role, or only an insignificant role, in creating the existential requirement they are under. Quite the opposite: it is only by experience of and serious reflection upon the independent realities of love itself, and of evil and the suffering children, that believers or unbelievers can properly take their stand and thus truly be under the requirement they take themselves to be under (so they can be mistaken about that requirement). Nor does my denial of universalisability entail that these requirements are really only the expression of emotions, attitudes, policies and so on. Existential reality is no less real than any other. (I discuss this in the next chapter.)

But what about the objection's demand that there be *independent grounds* (as opposed to a motive) for believing that God is (or is not) a moral agent or causal force? Well, if we are talking about whether the *entities* people regard as God are or are not moral agents or causal forces, then it is simply built into them that they are or are not. The omni-God is stipulated to be a moral agent and causal force, and love itself by its nature is not. Perhaps the question is whether we have independent grounds for believing these entities *exist*. In the case of the omni-God we are familiar with independent grounds for believing in its existence: the standard arguments for the existence of God. In the case of whether love itself exists the situation is different. It is closer to something we non-inferentially experience – like the physical world – than to a hypothesis we confirm or disconfirm with evidence. Its logic is very different. I discuss this in the next chapter. Finally, perhaps the point is that there are no independent grounds for holding that love itself is to take precedence over the burning children. That I have already conceded in holding that this is a clash of incommensurable views, irresolvable from any neutral (independent) vantage point. But as I have also said this is not to say that there cannot be intelligent, perceptive and helpful discussion between the two parties, that they are reduced to emoting, propaganda and the like. But I concede that lack of space prevents me from saying much about what that sort of discussion is like, though some parts of the book – including the first, second and final chapters – may to some modest extent exhibit it in places.

To sum up my position, there is no universal truth about whether *everyone* must give their allegiance to love itself over the burning children, and thus no universal truth that there is a true God. The most I think we can *universally* claim is that God and Ivan's compassionate indignation for the victims of evil have an equally powerful and incommensurable claim upon us. Nonetheless both believers and unbelievers *are* responding to universal truths about reality, to 'objective' features of it. Both are responding to a reality, something of which it is universally true that it is 'really there': love itself and the victims of evil. Equally in both cases there is no universal truth about which is more important, which should be given precedence in an overall judgement of God and evil.

> Objection 5. *In the previous chapter you allowed the possibility that A must believe that God's reality is consistent with the existence of evil, and B must believe that it is not, and that both A and B comply with all the conditions of ideal judgement. But surely either the proposition that God exists is consistent with the proposition that evil exists or it is not. The consistency of propositions is an objective matter of logic. To deny this is idealism, or relativism, or at any rate something very bad indeed.*

One minor point first. As Plantinga has shown us there are more propositions that must be added to the set and considered before we are in a position to declare that *God exists* and *evil exists* are consistent or inconsistent. But at least one of those propositions must be a moral or more general value one (in addition to *evil exists*, which is the judgement that some existing things are evil). A, who believes that God and evil are consistent, will include in the set a value proposition that renders them consistent (in the vein of the last chapter, that love defeats compassionate indignation), and B, who believes they are inconsistent, will include a value proposition that renders them inconsistent (denying that love defeats compassionate indignation). So it is misleading to say that '*God exists* and *evil exists* are either consistent or they are not', for the question cannot be answered without specifying a larger set (or perhaps the answer is that by themselves they are consistent, but that the set consisting of only them is not the relevant set to consider).

That by itself is not sufficient to answer the objection though, for it remains consistent with A asserting universally that love defeats compassionate indignation and B asserting universally that it does not: they cannot both be right. But the point is that their assertions are *not* universal, though of course in casual speech they might speak as if they were. On the account I am giving, what A should say is '*I* must put love ahead of compassionate indignation' and '*I* must love God despite evil.' A says nothing about what others must do. What B should say is '*I* must put compassionate indignation ahead of love' and '*I* cannot love God given evil.' And B says nothing about what others must or cannot do. A and B are declaring an allegiance, to God and to the burning children respectively. Consequently I am not committed to the idea that the consistency of propositions can vary from one person to another. What I am committed to is a denial of the substantive universalisability of overall judgements about God and evil – but that is not what the objection purported to dispute.

I also hold that A can be right when he says that these features of the world require this stand of him *and* B can be right when he says that they require the opposite stand of him, and both can acknowledge this is the situation. Moreover there is a sense in which they can be appealing to the *same* features of the world (are in the same 'relevant circumstances') to justify their stands. That is what it means to deny universalisability. But now how can the world, the very same features of the world, justifiably require just one response from A and just one, but *another* and *opposite* one, of B? At most, shouldn't A and B *both* be bound by *both* contrary requirements in the manner of a dilemma?[12] No. The situation need not be one where the same features justify two conflicting responses binding on all. Situations can be *ambiguous* and ambiguous *as a whole*, in the gestalt manner of the duck–rabbit. Here any agreed description of the case falls short of justifying either interpretation or both as *universal* moral requirements, that is, as ones binding on everyone in the relevant circumstances. But it does justify each interpretation in the sense that each is one a person can be subject to as an *individual* existential requirement, that is, as the reader will recall, a requirement that no one else need be under, a personal existential necessity. But since neither interpretation is a universal requirement it is not a case where both A and B are under the same requirement or requirements. While it is true that discussion of the case cannot resolve it in the sense of establishing a universal requirement, discussion can reach a universally binding conclusion to the effect that only certain versions of belief and unbelief are consonant with the conditions of ideal judgement and available as individual requirements. There is no warrant for saying this position is irrationalist. (Of course, it is an *existential* discussion, rather than an impersonal and objectifying one, but that in itself does not establish irrationalism.)

In this respect the simplicity of the duck–rabbit example might mislead. It suggests that one just switches between gestalts randomly, or at will, or by simple re-juxtaposition of viewer and object, and that there is little or no room for intelligent reflection and discussion. The case of God and evil is closer to two highly experienced and capable art critics each giving one of two convincing but incompatible and incommensurable interpretations of a painting. Their disagreement may be irresolvable, not due to the limits of their ability, but due to the nature of the case, the same nature which licenses just these two interpretations. Yet intelligent discussion between them of the painting may, without useless repetition, continue indefinitely and it could meet all the standards of ideal judgement. It would not be helpful to say they were *only* declaring allegiances or expressing attitudes and were not talking about any real properties of the painting. The painting *itself* is ambiguous, licensing two interpretations and mandating none. I am suggesting that the case of God and evil is also ambiguous, between putting God ahead of the burning children and putting the burning children ahead of God. What is not ambiguous though – at least when we free our perception from the distorting effects of evil – is the reality of the things a person must choose between: the reality of evil and innocent suffering on the one hand, and on the other hand the reality of love itself.

# 6
# The Real God

## 1. Two God's-eye views

In Christian understanding God and human beings are likened to one another – *in certain respects*. The previous three chapters have tried to elucidate some of the respects in which the likeness is a sound one and some in which it is misleading. In the previous chapter I argued that believers do not regard God as a moral agent or person, or indeed any other kind of causal force. But then how is God capable of love? The question is misleading. God is not capable of love. But this is not because he is *in*capable of it. Rather, God *is* love, as opposed to an agent performing loving acts.[1] But what does it mean to say that this God of love itself exists independently of human beings and the world (as we normally take God to do), that, as I have said, God is a kind of reality, an 'existential' reality? Here I have space only for the sketch of an answer, but the reader has a right to know where I am coming from.[2]

Philosophers often talk of and aspire to a 'God's-eye view' of the world. They mean a perspective on the world that is unconditioned by embodiment, by individual or social history, or by spatial and temporal limitations. Much of this book is deeply critical of that aspiration in the work of philosophers of religion. Despite this, there is another sort of God's-eye view that I am sympathetic to. The conventional philosophical understanding of the God's-eye view is one operating in the *impersonal* mode of thought outlined in Chapter 4. That view is one affording a description of reality that is impersonal, a matter of expertise, that does not require authenticity and that endorses the formal universalisability of judgements. Modern materialism's 'completed science' is an example of that description. Certain forms of theistic metaphysics – for example, that which might seek support from the arguments of 'intelligent design' – while not detailed descriptions of the world as a whole, are nevertheless world pictures of a very general sort in the impersonal mode.[3] Not everything in the category of the impersonal falls in these camps though. As I said in Chapter 4 mathematics and black-letter law are other realities that satisfy its defining tenets.

In contrast, there is an understanding of the God's-eye view that is existential in the Chapter 4 sense: its manner of thought is non-objectifying, is not subject to expertise, requires personal authenticity and does not endorse the formal universalisability of judgements (though there may be substantive universalisability of some judgements). Sometimes it is called a view of the world *sub specie aeternitatis*, or a view of the world from the perspective of eternity. What we see from the impersonal perspective of the first God's-eye view is the world understood in terms of objectifying factual description. What we see from the God's-eye perspective of eternity is the world understood as possessing a very different kind of significance. For example, the impersonal perspective sees the fact that we die as a purely biological phenomenon about which we might ask certain sorts of causal questions: what causes death and how might we prolong life, and so on? The existential perspective sees death as a phenomenon raising questions about the meaning of our lives: what sort of human being have I been, have I wasted my life, how can I spend what remains of it in a worthy way, and so on? The impersonal perspective understands the magnitude and contingency of the world at large as requiring another set of causal explanatory questions, perhaps very general cosmological or metaphysical theses. The eternal perspective understands them through such responses as awe, wonder, a dizzying sense of our own contingency, a requirement for gratitude and so on. The existential significance is that revealed from the perspective of a standpoint – eternity – that is *not* subject to these 'Big Facts' (as they are sometimes called). We perish in the world (the impersonal, objectifying physical world) but the *significance* of our lives does not; that each human life is sacred is not a truth that varies with time or tide, or that is subject to fate. Our careers, aspirations and hopes prosper or fail and ultimately are extinguished in the world, but in eternity the moral significance of an act of kindness or of cruelty is never diminished or affected ('it lives for ever', as we sometimes say). Our bodies become dust, our lives are forgotten, in the world, which continually passes on to new things, but in eternity no life is forgotten or un-memorialised. The world is the possession of big-shots, tyrants and tycoons, but eternity the home of the humble and meek. The world is prisoner to lies, eternity the home of truth itself where all our deceptions are stripped away. The perspective of eternity is the perspective of a pure love, love 'itself' we can say, because eternity embodies the essence of this love: that it does not distinguish on the basis of power, money, prestige and other 'worldly' criteria. From this perspective there is no distinction of prince and pauper, duke and dustman; it represents a spirit that does not weary or falter with time, chance and temptation but is always steadfast, that is truthful and just regardless of circumstances, that is not taken in by human chicanery, and so on. The impersonal, objectifying God's-eye view is one we try to occupy by divesting ourselves of attention to individual things and by rising as far as we can to a perspective that is as general as possible. There is a certain generality in the eternal perspective too (the equality inherent in each human life being sacred) but it is of a sort which demands attention to (and which can be understood only through) the individual human lives (and other things) in our own locality: no one can appear to us as merely a specimen or example, as merely *representative*, whereas that is exactly the significance an individual has from the impersonal perspective. Our sense that those remote from us in time and space are every bit as sacred as our family and friends is mediated through an appreciation of the sacredness of family and friends and all those who cross our path.[4] We can enjoy the eternal perspective, can live in its light right now – can participate in the life of God – insofar as we can be freed from subservience to the treadmill of profit and loss, can ourselves be truthful, steadfast, patient and so on, as if not subject to the forces of necessity and chance. Spiritually, if you like, we can live in eternity here and now. This does not mean there is some spooky Cartesian bit of us that is not subject to physical laws or that after we die we will, physically or 'spiritually', go somewhere where we can continue to celebrate our birthday each year without end. Such a place is not eternity in the sense I am talking of. It is just an extension of the world understood in the *impersonal* sense. Where we 'go' is to eternity, but that is not some analogue of going to Melbourne.

The reality of God is the reality of that eternal perspective; if you like, of the 'place' from which, or in the light of which, we see these existential meanings. But we need to pay close attention to *context* in elucidating what this means. The question of God's existential reality must be divided into two. First, there is the question of the reality of existential phenomena in general – the sorts of truths that I was just mentioning – as opposed to the position that these are not truths at all, but merely expressions of attitude and feeling or something of that sort. The second question is whether the eternal perspective from which we see them is real independently of human beings and of the physical world as a whole, as God is normally taken to be. I shall deal with the first fairly briefly and concentrate my discussion on the second.

## 2. The reality of the existential

The key here is to recognise that there is no single, univocal sense in which things are real or assertions true. There are different kinds of reality. In one way there are as many different kinds of reality as there are things that are real – a magpie is real in a different way than a starling. But there are also general categories we can recognise.

The first is the category I call 'impersonal'. Within it we can in turn identify a number of sub-categories. The Eiffel Tower is a case of straightforward physical reality, the juxtaposition of visible, audible, tangible physical bodies in space and the causal relations between them. The reality of physical objects consists in their being 'out there' in a literally spatial sense. We encounter this reality, and learn what it means to speak of being 'real' as a physical thing, by literally bumping into it, manipulating it and so on. There are also broadly empirical phenomena, such as sub-atomic particles, which cannot be seen or pointed to in this way, but they are still impersonal phenomena because they are phenomena we meet and understand primarily through the objectifying practices of proposing causal hypotheses, predicting and (dis)confirming them by exact observation (of the particles' effects) and so on. This is as opposed to an understanding in terms of, say, their aesthetic or existential significance (think of a poem written about an electron, perhaps using its empirical elusiveness – its lack of a determinate position and so on – as a metaphor for the contingency of the empirical world). Certain sorts of arguments for the existence of God – ones employing intelligent design, for instance – clearly are moving in the 'conceptual space' of empirical and scientific explanation broadly construed. God appears in these theories as a hypothesised entity which may be unobservable directly but which is still detectable by confirming the causal consequences of the hypothesis.[5] Traditional metaphysical arguments for the existence of God – the contingency argument for example – strive to transcend the empirical, but they still employ, perhaps in its most general form, the intellectual apparatus of positing God as a kind of theoretical entity, a causal explanatory hypothesis for an observational fact: the existence and the contingency of the empirical world.[6] That is a rough overview of *some* of the contents of impersonal reality, those which share a causal explanatory structure.

Others (not having that structure and each forming a sub-category of the impersonal deserving its own treatment) include mathematics and law (at least black-letter law) and no doubt others I have not thought of. Thus I have to admit that the category of the impersonal is in one way something of a grab-bag. But its sub-divisions remain united – for the purpose of distinguishing them from the moral and the existential – by the features identified in Chapter 4. To repeat myself, the practices and judgements concerning them are all objectifying (that is, no moral or existential issues are internal to these practices), they admit of expertise, they do not require personal authenticity, and their judgements are formally universalisable.[7]

The reverse of these features characterises moral reality, which concerns the truth of principles and judgements about human conduct and ideals of living. We do not encounter moral reality by (literally) seeing it and physically bumping into it, or by forming hypotheses about it, or in the ways that characterise mathematics or black-letter law. We encounter it through such things as guilt and remorse, sympathetic feeling and the impulses to indignation and blame or praise and reward. We acquire moral vocabulary by hearing it used in these contexts and emulating that use. The line between the moral and the existential is not sharp. As well as requiring us to ask straightforwardly moral questions about our conduct, morality (unless artificially restricted to legalistic rule-following or the sorts of impersonal, theoretical conceptions of it found in a certain sort of moral philosophy) requires us to meet many of the existential conditions of ideal judgement I identified in Chapter 4. Am I being serious or frivolous? Am I being honest with myself or am I rationalising? Am I being a true friend, spouse, parent, citizen and so on? That is to say, morality is not technical or objectifying. Moreover it does not admit expertise and moral insurance (I cannot pass my moral responsibility to another when I rely on their advice), it requires personal authenticity, and it is not committed to formal universalisability of judgements. So moral reality and the human practice through which we encounter it, and which gives us our understanding of that reality, are not impersonal.

Third, there is what I have called existential reality. It is not moral reality in the sense of truths about how we should treat one another, though it is closely related to moral truth, providing a sort of deep background to it. For example, that human beings are sacred is not a moral truth in the sense of being itself a principle of conduct or ideal of living (it is consistent with a wide variety of these, though not with all).[8] But even less like morality are such things as grief and hatred, joy and laughter, the importance of our children to us, that we can curse the day we were born and shake our fist at the universe or get down on our knees in sheer gratitude for being alive, that we are inclined to pray when we are in desperate straits, that we can feel uncanny when, lying in the dark, we think about the dead, or wonder why terrible things happen, or why we or anything exists at all. These are all human responses to, encounters with, the existential significance of the world. That significance is a distinct kind of reality. As with moral reality it is not technical and objectifying, it does not admit expertise, it requires personal authenticity, and it is not committed to formal universalisability. It is not an impersonal reality. It is existential.

I call it 'the reality of the eternal'. Just as impersonal reality is one kind of reality (with sub-divisions as we have seen) and moral reality another, so this existential – or *religious* – reality is another: the kind of reality we meet in *these* practices and responses, just as we meet moral reality in indignation and remorse, or the various impersonal realities in the ways I described. They are all kinds of reality in that they bring with them their own forms of a distinction between the true and the false, the real and the illusory; they each resist fantasy, wishful thinking and so on *in their own distinctive way.* For physical reality it is a matter of veridical and illusory sense perception. We learn this distinction and the language to express it by correcting our misperceptions by looking again in a better light, when we have sobered up, by having others look and so on. In science and metaphysics that deals with theoretical entities, or in mathematics or in law, there are different ways again of making the distinction. In morality we learn to distinguish true values from false – and the language to express the difference – by attention to conscience, sympathetic feeling, the good example and instruction of others, and so on. In existential matters we learn to distinguish responses to the 'Big Facts' (of mortality, contingency etc.): those responses which are proud from those which are humble, those which are honest from those which are in bad faith, those which are serious from those which are frivolous, and so on. Here, as with morality, life experience and the influence of others are vital, though the subject matter is somewhat different. In existential matters we are concerned not so much with conduct towards others as with things such as the momentous meaning that human life has for us in the first place, the beauty of the world and the sheer inexplicability of it existing at all, our frightening vulnerability to random fluctuations of good and evil, and much more.

The great mistake is to take the impersonal conception of reality, and oftentimes even the broader empirical conception (the one dealing with causal explanatory theoretical posits of observable phenomena), as the mark of reality *simpliciter*, and then to try to fit *everything* real under that model. A dialectic familiar from discussions in meta-ethics (relieved to some extent by the more recent interest in redundancy and minimalist theories of truth) plays itself out. Either the contested entity or property is configured as a sort of pseudo-physical object or theoretical posit existing in a nether-world of such objects (for God a 'spiritual' world) or this is deemed too weird (since not scientifically naturalistic) and the entity or property is 'eliminated' in favour of some sort of non-cognitivism or anti-realism. In philosophy of religion this dialectic is not so explicit, but it is pervasive. However, there is something weird about moral realities and existential realities only if we insist on construing them as pseudo-empirical objects (I use that expression to cover both directly observable objects and theoretical posits) rather than letting them be what they are. The problem is that we have in mind a picture like this. Science has investigated the impersonal, empirical world very thoroughly and arrived at a comprehensive and unified picture of it which – it turns out as a contingent matter of fact – does not include semantic, mental or moral, and by extension existential phenomena except insofar as they reduce to or supervene upon the empirical phenomena. From that scientific worldview moral and existential phenomena that do not reduce to or supervene upon the physical appear distinctly odd. They spoil the purity and sweeping simplicity of the naturalistic picture. They should be 'eliminated' from our ontology – our inventory of the kinds of things that exist – and talk about them explained non-cognitively as expression of attitudes or some more or less sophisticated variation on that theme. But that picture is mistaken because it tacitly assumes that there is a single, neutral, univocal, context-less sense in which things can be real, and so a single, authoritative and exhaustive inventory of real things that could be drawn up. However, in truth, far from being neutral, it is party to the impersonal, objectifying conception of reality, and even to the empirical object version of it, advancing this disguised as the supposedly neutral conception. On this view when we talk about moral values or spiritual, existential truths we are taken to be positing things that exist in the impersonal way and thus bidding for their inclusion in the canonical inventory of impersonal reality. If they are included but without reduction or supervenience (so that they are primitive elements, along with fundamental particles), then the naturalistic ambition for that inventory is a failure: the inventory has gone weird. The alternative picture is that moral and existential realities are not candidates for inclusion in the inventory of impersonal, objectifying reality, let alone empirical reality, because they are not impersonal, objectifying phenomena: the sense in which they are real is not the impersonal one, but the moral one or existential one respectively. Thus they do not *compete* with electrons and protons and quarks for inclusion in a single, *context-less* world picture – there is no such picture – but have their own respective pictures. Consequently the naturalistic picture of the world is *not* breached by supposing that non-reducible or non-supervening moral and existential phenomena are real – physical, moral and existential phenomena do not *compete* with one another – since that picture is indexed to a context, the context (or contexts) of our *impersonal* relations to the world, and moral and existential phenomena do not belong to that context: they have different contexts of their own and different pictures of reality.[9] So it remains perfectly legitimate (and perhaps true; I do not judge that) for physicalists (as opposed to dualists or spiritualists) to claim they have the correct account of reality, so long as they mean *impersonal* reality. But if they claim to have the correct account of reality *simpliciter*, they over-reach.

Of course, famously, there is also a conceptual argument for the weirdness of moral phenomena realistically construed. Realism naturally goes hand in hand with cognitivism, the view that moral propositions are truth-valued. Then the worry is that this cognitivism is inconsistent with the conjunction of the seemingly plausible assumptions (i) that moral views are intrinsically motivating and (ii) that motivation requires two distinct states, a belief and a desire. If cognitivism and (i) are true, then it would seem that moral views are beliefs and that such beliefs are sufficient for moral motivation, contrary to (ii). But if (ii) is abandoned, then it seems to follow, absurdly many philosophers think, that moral realities have an intrinsic 'to be/not be done-ness' built into them. Plausibly, a similar argument could be constructed for a realistic view of the existential. I believe this argument also rests ultimately on the same mistaken assumption of a single, univocal sense of being real. But I shall not argue that here. The purpose of this section was to give the reader the gist of my 'quietist' position rather than to defend it in detail. That gist is needed for my main concern, the stronger claim that the existential reality of God is independent of the existence of human beings and the physical world.

## 3. Does God exist independently of the world?

My argument in the previous section invites an obvious objection. If different kinds of talk about reality get their sense from the different contexts of human activity in which a word such as 'real' is used, then isn't there a serious risk the position amounts to some form of reductionism, treating God as if he were simply morality or some aspect of human psychology: perhaps even a part of a human religious practice or language game? I hope I have said enough to distinguish the *subject matter* of religion from morality, at least roughly. The suggestion that my position treats God as a property of human nature, practice or language game (so that God is dependent on humans for his existence) confuses the following two claims, or takes the first to entail the second:

> Claim 1. *The sense of the language we use to talk about things – including the words 'true', 'false' and 'real' – and thus the sense of the distinction between truth and falsity, the real and the unreal – is given by the way words are used by human beings in the various contexts of their lives (principally, for our purposes, the impersonal, moral and existential contexts).*
>
> Claim 2. *All we talk about, or all language refers to, is human practices or human nature, or even human language itself.*

I assert (1) and deny (2), quite consistently. As I explained above, the sense of the distinction we draw between veridical and illusory sense perception – what talk of such a distinction means – is given by our practices of correction in looking, hearing, tasting and so on. This hardly means that when we talk about tables, chairs, mountains and buildings we are talking about human practices or language. Similarly the fact that the sense of the distinctions we draw between right and wrong, virtue and vice, is given to us in our experience of conscience, compassion, moral example and instruction, and so on does not of itself mean that we are talking merely about these experiences and practices (considered simply as psychological phenomena), much less that we are talking only about moral language. Finally, in relation to religious reality, children are instructed in prayer, worship and other practices that give them the distinctive sense of God's reality. So again in this case, as in the empirical object and moral cases, there is no reason to think that believers are talking only about their own practices or language games simply because the sense of 'independent' is given through the place of that language in a certain domain of human life. Of course, as I have been saying, the nature of that independence is different in each case.

But this general point, even if granted, might seem to be inadequate in the present case. For haven't I said that existential reality is the reality of certain significances possessed by human life in particular and the physical world at large? But that makes existential realities properties of the physical world, so that if the physical world had never existed neither would the existential have.[10] So if God is to be located inside the existential he cannot exist independently of the world, as normally supposed.

My reply is that actual *particular* existential truths – the sacredness of these people, the significance of this world's contingency, the terror of these evils – are indeed properties of the physical world and that they perish with it and would not have existed without it. But God is not to be identified with these particular truths. As the previous chapter has already suggested, he is something closer to the Platonic form of whatever it is that is instantiated, manifested, in particular good things. I have called that thing love itself, and I do tend to regard that as its, or his, most central characterisation. But he has many faces. He is goodness itself in a sense that has love as central to it. And, as Plato realised, from the perspective of this goodness our illusions and pretences and rationalisations – the shadows of our worldly cave – are stripped away: thus God is also truth itself. (Love wants to love people as they really are, unconditionally, so that there is no need to airbrush them: it cannot abide untruth.) Thus understood God would indeed be there even if the physical world were not. Love itself, goodness itself, truth itself – as opposed to their particular instances – do not perish or change. Thus we can say they – God – exist in eternity.

We will not understand this, however, if we assimilate it to the common caricature of a Platonic form. That has all forms existing *in the same way* as if their nature as the forms of *goodness*, or *redness*, or *triangularity* was incidental to the *kind* of reality they have. That way – by now the reader should be expecting the theme – is the impersonal and objectifying way. The forms are conceived as pseudo-empirical objects existing in a pseudo-empirical world (camouflaged by calling it a 'spiritual' or 'Platonic' or 'abstract' world) but most importantly as impersonal entities and thus as candidates for inclusion in the canonical inventory of types of impersonal things. Their inclusion again threatens the neat, non-weird attractions of naturalism, and fuels the debate over universals, with its search for naturalistic or nominalistic alternatives in a manner paralleling the debates over morality. But this flattening out of the reality of the forms (in a way which seems almost to treat existence as a property) is a mistake. Triangularity has an inescapable *geometric* reality, so that we encounter it through the practice of geometry and learn what it means to talk about 'triangularity' and its 'reality' through the use of those words in the context of that practice. Similarly for redness and our life with colours and associated colour language. And the same goes for talking of love, goodness and truth – in themselves – as realities: we encounter them and learn what it means to speak of them in appropriate human contexts of love, goodness and truth. These are moral contexts shading into existential ones, the latter in full fruition when we speak of God's reality, the sense of that speech coming from its use in the context of prayer, worship, confession and so on, as well as the wider background of moral and existential contexts in general. As before for particular existential realities (in the previous section), once we see that God's eternal reality is not objectifying, that it is not positing something in competition with empirical objects for inclusion in a single, definitive inventory of what is real, we can perhaps see that there is nothing here to regard as weird. In the same spirit, eternity is not the implausible sempiternal notion of going on and on for ever, crossing off the hours and days as they pass. The eternal is not there before human civilization and after it, like the Sun. It does not come *before* or *after* anything. It is not a temporal notion of duration at all, quite the opposite. That is an impersonal, objectifying notion of the eternal. We are dealing with an existential one.

So on this account God does indeed exist quite independently of the physical (and mental) world. But it is not a spatial, temporal or causal independence, or any kind of independence within the impersonal picture of reality. It is the conceptual independence of belonging to the existential realm of reality instead of the impersonal one. As I have explained, this does not entail that 'God exists' *means* the same as (is synonymous with or can be translated without loss into) some statement exclusively about human reactions and practices, or that when we are talking about God we are talking about those reactions and practices. No more than the fact that the sentence 'The table is made of small particles with a lot of empty space between them' gets its sense from our scientific practices means that the statement is about those practices. No, we are taking about God and about the table respectively. The suggestion otherwise just repeats the confusion of claims (1) and (2) above.

This line of thought has sometimes had its gist expressed by saying God is not an *object*, *thing* or *entity*. That can mislead because the words are so broad and content-less. They can be used in any context to indicate a topic of discussion. But what people who have said this were getting at (or at least what they should have been getting at) is that God is not an *impersonal*, *objectifying* kind of thing. He is not an item, like the Sun, to be included in an inventory of items that make up the world understood in the impersonal sense. The negations of classical Christian theology – that God is disembodied, simple, outside time, immutable, impassable and so on – are not attributions that make up the nature of some mysterious objectifying object. If I say God does not have a body, that is not a way of specifying a body he has and *nor is it a way of attributing some non-bodily property or power* (or an 'immaterial' nature). Similarly, if I say that God is perfectly simple – all his properties are identical with one another (and identical with him) and he is not composed of any parts, states or processes – this is not a way of specifying any parts, states or processes and *nor is it a way of attributing some kind of property or power that does not depend on parts and processes.* And so on *mutatis mutandis* for the other negations. The negations are not attempts to describe or attribute a positive impersonal nature. They do the exact opposite. They are reminders that the impersonal domain is the *wrong place* to look for God. As I like to put it, they are conceptual 'Stop' signs, or perhaps conceptual 'You Are Going the Wrong Way: Go Back' signs (the ones you see, at least in Australia, when you enter a freeway via an exit road).[11] They are there to tell us that asking what God's body is like, or what parts he has, or what states or processes go on in him is asking the *wrong questions*. God is not a being of *that* (creaturely) sort, not something talk of which gets its sense from the impersonal kinds of human activities.

## 4. Objections

There are many kinds of objection which forget or ignore the point about context. One would be to insist that eternity is not a kind of reality at all. Indeed, the thought might go, it is the paradigm of what is *unreal*, the paradigm not of a thing or entity that is there, but of *nothing*, of sheer emptiness. It is just a colourful way of talking about a viewpoint which a human being may or should adopt. It is simply a possible human perspective, and perishes with those who from time to time adopt it. There is no reason to think that anyone or anything permanently occupies the point of view in the way I have said God does, no reason to think the point of view has any reality when a human being is not occupying it. But the objection forgets what I have been at pains to stress: that what 'real', 'there', 'exists', 'thing' or 'entity' means is not univocal but varies with context (or if there is an underlying univocal meaning, then it is too weak to help in these disputes). We have practices of an objectifying sort for determining whether there is any furniture in a room, for example. These are practices of looking, counting, using pieces of furniture in the appropriate way and learning the language that goes along with all this, which enable us to understand

and answer such a question. Also in an impersonal vein there are other, more sophisticated observational, explanatory and predictive practices for examining scientific questions. And we have practices and responses of a very different, moral and especially existential sort which give sense to disputes over whether there exists an eternal realm beyond the impersonal, physical world, and whether in it there dwells perfect love, goodness and truth: God. These are such things as prayer, worship and confession, but even more fundamentally such things as conscience, the fear of death, the capacities for gratitude for or resentment at our existing at all, especially given the reality of evil, and so on. If physicalists are right, then from the impersonal point of view there may indeed be 'nothing' left after the physical world has been stripped away. But from a religious form of the existential viewpoint, this 'nothing' may be the most important thing of all. 'Things' matter to us in different ways. There is no reason to think that any of these ways, or the descriptions associated with them, is more fundamental than any other.

It is important to see that this position *does not guarantee the existence of God* any more than my account of the reality of tables and chairs, or protons and electrons, guarantees their existence.[12] It is quite neutral on that. It is trying only to delineate what it *means to say* that there is, or is not, a God. A person might accept it and remain entirely sceptical about whether there is such a thing – for example, because they think that our existential experiences are the illusory product of class warfare or childhood neuroses. This point is a crucial move in meeting the common objection that the sort of position I have defended would license any old piece of nonsense. But I am not passing judgement on any substantive existential claim, and no particular judgement on any case is implied. I am describing what I take to be the nature of debates people actually have, the sorts of considerations that are relevant to them and so on. Whether tachyons exist is a matter for investigation in the appropriate impersonal ways. An account of those ways does not prejudice the result of those investigations. Whether ancestor worship is a true religion has to be investigated in very different ways, since 'true' here has, or at least also has, a crucial existential meaning, but the principle remains the same: an account of those ways, an account of existential meaning in general, should not prejudice the substantive issue.

It might be objected that I am putting the cart before the horse when I claim that the meaning of reality-claims depends on human practices. For the meaning and point of those practices (be they impersonal, moral or existential) depends on the assumption that their objects (the physical world, morality, God) are real. That assumption *justifies* the practices, which are otherwise arbitrary or pointless, or at least expressions of attitude in a sense which implies they are not candidates for truth. But the objection just repeats the confusion of claims (1) and (2) from Section 3. Certainly someone who prays assumes, or at least hopes, that God is real. Certainly the prayer is pointless (or at least does not have its usual point) if God is not real. But it does not follow that the meaning of 'God is real' is determined independently of those practices, which include our responses *to the reality of love itself.* The practices *are in large part formed by that reality* (assuming it exists), just as our practices with physical objects are partly formed by *their* nature. So it is not as if the human practices are some sort of private activity, or are in some way sealed off from the world, so that the world, including the referents of our terms, does not enter into the determination of meaning. Perhaps an appreciation of this point will help head off the charge of 'linguistic idealism'.

In a recent discussion of D. Z. Phillips's view on the nature of the eternal, John Haldane puts a version of the objection just discussed:

> Claims about surviving death are interpreted as expressions of a religious outlook on this life, and other claims of an unmistakably religious sort are then interpreted in the same way. 'Religious' however, is itself denied anything but an attitudinal reading whose distinctive character either begins to evaporate or is fixed by reference to attitudes to religious stories and images. What makes these 'religious' once more appears to be the attitudes taken towards them, ones of reverence and awe, say. But this seems to get things back to front, or at least to be inaptly unilateral; for in discriminating between different attitudes we need to make some reference to their proper objects. Phillips wants to say that 'God' is to be interpreted in terms of 'Godly' attitudes (understood very broadly) whereas the characterisation of such orientations, along with other intentional attitudes, is defeasibly to be given by reference to their *objects.* Certainly one may allow some influence in both directions, but to allow it in only one direction seems premature and close to stipulative. (Haldane 2007, p. 258; original emphasis)

This is a particularly subtle case of the confusion of claims (1) and (2). It is one thing to assume that reference transcends language and other human practices in the sense that 'God' refers to something beyond them (and the objectifying world). That should be uncontroversial. It is quite another to maintain that our managing to refer to *this* rather than *that* can be accomplished independently of the sense conferred on our words by their use in our practice. Quite another, that is, to say that what counts as a 'proper object' of reference, and what sort of reality it has, is determined independently of that use. That is magic. But it is the meaning Haldane needs to sustain his argument. The proper object here is, as he acknowledges, a *religious* object, but that is not much help unless we know what is meant by 'religious'. Haldane treats this as obvious. It is, he says on the same page, a 'metaphysical' object, and on the next page he calls it a 'transcendent reality' and claims that talk of it makes 'ontological presuppositions'. A lot of weight is carried by the rhetorical force of these phrases, for in the Platonic, existential sense I have outlined – which I take to be on the whole in the spirit of Phillips's work – one can perfectly well talk of a metaphysical object, a transcendent reality, and so on, if that just means something beyond the objectifying world, and also beyond what Haldane calls, rightly condemning it as superstition, belief in a 'supremely powerful agent within the universe' (but invisible and so on, I assume he means) and in 'prayer and the rest' as 'quasi-empirical processes of influence and exchange' (p. 258). Equally one can agree that the object itself, in our encounter with it, influences our view of what our attitudes should be and what they should be directed towards,[13] so long as we remember that these are *existential* attitudes, that encounter with God is an *existential* context: so long, for example, as one remembers that God is something to worship and love, or to fear and rage against, and so on, and not something to measure or observe through an instrument or include as a hypothesis in a scientific theory (or something on which to perform some sort of simulacrum of all this). I do not know whether the existential sense would satisfy Haldane. But if not, this is because the rhetorical force of those phrases is working overtime and pushing him into the magical supposition of a 'proper reference', and a sense of what kind of reality the referent has, that is just given to us quite independently of the relevant existential human context and the judgements of propriety that involves: think again of the issue of idolatry.[14] In practice though he either treats this reality as something impersonal, and falls into the very superstitious position he condemns, or else is talking about something I for one cannot make any sense of.

Another line of objection concerns my denial that God is a causal force. If the argument of this book is sound, there is no escaping the problem of evil if God is a moral agent. But I have gone further than denying he is a moral agent. I have denied he is an efficient causal force. But, the objection goes, can it really be denied he is an efficient causal force without departing radically from historic Judeo-Christian faith? Christians affirm that God created the world and worked miracles. How can these beliefs be retained if God is not a causal force? Believers do not escape the problem of evil just by denying that God is a moral agent or person. X does not have to be a moral agent for one to draw conclusions about X from its being the cause of Y. If a food makes us sick we can conclude it was contaminated. If water in the radiator of our car damages it we can conclude the water contained impurities. Similarly, if an omnipotent being creates a world with the sort of evil in it that this world has, then (in the absence of just that sort of morally sufficient reason which theodicy seeks) we can conclude that the being is not 'love itself' or 'perfect love'. It is irrelevant whether or not the being is a moral agent and irrelevant whether or not a person responds with love or resentment. The point is that the descriptions 'love itself' and 'perfect love' cannot be true. But the denial of God's causal power seems hard to square with historic Christian belief.

Take creation first. We say that God created the world. But can we just assume that the logic of this is not importantly different from the logic of 'the man built a house', 'birds make their nests', 'Plato created a world of ideas' and so on? Especially when we are talking about a being who, in the predominant tradition of Christian thought, is disembodied, eternal, immutable, impassable and simple. There is no describing the processes (physical or mental) by which God creates. Causation becomes so foggy in this context that it is unclear how helpful the word is in explicating creation. Furthermore, if I am right in claiming that the logic of Christian belief is asymmetrical, praising God for good but not blaming him for evil, then we seem even further removed from being able to make sense of creation as a causal phenomenon.[15] In contrast, the view that God is love itself can avoid the problems of the causal account. Love itself is encountered through its manifestations in the good things that befall us and the good things that we do. Of the former, the most important by far is simply the bald fact that we and the world exist at all. The instantiation of love itself as the existence of the physical universe *is* creation. A sense of the sheer remarkableness of this is perhaps the most potent source of moral and spiritual life, and we have constantly to fight against the deadening of it. That manifestation of God, and our response of grateful love (or resentment) to it, is what gives sense to talk of God as the alpha of the universe, our origin, our Creator. Intelligent design worships at the altar of a very different God.

But on this view how do we account for the existence of evil? Since evil is not a manifestation of God – of goodness itself – then it seems there exist states of affairs that God did not create. My answer is two-fold. First, I distinguish creating objects from creating states of affairs and hold that creation requires only creating the former. Every physical object is in itself a good thing: each manifests love itself. So, in the sense I have described, God is the creator and sustainer of everything that makes up the physical universe (and moral and existential phenomena, but let's concentrate on the physical universe). In that way God is the creator and sustainer of the physical universe period: even though – not being a causal force – he is not responsible for the particular arrangements, the states of affairs, physical objects enter into, some of which are good (and manifest him) and some of which are not. My second answer relies on the assumption – made elsewhere in the book – that good, including love, cannot exist without evil, physical and moral, and indeed the serious evil we find in the actual world. The momentousness of human life, with its capacities for love, compassion and so on, depends upon our vulnerability to serious evil.[16] But as I have admitted before, this assumption is too big to be properly defendable within the compass of an already crowded book.

Against all this someone may grant the general semantic point about the human context of words' use and meaning that is central to my position, but just flatly deny that existential contexts are the only or the main context conditioning the use of 'God' and other religious words. They might point out that people *do* debate the existence of God without *any* reference to existential questions at all (in my sense of 'existential'). It is certainly true that these debates exist, and while they tend to be the activity of philosophers and other intellectuals I do not deny that – at least prior to reflection – many laypeople would agree that the intellectuals are debating the existence of the same God that they do, or do not, believe in. One may point, for example, to the large number of lay Christians in the United States who reportedly are supportive of intelligent design or even creationism. But this is not enough to show that the existential account is mistaken. The argument assumes that people's beliefs are to be identified with their *opinions, theories* or *speculations*: what they will or might *say* if they start to philosophise. But opinion (as I shall call it) is not the only form of belief. There is also *practical* belief: what people *do* – more broadly, what their life is like and the place of their non-speculative use of religious language in it – rather than what they say. And as I have emphasised before, in difficult matters like these it is very easy for the two to come apart: the phenomenon of dissociation. To take an example of Phillips's some distance from religion, if we asked people in the street about the nature of thinking, 'a confused Cartesianism would be returned with a thumping majority' (if the people in the street happened to be professional philosophers this would remain true, but with the brain substituted for the Cartesian soul). Phillips (2007a, p. 78) comments that we cannot do philosophy by Gallup poll. But the present point is that there is a sense – the practical one – in which the people in the street are not confused about the nature of mind at all. In their daily activities they attribute mental states to themselves and others (and act and respond appropriately) in generally accurate ways that only an eliminativist about the mental would impugn. It is just that they struggle – as we all do, however long we have studied the question – to give a clear and accurate discursive philosophical account of what in practice they fluently understand. The same distinction applies to religion. If asked to give their opinions about God, they may come up with a crude anthropomorphism. They may say, for example, that prayer and God answering it is a matter of what Haldane calls 'quasi-empirical processes of influence and exchange'. But if they persist in prayer despite its repeated failure to make any detectable difference to the way the empirical world goes on, if they have no interest in those experiments which study the illness recovery rates of patients prayed for against a control group not prayed for, and so on, then despite what they may say, there is good reason to think (and it is not necessarily patronising to do so) that their opinions are not an accurate representation of their practice: of their *actual* faith, the real meaning and point of prayer in their lives, which is not to secure some effect in the empirical world, but to glorify God, to express their hope of good things but their trust in the reality of God however the world goes on. Someone like Haldane, who acknowledges that some philosophers hold (in their theoretical beliefs) superstitious (his word) views of God, should appreciate the point. It is the basis for saying that when we criticise a philosopher's *opinions* we are not criticising *them* or their personal, *practical* faith.[17]

But my case does not rest entirely or even mainly on this empirical claim. More importantly I hold that there is a central *logic* to Christianity (or any real-world movement or tradition or institution) that is not a simple function of its empirical manifestations, which sometimes may seem to run against it. I have in mind the way in which we might talk of a central logic or general moral thrust of, say, an institution such as the common law, and associated political and constitutional practice, a thrust that may legitimately lie at the heart of a tradition even despite very considerable departure from it in practice and certainly in theorisation about it (recall also the cricket example from the previous chapter). I think that the idea of God as love itself, and of our love of him as unconditional, is at the heart of Christianity in a way in which causal power is not. There are impersonal contexts in which we learn words such as 'create', 'make', 'act' and so on, and there are religious contexts in which we learn a different (but related) use for these words. In the former case we can normally verify or falsify any hypothesis about a cause of some observed effect. The hypothesis that human characteristics are passed from parents to children by internal information-bearing entities called genes was verified by the discovery of the DNA molecule. The hypothesis that a perturbation in the movement of the planets can be explained by the existence of another heavenly body can be verified or falsified by telescopic observation. The hypothesis that Jones was the murderer is verified when a witness turns up. And so on. Of course sometimes there are reasons why we cannot directly verify a hypothesis. Some of those reasons are accidental, such as an object being too old to get an adequate DNA sample from, or the right technology not having been developed. Others are impossibilities (I assume), such as travelling back in time to observe the Big Bang or seeing what happens on the other side of a black hole. But accidental or in some sense necessary, these reasons all belong to the impersonal category of understanding. These are objectifying, technical reasons. In contrast, if God is a quasi-cosmological hypothesis about the causal origin of the world (whether inferred or revealed), why cannot we verify *that*? However, *the very idea* of verifying God by sensory observation, however technologically enhanced, makes no sense. God is not *that* sort of thing: anything that can be perceived like that is a creature, not the Creator. Even the strictest 'fundamentalist' recognises intuitively that Yuri Gagarin was making a category mistake when he said he had been into space and had not seen God. Whatever he did not see it was not God. You get no closer to God by going into space or back or forward in time or even by being brought back to life after you die. God is a *spirit* and not something we can see, touch and so on. But this is not because he is a very subtle spirit, too subtle for even our most refined instruments to detect. That would be just another objectifying reason he could not be seen, implying he was an objectifying kind of object. We cannot see him or touch him because he is a spirit, a spiritual reality, in the sense of an *existential* reality. (That spirit can enter and inspire our lives, but the entrance is not a *causal* phenomenon, the way radiation may enter our bodies. Rather it is the instantiation of the spirit, of love itself, in our lives.) Perhaps all parties will agree that God is not an *empirical* object, and thus that his unobservability is not like that of sub-atomic particles, something for which we could give a *scientific* explanation. But my point is that there is a tension between agreeing to that and nevertheless treating God as a hypothesised theoretical entity causally explaining observable phenomena, whether those phenomena be as particular as explanatory gaps in evolutionary history and the fine-tuning of the universe or as general as the bare existence and contingency of the universe. If we hypothesise the existence of some as yet unobserved cause of some observed phenomena, then either (i) it needs to be possible that the cause can be confirmed by observation in the future or (ii) we need to have an *explanation* of why it cannot even in principle be observed. In God's case that explanation cannot be scientific (the way it is with sub-atomic particles) without reducing him to an empirical phenomenon.[18] So what is the explanation? It is no good merely to say that God is defined as immaterial. That is just another way of saying that we cannot even in principle observe him. We can argue that contingent reality requires the existence of a necessary reality on which it depends, and then try to show that a necessary being cannot be empirical (for then it would still be contingent) and derive the various divine negations. The problem here is that if we construe the necessary being – as unfortunately many philosophers tend to do – *as having an impersonal and objectifying reality*, then it is not clear why the necessary being is not simply (as an earlier objection to my argument had it) *nothing* at all. After all, nothing (or nothing-ness, if you prefer) seems to possess all the negative properties of God: it is simple (contains no parts or processes), it is outside time and space, it is not subject to change and does not suffer forces acting upon it, and so on. View God's reality as impersonal in the way tables, chairs, lions and sub-atomic particles have impersonal reality and he is in danger of not existing at all. But there is an alternative, *existential* construal of the contingency argument. That would begin with an existential understanding of what contingency is, one relating it to the sort of sense of the world's perishability and our mortality expressed in Gerard Manley Hopkins's words 'the blight man was born for' ('Spring and Fall' in Hopkins 1953, p. 50). The argument would proceed to the existential reality of God as love itself, existing 'in eternity', as something not subject to change, not datable or with an age or history, without parts or processes, and certainly not observable, and so on (the divine negations). God's power as the Creator of Heaven and Earth (creation's dependence on God) is then understandable in the way I have indicated as the instantiation of love itself. But of course, this *just is* my position, in which God is no longer a causal force in any sense that warrants the words. I do not know that I can show there are no other possibilities here, and I concede that the matter requires more discussion. But in the existential position we have a principled explanation of why God is real yet is not an empirical object, and one which has the advantage of not admitting inferences from the existence of evil to the nature of God. The thrust of all this is to back up my claim that the *central logic* of faith bends towards the denial that God is a causal force, so that it is quite principled to maintain that denial. It is not just an *ad hoc* expedient for escaping the problem of evil.[19]

There is a second argument in support of that claim about the central logic of Christian faith. If philosophers and scientists did ever agree in proving or discovering the existence of a disembodied, super-powerful being who made the universe – John Bishop's omni-God – no doubt we would (overlooking the problem of evil!) have good reason to be very grateful to him/her/it, just as we can be to human benefactors. But that gratitude and praise *would have to be apportioned according to the being's merits*. This would mean praising God as 90 per cent good or 80 per cent good or some other estimation. 'How great thou art,' we sing. How great? Eighty per cent great! But there is no religious point in this. Believers who cannot love unconditionally in response to evil become unbelievers, not adherents of a better-than-average or just-good-enough God. Such a God is distinct in principle from the worship and love of God as love itself, a worship and love which are *not* proportional to the good and bad in the world, but *unconditional*.[20] It is this unconditional love of God that is at the heart of Christianity, is its central logic, not causal power.

So, on my account, the logic of Christian faith is such that when we say God is not physical but spiritual we do not, or should not, mean he is some sort of non-empirical but still objectifying thing, existing in a sort of objectifying shadow world of the empirical world. We cannot turn God into a genuinely spiritual – that is, existential – thing by prefixing 'im' to 'material'. God is not a material thing and he is not an immaterial thing either, for both those notions (at least as used in the sort of philosophical account of religion I am criticising) are impersonal ones. Rather God's reality is existential. One encounters God through prayer, worship, conscience, angst and not least the shock and humility of realising we are not able ultimately to be captains of our own fate. It is often said or implied that without God's being a causal force, Christianity is worthless. This seems to me an astonishing mislocation of its real significance.

The same reasoning applies to eschatology and the fulfilment of prophecy generally. These do not in themselves establish the reality of God – not if they are understood as the coming to pass of a series of impersonal and objectifying events. If at some time in the future we found ourselves brought back to life with our old bodies somehow reconstituted but in a form no longer susceptible to decay and dissolution – if indeed something like this happened to the whole universe – that would certainly prove the world was causally wired up in a certain sort of astonishing way. If it turned out that this wiring was causally created by some sort of person with mega-powers, then so be it: another objectifying fact. As it happens, given what the world is like we could hardly conclude that he is love itself: that is just the problem of evil all over again. But that is *not* the main point. The main point is that even if his record were perfect, what we love and worship in what he has done is not primarily the results he has procured, much less the causal power to procure them – indeed there is something seedy about being in awe of sheer causal force: it is an attitude either cringing or ambitious, or both – *but rather the love that his actions manifest*. And the logic of that leads us on to a sense of encounter with that love that transcends this particular manifestation of it. Now of course it is important to know that we are loved by this or that individual, including perhaps my mega-powered being. The last thing I want to suggest is that we should be so falsely pious as to spurn the worldly consolation of human love or tangible goods in the name of something higher. But it is not always realistic. There was precious little such consolation in Auschwitz and Dachau. If there can be hope or faith in that sort of depth of evil, it is the knowledge that, no matter how bad things are, *in the light of unconditional love itself we are sacred*: we matter – infinitely and eternally. This is the only thought with the power to defeat the worst evil in our lives, if anything can. Even the hope that the ruling causal powers of the universe will make things turn out well in the end cannot do that, not only because of doubts about the prediction being realised, but because some evils cannot be defeated by providing greater goods, as I hope my discussion of that idea has helped show. This I believe is one of the things that Christian faith of the right sort – as opposed to worldly resources – distinctively offers. It takes the measure of evil. And again it is much more central to that faith than causal claims.

Or consider miracles. Even Jesus himself knelt to pray as if to something greater than himself, to something he uniquely embodied in human form but still transcending him considered as a human being. If that love were a causal power it would make sense to say the resurrection proved Jesus's divinity. But it doesn't. Considered just as an impersonal causal phenomenon the resurrection could be the work of the devil. It is only *already* seeing God as uniquely and supremely present in Jesus which can reveal any of the miracles as an act of God. But then it can't be causal power which establishes Jesus's divinity – an inference from effect to cause, notice, in the manner of hypothesising a theoretical entity – for that is just what the miracles display in spades on a purely objectifying understanding of them. Rather what establishes Jesus's divinity if anything does is the authority of the love in him, and the authority of that love is demonstrated on Calvary: whatever the resurrection means it would be nothing revelatory of love itself without Calvary.[21] Simply as causal force it is consistent with brutalism. But doesn't the beneficial use of that power demonstrate love? Even putting aside the problem of evil, it does not. Above I wrote of a mega-powered being whose perfect moral record manifested love. That was fine for the point I was then making, but I was being rather generous. The truth is that an omnipotent person bestowing largesse on all and sundry is rather like a billionaire who pours money into philanthropy at no cost to himself. It costs him nothing significant and is consistent with vulgar narcissism. What it means to speak of God in personal language is shown in the incarnation, and what it means to speak of his love as a person is shown on Calvary: God's – love's – greatness is his *humility*, and his power is manifested in his *suffering* at the hands of *worldly* power. And this love is not something you infer from observation, in the manner of postulating a theoretical entity to explain observed phenomena, in the manner of one kind of impersonal reality. It is something that you simply see in his actions and demeanour, as you do with anyone. It can be seen too in the world. The Psalmist declares that God's handiwork is visible in the heavens above. But he is not inferring the existence of a cause of those heavens in the manner of intelligent design. He is praising the love that is non-causally manifest in the extraordinary fact that such a beautiful world exists.

But if this is true, then the idea of God as a causal explanatory hypothesis, a cosmological thesis, is no better able to be preserved through appeal to causal forces that transcend those of nature than it is through appeal to natural ones themselves. Events (miracles, fulfilled prophecies), natural phenomena (the beauty of the stars, of nature at large): to see any of these things as revelatory of God you *already* have to see

them, or the human who performed them, as manifesting God, as manifesting love itself. But then no confirmation is needed, and where no
confirmation is needed no unobserved or unobservable cause is being
postulated. God is not *that* sort of impersonal and objectifying thing.
But if he is not that sort of thing, if he is not the sort of thing we
know by drawing inferences about him from the world and its details,
or testing hypotheses about him against the world and its details – but
rather the sort of thing we personally and existentially encounter in
experiencing goodness and love – then we are not required to draw any
conclusions about him from the reality of evil. It is God who enables
us to see the world and know it properly, not the world which enables
us to know God. Once again, the perspectives of belief and unbelief are
incommensurable.

Notice, importantly, that nothing I have said actually involves the
*denial* of any impersonal, causal claim. It does not in itself deny the
existence of an omni-god (to give it its appropriate lower case), though
it does deny that he is God. It does not involve the denial of any miracle, however literally understood, or even of a birthday-celebrating,
temporal afterlife. But it does deny the prime importance these things
are often given. It is possible in principle for someone believing in the
omni-god's existence to agree with the substance of my position – and
this will be the sticking point – so long as they acknowledge that the
omni-god is in fact a creature, an especially important loving one perhaps, but not God with a capital G. God is what *shows in* the omni-god's
existence and life: the love itself which transcends any instance of it.

## 5. Conclusion

Theodicy rightly teaches us that the experience of evil can be the source
of spiritual growth. However, it wrongly tries to make it into a justification for God's creation of a world with so much evil. It also holds out
to us the prospect of a future eternal beatitude: eternal in the birthday-
celebrating sense. That is of course related to spiritual growth, but there
is also no doubt that theodicy tends to emphasise that it will be a state
of happiness in the psychological sense, certainly a state free of pain or
suffering – and it makes the expectation of that condition essential to
our relationship with God. But this misunderstands the nature of that
relationship and the role of evil in it. Such expectations are always in
danger of taking on an essentially worldly form, especially if the problem of evil tempts us to use them as a ground for God's exoneration.
What we really *can* most deeply learn from evil is precisely *to have no*

*such expectations*. God is the centre of the world, not us (Mulhall 1994, pp. 66–8). If people can be described as blessed by terrible sufferings at all, it is in the sense in which Simone Weil wrote of those she called 'the afflicted' as especially loved by God, for (my interpretation may be disputed) they alone can see the world stripped of the illusions our ego clings to, and thus can see God and depend on God alone.[22] Chief among those illusions is the hankering to dilute evil's threat by finding in it some instrumental purpose more agreeable to us. But the *pointlessness* of evil is essential to its horror. The only thing equal to and greater than it is the equally gratuitous reality of the goodness and love that God is. As Iris Murdoch says, writing of the capacity of great art to do justice to reality, it does so 'by a juxtaposition, almost an identification, of pointlessness and value' (1991, p. 87). And that means seeing it in the light of love, truth and as she said (giving it primacy) The Platonic Good itself. In contrast she would no doubt have classified theodicy as one of her 'consoling fantasies'. Theodicy is thus self-defeating. By seeking to find a function for evil it keeps us from the recognition of its pointlessness that we need to be free from its thrall. So it feeds the very discontent it seeks to relieve.

Good I have said is as gratuitous and pointless – as *non-instrumental* – as evil. That means its superiority over evil cannot be a *causal* superiority. It is enormously tempting to think the assertion that good is stronger or greater than evil can be made in terms of some neutral, common measure – and then to take that measure to be raw power. But there is no neutral criterion. Raw power is a criterion already biased on the side of worldly things. The superiority of the love is a *spiritual* or existential superiority – and can be seen only by someone who at least in some degree already sees things from that perspective. The problem of evil is a battle inside our hearts between two incommensurable perspectives. That battle is existential and it is what this book has tried to describe as the real, reconfigured problem of evil. That we cannot infer God's nature from the world does not mean there is not a struggle between God and evil, so it does not mean the problem of evil is resolved. It is resolved in God's favour for someone only if they find that the worship of love itself is not something they have to, or even can, abandon in the face of evil. But that is not an easy love to accept or even to see, for the world is shot through with evil. Perhaps we can see it clearly only on the Cross. It is a hard love. A frightening love.

# Notes

## 1. The greater good

1. In the entire 24,000 words of Michael Tooley's (2009) entry on 'The Problem of Evil' in the authoritative on-line *Stanford Encyclopedia of Philosophy* – an article intended to represent the state of the art – there is not a single mention of Dostoevsky or Ivan Karamazov, or of any of the radical anti-theodicy ideas canvassed in this book. Likewise, only on the last 2 pages of his nearly 400-page history of the problem of evil, *Evil and the God of Love*, a contemporary classic, does John Hick come to Dostoevsky, despite describing his challenge as 'the gravest of all ... to a Christian faith in God'. His only strategy in reply is to hold out the hope of a 'future good so great as to render acceptable, in retrospect, the whole human experience' (1978, p. 386). But, as we shall see, the radical-ness of Ivan Karamazov's challenge consists in rejecting exactly this line of thinking, so that Hick's reply begs the question. (Hick does briefly discuss the objections that theodicy is impious and lacking in compassion; 1978, pp. 6–10.) There are honourable exceptions. Anglophone philosophers who have taken Karamazov-type anti-theodical ideas seriously include Tilley (2000), Vardy (1992), Phillips (2001, 2005), Sutherland (1984), Scott (1996), Gibson (1973), Levine (2000), Roth (2001), Mulhall (1994) and Trakakis (2008), from whom I have borrowed the title of this section and to whose general discussion of anti-theodicy I am greatly indebted. Among Anglophone theologians Williams (1996), McCabe (1987) and Surin (1986) are three who have explained their rejection of theodicy in print.

2. Alvin Plantinga compares God creating a world in which people, including presumably children, will suffer as some people suffer in this world (he sets no limit) to a mother insisting her child 'take piano lessons or go to church or school' (2004, p. 24). The speed with which Plantinga takes it that the routine acceptability of the example can be extended to cover the horrendous suffering we find in this world – including that of children – takes one's breath away. (In the context his main idea is that people would consent to suffer in this life if they had God's knowledge and goodness, as children would consent to go to church or school if they had their mother's knowledge and goodness. As he makes clear, the idea of consent does not in itself include the idea of benefiting from the suffering – he adds this separately – but the example surely suggests just that as part of the justification for consent. I discuss consent below.)

3. Thus Richard Swinburne defends God against evil partly on the ground that it is a good for the victims of evil that their suffering enables them to be 'of use' to the moral development of *others*. He supports this with the example of a soldier being of use to his country (1996, pp. 102–3). If certain conditions are satisfied it is perhaps an honour for soldiers to serve their country, but that is not a justification, or part of a justification, for sending

them to war. The justification is that the war is a regrettable necessity for avoiding some worse evil. But God's creation of this world is not a lesser evil. Elsewhere Swinburne (2004, p. 262) does write that there are 'limits' to the evils a benefactor may inflict on a person in the early stages of their life (so long as the life as a whole is on balance good). But whatever limits he has in mind, all the suffering of this life is inside them. Given what that includes, one is inclined to ask Swinburne: just what do you think *is* unconscionable? On Swinburne's views see also Keller (2007, pp. 20–3).

4. Theodicy makes it axiomatic that we can benefit spiritually from evil, but it betrays the truth this contains by making it a justification for creating a world with that evil in the first place. An egregious example of this is the position – popularised by C. S. Lewis (1957) and also held by Eleonore Stump (1990) – which emphasises the role that suffering can play in rebuking our pride and reminding us of our ultimate dependence on God. It is a profound truth that suffering can do this. But we vulgarise that truth by turning it into a justification of God creating a world with that suffering. That is making God out to be the worst sort of tyrant: a Lord who tortures his vassals to wring submission out of them. That can, at best, produce only an insincere submission. But the notion of an insincere submission to God himself (as opposed to an insincere submission designed to fool other humans or even yourself) makes no sense. As Huckleberry Finn said, 'You can't pray a lie.' The underlying problem here is a conception of God which makes it possible to understand his reality without having specifically *religious* responses towards him, which treats those responses (such as submission) as only externally and causally related to understanding his reality. I discuss these matters in Chapters 3, 4 and 5.

5. A subset of this type of case are the religious and political fanatics who would sacrifice their own children to some scheme of general human improvement, to make a good world better. They are so absorbed by career-ist ambition or fanatical hatred that the normal parental love they would have for their children (not to mention normal human sympathy for suffering in general) is lost. The Bolsheviks and the Nazis, who coldly killed for the sake of putative greater goods, surely were in truth moved by passions of contempt and hatred, not just the desire for some future good. Moreover they surely understood their actions as aimed at escaping great disasters (rapacious capitalism, Jewish racial pollution and so on) rather than, say, improving the lot of those already relatively well off.

6. For example, the refusal to mix bodily materials by transplant and transfusion can be seen as a form of respect for bodily integrity and personal individuality. These cases are thus quite different from that of God as understood by theodicy, where the justification for creation is the instrumental one of securing a future good. There is no *violation* of anything valuable if God does not create, or creates only a vegetative world, just the *forgoing* of something valuable that he would like to realise.

7. Possible objection from a theodicist: neither God nor human parents have to agree that their children *will* be subjected to serious evil in return for a greater good and compensation, only that they will be exposed to a *risk* of it. But this is little better if the risk is either very high or unknown (would or should parents hostage their children's lives to an unknown, possibly

high, risk of serious evil?). (See further discussion of this in Section 4.) So we would have to assume that God knew the risk of serious evil entering the world (the Fall) to be quite low, an assumption not all theodicists would be happy with (such as those who believe God foreknows the free choices of all created agents, so there was no uncertainty for him about the corruption of this world). But even granting this low-risk scenario as a logical possibility for God, the claim of mainstream theodicy is not about the justifiability of creating a world with a certain risk of evil, but about the justifiability of creating a world with evil. Theodicists say time and again that the greater good outweighs the evil *itself*, and rarely does risk enter the picture. In any event, I bring a quite different argument against low-risk theodicy (and any theodicy) in Section 4.

8. It is not enough even if the ideal observer says only that one *can* consent, since (i) it remains the case that we do not, and (ii) in the relevant moral sense parents *cannot* consent to their children going to Auschwitz. The relevant sense is that of moral necessity (see Chapter 4).

9. To say one is better placed to judge the matter after getting in all the evidence, the good and the evil, looks awfully like saying one is better placed because one has ascended to the ideal observing position. In any event, if the actuality or imminent prospect of suffering can distort our judgement, then why cannot the actuality of good? Could we have just been bought off if we consent?

10. The term 'morally sufficient reason' is due to Nelson Pike (1990). Pike originated the defence strategy in the early 1960s, but his version of a defence was weaker than that described in the main text. He held that the atheist's 'argument from evil' does not succeed because its proponents cannot show that the non-existence of any MSR is a *necessary* truth. If the atheologian cannot show that there logically cannot be an MSR, the logical version of his argument fails. On this approach there is no need for the theologian even to speculate about possible MSRs. Alvin Plantinga later pioneered the stronger form of defence with actual speculations (see Plantinga 1974a, 1974b). More generally, the theodicy/defence distinction, among many others found in the literature, is drawn in different forms by different authors. Consequently no account of them is likely to please everyone.

11. If those two propositions are inconsistent with one another, then (as Plantinga explains) that inconsistency can rely only on other propositions that are *necessarily* true (as any inconsistency relies, say, on background laws of logic). It cannot rely on any *contingently* true propositions, for then the inconsistency would be between *God exists* and *evil exists* and those other contingent propositions.

12. Other non-moral or minimally moral starting points include rationality (in various forms), self-interest, flourishing and the theoretical virtues of simplicity, elegance, explanatory power and so on that govern processes such as reflective equilibrium.

13. Witness, for example, the way in which Graham Oppy (2004, pp. 72–5), attempting to find fault with Plantinga's moral assumptions, confesses to being unable to make much progress, concluding that he cannot see any persuasive argument to back up his 'intuitive' (that is, philosophically

untheorised) moral judgements. The reason for this is the drastically limited conception of justification on which he relies.

14. If he could alter it, then he was surely duty-bound to minimise it and that puts us at the point this line of thought will shortly get to anyway: the case where God knew the risk to be very low. I assume he could not eliminate the risk.

15. I shall call it a 'theodicy' even though it could be presented as a defence. In general, since that distinction makes no difference to the argument of my book, I shall from now on usually talk of 'theodicies', using the term to include defences.

16. For general discussion of the issues here see Williams (1993) and Gaita (2000b).

17. I have to admit that I do not have the space to give an argument for this crucial premise here, so must rely on whatever *prima facie* plausibility my readers will take it to have.

18. The impersonal conception of thought can allow that the conclusion ideal thinkers would agree in reaching may be a suspension of judgement, or a judgement of probability, or the acknowledgement that a range of positions, even ones inconsistent with one another, is legitimate. But whatever conclusion is reached, it is mandatory on *all* ideally rational and properly informed beings; it is just the conclusion such ideal thinkers would converge on. The range of conclusions has of course to be *limited*, on pain of the impersonal thinking being of no profit.

19. It might be denied that theodicy requires the parents to give any such consent. Greater good thinking gives the objective moral *justification* for humans being permitted to have children despite evil, but, so long as their actions conform to what that justification requires, the parents' *motive* for having children can be anything at all, including love. They can even actively disbelieve in the justification. God must believe in the objective justification (since he is omniscient), but even he can have it in the back of his mind, so to speak, allowing his creative love to drive his actions so long as they do not trespass beyond what the objective justification sanctions. In response one may wonder, first, whether we do not need very strong initial grounds to accept moral theories whose account of justification departs from the pattern of human motivation in this drastic way. But quite apart from that, the appeal to the motivation/justification distinction is of no avail in this instance. The question at issue is whether it is all-things-considered permissible for terrible evils to be inflicted on children (and people in general) if it is the only means to greater goods, and if compensation is provided, and if (usually hypothetical) consent is given – and, we may add for good measure, if the motive of the parents is love (rather than the greater good) and if from that love they refuse to acquiesce in the evils. Theodical morality says *yes*. Parental love says *no*. The question is: which of these is the right criterion to judge by? The introduction of the justification/motivation distinction gives people favouring the parental love criterion no reason to change their mind. They do not find the idea of such evil being inflicted (or being allowed to be inflicted) any more permissible because the conditions of that permissibility include some caveats about parents' own motivations and protests. (On another matter, one might of course call parental love

itself a kind of morality. But in the context, the move is merely verbal. The substantive contrast is between the greater good, ideal observer morality of theodicy and parental love – regardless of whether you call the latter a 'morality' or not. I elaborate on the distinction I am after, which I express as one between morality and love, in Chapter 3.)

## 2. The intellectual and the existential

1. Remembering, as I wrote in Chapter 1, that the universally valid resolution ideal thinkers would agree in reaching may be a suspension of judgement, or a judgement of probability, or the acknowledgement that a range of conclusions, even ones inconsistent with one another, is legitimate, though no one is mandatory.
2. Other than in the case, mentioned in the previous note, of a limited range of resolutions all of which are permissible. But the limits are universally binding.
3. For other examples of this doctrine of the separation of the intellectual and the existential see Langtry (2008, p. 1), Plantinga (1974a, pp. 28–9 and 63–4; 1974b, pp. 35 and 195) and, in a more equivocal version, Hick (2001, p. 49). Peter van Inwagen allows that theoretical discussion of the problem of evil 'may provide materials the pastor can make use of' (2006, pp. 10–11). But the issue is not only or mainly about the relevance of philosophers' writings to the victims of evil, for the victims can certainly find solace without the help of philosophers. It is more about whether the victims' suffering is relevant to the philosophers' writings, whether the philosophers are listening to the burning children. Despite what he says about the provision of materials for pastors, elsewhere in his book van Inwagen expresses considerable hostility towards any attempt to inform intellectual discussion of the problem with existential concerns. For one example, witness his criticism of Susan Neiman, which I shall discuss in the next chapter (van Inwagen 2006, pp. 15–17). For another, even when expressing himself what is patently a moral criticism – of the doctrine that evil is not real – he is at pains to convince the reader it is only 'intellectual' criticism. The gist of the criticism reads:

> If we think of soldiers making mothers watch while they throw their babies in the air and catch them on the points of their bayonets, or of the ancient Mesopotamian practice of moloch – of throwing living infants into a furnace as a sacrifice to Baal – or of a child born without limbs, we shall, I hope, find it impossible to say that evil is not real. (p. 60)

It is hard to see the point of an intellectual/moral distinction which would classify that passage as appealing only to people's intellectual capacities and not at all to moral ones.
4. Davis (2001b, pp. 84–5).
5. Davis writes that heaven will make 'all previous suffering such that the pain will no longer matter'. The full quotation, which Hasker (2008, p. 45, n. 45) reproduces, reads thus:

> The biblical vision is that despite the pain that all people have endured, and despite the horrible pain that some people have endured, the vision

of the face of God that we will then experience will make all previous
    suffering such that the pain will no longer matter. (Davis 2001b, p. 85)
Hasker, criticising Phillips, expresses astonishment that this passage could
be read as minimising human suffering. Certainly Davis acknowledges the
depth of human suffering. But the question is whether that is compatible
with saying that one day it will no longer matter.

6. There is an irony here in that, while they usually disavow practical and
existential problems, greater good theodicists treat the problem of evil as
though it were a practical problem: the problem of finding enough good to
outweigh the evil, and in the particular case at hand, enough good to erase
psychic pain.

7. The original is in Davis (2001c, p. 104).

8. Hasker is quoting Roth (2001, p. 31), who in turn is quoting Wiernik himself.

9. The original is in Roth (2001, p. 33).

10. Redeemed perpetrators, presumably, do wish the evils away (since it would
be inconsistent with remorse not to do so) but she can say they can come
to accept and forgive themselves, and to be reconciled in forgiveness with
their victims.

11. For very penetrating criticism of Adams see Williams (1996). This is a wonder-
ful paper, perhaps the best discussion of evil for its length that I know of.

12. It is worth noting here that in many cases it will be impossible to *confine
one's A-consent to one's own suffering.* If I A-consent to my own suffering, very
often I thereby effectively A-consent to others' suffering – do not wish *their*
suffering out of *their* lives – for I have suffered *through seeing them suffer.* Is a
mother supposed to cease regretting that she suffered seeing her child die
painfully of cancer? Are genocide survivors, a good part of whose suffering
is knowing how many of their fellows did not survive, supposed to cease
wishing they had never had to suffer that? If they cease to object to their
own suffering, they unavoidably cease to object to that of their child or of
their fellows who did not survive. (Unless the suffering of the others was
merely an illusion God inflicted on the mother or the survivor. But why is
the suffering of others an illusion and not their own? In any event, I take it
that God is not a deceiver.) There are many other examples. It is one thing
to cease wishing horrendous evil out of *one's own* life, quite another to cease
wishing it out of *others'* lives.

13. Since I shall be arguing it does not, the stronger claim that a majority of victims A-consenting is sufficient to exonerate God is automatically covered by
my argument.

14. Adams (1999, ch. 8) does say there may be alternative theoretical exonera-
tions of God to her own. Consequently she does not believe philosopher–
victims *must* satisfy themselves about universal A-consent before they can
make their personal decision. I'm not sure this helps her much. Critics
remain entitled to explore the consequences of her theory, the situation
someone would find themselves in if they took it as their solution to the
problem of evil.

15. The appeal to eschatology goes hand in hand with greater good thinking. Its
essentially unknown and speculative nature offers a blank cheque for entry in
the credit side of the universe's ledger, an entry in effect stipulated to overwhelm

anything that could be in the debit side. Adams's incommensurate goodness of the post-mortem beatitude is too indeterminate a philosophical abstraction to have any known concrete relation to a person's actual life, and for just that reason can conveniently be bellowed up into a cure-all for every ill, without any real attention to those ills. Precisely because no one has ever experienced the post-mortem beatitude and returned to give us their testimony of it, there are no actual witnesses, or imagined examples nourished by accounts of such witness, for theodicists to be held accountable to, and therefore nothing to check their speculation. There is no *concrete* phenomenon we can point to (as we can with good and evil experienced in this life) which can be a focus for discussion. No one knows what incommensurate goodness is; it is just 'whatever will do the trick'. Is Ivan supposed to sell the suffering of children for something he-knows-not-what? To think that the mere *meaning* of the word 'incommensurate' refuted him, that the matter could be settled by *stipulation* (it 'seems to me to reflect an insufficient appreciation of what "incommensurate" means') just evades his point and is in danger of obscurantism. For criticism of post-mortem goodness theodicy very similar to Ivan's, but directed at Stephen E. Davis, see John K. Roth's (2001, esp. p. 33) 'theodicy of protest'.

## 3. The problem of evil and the problem of the slightest toothache

1. One may, of course, very plausibly challenge the coherence of the scenario: human beings, unless treated as merely a kind of ape and maybe not even then, necessarily have goods and evils distinct from pleasure and pain. But we can ignore this for present purposes. Notice too that Swinburne's argument assumes that none of the pains are necessary means to pleasures that outweigh them. This also makes no difference to my argument.
2. I borrow the terms 'personal' and 'pastoral' from Peter van Inwagen (2006, p. 5).
3. Pike (1990, p. 40), van Inwagen (2006, pp. 12–14), McCabe (1987, p. 31).
4. It is true that various philosophers writing on God and evil recognise serious evils as giving rise to problems peculiar to them, and also true that discussions of the evidential version of the problem of evil have focused attention on the scale and seriousness of actual evils. But in general these discussions remain within a conceptual framework of greater goods theodicy, and within that framework the *de facto* assumption is that blemishes count as evils that must go into the calculus: they are just too minor, too obviously accounted for by greater goods, to be worth explicit mention.
5. Swinburne (1998, p. 4) acknowledges the linguistic point without perceiving its implications for his toothache claim. Van Inwagen (2006, p. 12) points to common usages such as 'a necessary evil', 'the lesser evil' and so on, which do not imply anything terribly serious. But everything here depends on context. In the context of the problem of evil, an *evil x* must have the sort of seriousness I am talking of if it is to be relevant, and, outside philosophy, we do use 'evil' in that way in such contexts, however blandly the word may also be used in other contexts.

6. This does not commit me to saying that only things seriously deserving to be called 'evil' threaten the goodness of God. 'Good' has uses that contrast with 'bad' as well as uses that contrast with 'evil', and the goodness of God includes many of the former uses as well as the latter. It is the extension of 'evil' to cover 'bads' which do not threaten the goodness of God that I am objecting to.
7. I am grateful to Chris Walsh for pressing this objection.
8. This is a variation on Alvin Plantinga's scenario, described in Chapter 1, of God being unable to create any world with a better balance of good and evil than that in the actual world.

## 4. The God of love

1. The idea that the authority of morality can be checked by other values (as opposed to checking itself) is of course controversial. For the case in favour of it see Williams (1981) and Taylor (forthcoming, ch. 4).
2. This condemnation is of course far from theoretical. Witness, for example, the moral views on infanticide of Peter Singer or Michael Tooley.
3. In fact, it is significant that human parents do *not* always do this. Recall the case in the first chapter of the religious believers who refuse certain life-saving medical treatments for themselves and their children.
4. Moral questions can of course be asked about whether one should prescribe a drug, draft a certain sort of contract or build a bridge in this place, and so on, but these questions are external to the technical expertise of a doctor, lawyer or engineer, which is why the general public have a big say in them (though of course the professionals will have a particular interest in the ethical questions and possess special knowledge relevant to them).
5. I am drawing a very stark line for the purpose of driving home the main point. There are of course aesthetic dimensions to engineering and architecture, and a humanistic understanding can be brought to bear in law and medicine. But I am singling out the technical and functional element of these disciplines, which the spirit of the times tends to emphasise.
6. I am of course assuming that the treatment of these existential questions cannot itself be reduced to technique, and I have not the space to argue that here if anyone wants to challenge it. A reader who wanted to challenge *that* is even further removed from my philosophical outlook than the average atheologist or theodicist. The latter seem committed to acknowledging that existential issues are not susceptible to technique by their own distinction between the intellectual problem and the existential problem for which they disavow any expertise.
7. Where the correct resolution of a problem leaves a range of permissible options some individual judgement will come into play in choosing between them, but the point is that this choice is no longer of an objectifying kind. Moreover there is a strong tendency in the objectifying mode of thought to regard such choices – and anything that cannot be settled in an objectifying manner – as arbitrary and non-cognitive: witness non-cognitivism in philosophical meta-ethics.

8. As Joe Mintoff has stressed to me, the transformed debate still requires the basic intellectual equipment of factual information, instrumental rationality and logical reasoning. These are involved even in thinking about the existential questions themselves. But this does not mean the debate will be specialised in the way the traditional debate is. I believe the transformed debate is within the reach of the intelligent, well-informed layperson, the generally educated non-specialist. The remaining technical elements are not so arcane as to be in practice necessarily the preserve of academic specialists. This is not to say of course that such specialists have nothing important to contribute to the discussion, especially when they are willing to broaden the terms of discussion in the way indicated.

9. This is consistent with the obvious fact that moral and existential truths can be stated glibly or hypocritically. The point is that they get their truth from what some human lives are like or approach being like and even in some cases can be like: they are truths about authentic human lives.

10. This is not to deny that we can and should have regard for people distant from us, or to deny that we can in some degree sympathise with them, but it is to deny that we can or should sympathise with them in the way we do with our family and friends.

11. See Taylor (2001, 2005a, 2005b), Winch (1972) and Williams (1981).

12. For fine philosophical explorations of what moral thought can be like when released from impersonal constraints see Diamond (1991, chs 11–15).

# 5. Is God an agent?

1. The sort of suffering I have in mind is something more than the ordinary run of human poverty or childhood illness and mortality I mentioned in the previous chapter. As far as these conditions go, and remembering their ubiquity until very recent times, if we make them a ground for condemning parents we might wonder, as comfortable liberals in affluent societies, where we can be reasonably assured of a good life for our children, whether our attitude might not be dangerously close to one which complains of the poor breeding too much. Still, there are circumstances – certain medical conditions with serious and constant physical pain and no drugs to alleviate it, for example – where, in the absence of countervailing considerations, there would be a serious moral cloud over parents who deliberately conceived a child they knew for sure would have the condition: a cloud dark enough that the appeal to love could not dispel it. Few human parents are in the position to have such knowledge, but God does not have that excuse. (Please notice that in the human case I have in mind only conceiving *versus* not conceiving; I have said nothing about abortion.)

2. Phillips (2005), Burrell (1979), McCabe (1987), Davies (2006) and Williams (1996) are just some of many philosophers of religion who (for various reasons) would agree that God is not a moral agent.

3. Love, in the parental image, is essentially creative. It favours existence over non-existence, life over death, creativity over destruction, and so on. At the creaturely human level this is a matter of efficient causation, of parents having children for instance. At the divine level it is something more like

the sheer gratuitous fact of there being something rather than nothing, and of our existing when we might just as well not have for all we can understand. Thus the antithesis of God is evil, destructiveness and ultimately non-existence, sheer nothingness.

4. We can speak of encountering God through evil only by the evil in some way leading to, or being overcome by, good (that overcoming does not mean primarily causal defeat in the way the police put criminals in jail: think of Calvary). We cannot see God in evil *in itself.*

5. This does not require causal interaction with good itself, as opposed to its instances. We can be nourished by our contemplation of fiction, for example.

6. But is it not the case that we owe our parents, even the very worst, some sort of regard, *just* in virtue of being our parents? I agree. But this is a bond of parent and child that goes deeper than morality, for it is not earned by behaviour or character: that is why it is not just for *good* mothers or fathers. This is parallel to that pre-moral bond between humanity and God that I mentioned at the end of the previous chapter.

7. Do not some people maintain a faith in God despite being unable to overcome resentment in their heart at life's evils? This actually supports my position. The word 'despite' is the key. It indicates that the central logic of resentment at the evil in the world is to destroy religious belief, and thus that a case where someone can maintain belief despite being unable to overcome serious resentment is an exceptional case requiring special explanation: this is someone who, despite permanently teetering on the brink of unbelief, cannot, so to speak, plunge the dagger into God's heart, cannot take the step which the logic of their situation is demanding of them. That is, they cannot finally *blame* God. If they are lucid in their understanding of their faith, they will realise that not blaming him is not a matter of finding conditions that excuse him – looking at the world, that is exactly what they *cannot* find – but of realising that praise (in the ordinary moral sense) and blame do not apply to him.

8. Could it be that the only way we can see love itself clearly, the only way to free ourselves of the distorting perceptions of evil, and in particular the scapegoating of love itself for evil, is for that love to actually be scapegoated in our midst, for us to see perfect innocence violated? That love itself and human suffering, the two rivals, actually meet and the rivalry is an illusion?

9. I should add, especially given my mention of meeting conditions of ideal judgement, that whether someone is a believer or an unbeliever is never entirely decided by reflection and reasoning. In the end it depends crucially on grace, not any merit of human beings. This is a reality of human life and the real substance to the doctrines of grace and predestination.

10. In the discussion of universalisability in the final section of the previous chapter readers might have wondered whether I distorted matters by concentrating on human beings and not God. It might be said that the relevant moral question for the problem of evil is not how *we* should respond to evil, but whether *God* has acted rightly in creating the world. The problem for us is to find, if we can, the correct answer to that question. I am now in a position to answer this concern. The objection wrongly assumes that

believers, like typical unbelievers, *judge* God, that is, see him as a moral agent. I have argued that this misrepresents believers' position. For believers, then, whether God has acted morally rightly is *not* 'the' question, and moreover, as I have argued in the main text, whether God is to be counted a moral agent or not is not the ultimate dividing line between believers and unbelievers.

11. On the whole issue of idolatry see Johnston (2009).
12. A and B may have no doubt whatever where they stand, despite perhaps feeling powerfully the pull of the other side, and in that sense the case is not a dilemma for them. There is not, for them, a dilemma about *what to do*. But the case will remain a dilemma in the sense that A must *bear the cost* (which they may recognise the full weight of), being morally bound as they are, and ditto for B. On bearing the cost (or what he calls 'suffering the consequences') see Phillips (2005, pp. 33–44).

## 6. The real God

1. Sometimes people say that God must be a person because we want the love of a person not just an abstract, impersonal love. Too true. Hence the importance of the incarnation. In my view the love of an abstract, disembodied Cartesian consciousness is no better than an abstract impersonal love.
2. Much of what I write here has been influenced by the work of D. Z. Phillips (1993, 2004, 2005). But see also Moore (1988) and (in defence of Phillips) Burley (2008a, 2008b), Ramal (2000) and Davies (2007). Gleeson (2009) is a less academic presentation of many ideas found in this chapter. For material critical of the sort of position I defend see Haldane (2007, 2008), Scott (2006) and Scott and Moore (1997). There is also much interesting relevant material in Moore (2003) and Moore and Scott (2007).
3. The anthropomorphic God of philosophers such as Swinburne and Plantinga is the crowning apex, the God of this God's-eye view.
4. Indeed, on the Christian account, the perspective of eternity can even be located as having meshed with the world in a particular man's life, lived at a specific place and time.
5. It makes no important difference here that he is regarded as a person and that personal – belief/desire – explanation is employed to explain how he produces his effects. Belief/desire explanation as we find it in contemporary philosophy of mind is impersonal and indeed quasi-scientific, through and through. Beliefs and desires are hypothesised causal states of an individual producing certain effects.
6. The proponents of these arguments themselves typically use the term 'cause' and other causal language, though they may stress that this is not causation in the empirical, efficient sense. I confess to having great difficulty grasping what they mean. I think there is a real question whether such arguments are using causal explanatory language in a meaningful way. There is a real risk of trading off the usual empirical sense of such language while denying one is doing so. (The real problem is that if metaphysical language does not have an empirical, moral or existential sense, then from what context of human life *does* it get its sense? I would argue that metaphysical argument

*by itself* does not constitute such a context. My fear is that this is another case of assuming a univocal sense of 'real' and 'true', which turns out to be the empirical sense in disguise.) Does this make me a positivist? I certainly share the positivist suspicion of metaphysics, but that is not enough to make me a positivist. I deny the central plank of positivist semantics: that the meaning of any statement is the means of its empirical verification, so that aesthetic, moral and metaphysical statements are cognitively meaningless, and presumably existential ones too. In contrast, something very like this assumption drives the mainstream debates about fitting mental, semantic and moral phenomena into an overall naturalistic worldview. These debates assume such phenomena must either reduce to, or supervene upon, empirical phenomena, or else be treated in some sort of non-realist, non-cognitive way. I mention them later in the main text.

7. Michael Scott and Andrew Moore criticise D. Z. Phillips for failing, by appeal to the practices of pointing to a thing or presenting it for sensory inspection, to distinguish God's reality from that of a physical object or something analogous to a physical object. They point out that sub-atomic particles would be in the same category as God by this criterion (Scott and Moore 1997, pp. 415–16). In the same spirit they argue, in effect, that representation *'according to the criteria of [sensory] likeness and similarity'* (p. 417; their emphasis) as a criterion for physical object-hood, and thus for distinguishing God from physical objects, would again put sub-atomic particles in the same category of reality as God. But my distinction between the impersonal and the existential is not vulnerable to this sort of objection and clearly distinguishes God from sub-atomic particles. Sub-atomic particles are invisible. God is neither visible nor invisible, since these notions (in their literal sense) have no application to him. However vulnerable the passages they quote from Phillips may be to their criticism, they overlook the significance of one sentence they quote: 'To say God is in the picture [Michelangelo's 'God Created Adam'] is a confession of faith' (Scott and Moore 1997, p. 416, from Phillips 1993, p. 44). A *confession of faith*: this – not to mention much else in his writings – surely suggests that when Phillips claimed God's reality to be very different from that of physical objects he had in mind the former kind of reality as being something like that I have called existential, however inadequate his explanation of it might sometimes have been.

8. The failure of attempts by philosophers to bring the notion, or some analogue of it, within the conceptual resources they regard as constituting morality (rationality or flourishing), or their outright rejection of the notion (most consequentialists), is telling. See Cordner (2005) and Gaita (1991, chs 3–4, 2000a).

9. The image of different inventories of different realities might mislead here, suggesting they are completely sealed off from one another. We can give impersonal accounts of moral and existential phenomena, or at least of our human responses to them: for example, there could be impersonal study of economic, psychological and other factors in the spread of moral and existential awareness. Equally there can be moral and existential evaluations of the significance of the physical world or of science as a human activity. There is a sense in which these are all descriptions of the same world (all the things there are) but that does not mean there is a privileged, context-less

description of that world. The aspiration to that assumes that language can get its meaning prior to or independently of its use, its 'place' as I like to say, in our lives, and that I think is a magical conception of language.

10. I am grateful to Craig Taylor for bringing it home to me that an earlier version of this chapter failed to address this point adequately.

11. Brian Davies (2006) has also used the 'Stop' signs image. We hit on it independently.

12. I mean that the existence of tables and chairs, or indeed of any impersonal world at all, does not *follow from* my account of objectifying reality. I do not mean to imply that we can coherently doubt the deliverance of our senses in normal circumstances.

13. In many cases this would be an understatement. The encounter with God blows away all our false idols and misconceptions.

14. Throughout his paper Haldane, though he professes to agree with Phillips about the importance of context, seems to me to treat words such as 'reference' and 'transcendent' as if they were exceptions, as if they operated regardless of context. The same is true of William Hasker (2010), who establishes nothing by accusing me of denying that the word 'God' has a referent. If he means it has a referent in the sense of an object understood on the impersonal model of reality, then I do deny 'God' has a referent. But that hardly means I deny it *simpliciter*. I have tried to explain what sort of thing 'God' refers to: something real in the existential domain. What 'reference' comes to may be different as well; for example, a causal account will not do.

15. It is doubtful that we can do that anyway. See Phillips (2005, pp. 5–13, 2007b), Hasker (2007, 2010), Gleeson (2010a, 2010b).

16. This is not a theodical claim: first, because I am not claiming that the dependence of good on evil justifies the evil; second, because I am not claiming merely that evil provides opportunities for doing or being good. Nor is the claim even just that, say, compassion necessarily requires suffering as its intentional object. The claim is that compassion cannot exist even as a disposition unless the world is one in which actual suffering is a common reality and the disposition commonly realised. It makes no sense to suppose that beings like us – capable of love and so on – could exist in a world devoid of actual suffering. A similar argument goes for moral evil, the reality of which also informs the fellowship and love humans are capable of, and indeed even our capacity to recognise one another *as* fellows.

17. I do not claim that the picture of believers' (and unbelievers') practice is a starkly black-and-white one favouring my account. Impersonal and existential matters get mixed together in practice (and opinion), and sometimes they are hard to disentangle. Some believers *are* interested in intelligent design and in the prayer experiments at a practical level. Some do retreat to wilderness compounds to await the end of the world. Perhaps in fact most believers' practical faith is of an impersonal character in *some* respect and degree: for example, they may get their hopes up in expectation of miraculous cures effected by prayer or relics. And of course there are *some* legitimate and crucially important impersonal claims in Christian faith: for example, that Jesus was crucified at Jerusalem in the first century AD. But

these do not bear on the dispute, between philosophers like Haldane and ones like me, over what it means for God to be real.

18. If we find absurd a scientific explanation for how we *can* see God directly (by building a thingummy-scope), then we should also find absurd a scientific explanation for why we *cannot* see him directly. It is not difficult to imagine a parody of that idea, similar to my Job parody of Chapter 3 against the idea of slight toothaches and the bitter taste of cough medicine counting against the goodness of God.

19. Didn't I discuss the *ad hoc* objection as objection 4 in Chapter 4? But there the issue was a purely *philosophical* one about whether I had independent grounds for denying God was a moral agent or causal force. Here the issue is partly a *theological* one about whether the denial is consonant with the Bible and historic Christian profession of faith.

20. Of course these relations with the being will be in part moral and existential, and we may recognise him as a person. But that does not compromise my claim that his *reality* is 'impersonal' in my sense of the word.

21. Thus some Christians get things exactly back to front if they argue that it is Jesus's divinity – considered as a causal power to work miracles, prophesy events and so on, a conception of divinity held independently of scrutinising his or anyone's particular life – which makes his life and teaching significant. Rather it is the significance of his life and teaching which give sense to what it means to speak of him as God.

22. Weil (1977, 2002). It is only with considerable trepidation that I broach the idea of terrible suffering as a 'blessing'. The danger of false piety here is enormous. In Weil, for all her greatness, I fear the development of a sort of spiritual aristocracy of affliction. See also Iris Murdoch's unfortunate comment that 'the attempt to be virtuous' is the *only* thing in life of any value (1991, p. 87).

# References

Adams, M. M. 1999. *Horrendous Evils and the Goodness of God*, Melbourne, Melbourne University Press.

——. 2001. 'Afterword' in Davis 2001a, pp. 191–203.

——. 2008. 'Plantinga on "Felix Culpa": Analysis and Critique', *Faith and Philosophy*, 25(2), 123–40.

—— and Adams, R. M. (eds). 1990. *The Problem of Evil*, Oxford, Oxford University Press.

Ahern, M. B. 1971. *The Problem of Evil*, London, Routledge and Kegan Paul.

Bishop, J. 1998. 'Can There Be Alternative Conceptions of God?', *Nous* 32(2), 174–88.

Burley, M. 2008a. 'Phillips and Eternal Life: A Response to Haldane', *Philosophical Investigations*, 31(3), 237–51.

——. 2008b. 'Phillips and Realists on Religious Beliefs and the Fruits Thereof', *International Journal for the Philosophy of Religion*, 64(3), 141–53.

Burrell, D. 1979. *Aquinas: God and Action*, London, Routledge and Kegan Paul.

Cordner, C. 2005. 'Life and Death Matters: Losing a Sense of the Value of Human Beings', *Theoretical Medicine and Bioethics*, 26(3), 207–26.

Davies, B. 2006. *The Reality of God and the Problem of Evil*, London, Continuum.

——. 2007. 'D. Z. Phillips on Belief in God', *Philosophical Investigations*, 30(3), 219–44.

Davis, S. T. (ed.). 2001a. *Encountering Evil: Live Options in Theodicy*, New Edition, Louisville, Ky., Westminster John Knox Press.

——. 2001b. 'Free Will and Evil' in Davis 2001b, pp. 73–89.

——. 2001c. 'Rejoinder' in Davis 2001b, pp. 101–7.

Diamond, C. 1991. *The Realistic Spirit: Wittgenstein, Philosophy and the Mind*, Cambridge, Mass., MIT Press.

Dostoevsky, F. 1912. *The Brothers Karamazov*, translated by Constance Garnett, London, William Heinemann.

Gaita, R. 1991. *Good and Evil: An Absolute Conception*, London, Macmillan.

——. 2000a. 'Goodness Beyond Virtue', in his *A Common Humanity: Thinking about Love and Truth and Justice*, 2nd Edition, London, Routledge, pp. 17–27.

——. 2000b. 'Guilt, Shame and Community' in his *A Common Humanity: Thinking about Love and Truth and Justice*, 2nd Edition, London, Routledge, pp. 87–106.

Gibson, A. B. 1973. *The Religion of Dostoevsky*, London, SCM Press.

Gleeson, A. 2009. '"My Kingdom Is Not of This World": Reflections on Archbishop Jensen's Jesus', *Modern Believing*, 50(2), 51–63.

——. 2010a. 'More on the Power of God: A Rejoinder to William Hasker', *Sophia*, 49(4), 617–29.

——. 2010b. 'The Power of God', *Sophia*, 49(4), 603–16.

Haldane, J. 2007. 'Philosophy, Death and Immortality', *Philosophical Investigations*, 30(3), 245–65.

——. 2008. 'Phillips and Eternal Life: A Response to Mikel Burley', *Philosophical Investigations*, 31(3), 252–60.

Harris, J. 1975. 'The Survival Lottery', *Philosophy*, 50(191), 81–7.

Hasker, W. 2007. 'D. Z. Phillips' Problems with Evil and with God', *International Journal for Philosophy of Religion*, 61(3), 151–60.

——. 2008. *The Triumph of God over Evil: Theodicy for a World of Suffering*, Downers Grove, Ill., InterVarsity Press.

——. 2010. 'Which God? What Power? A Response to Andrew Gleeson', *Sophia*, 49(3), 433–45.

Hick, J. 1978. *Evil and the God of Love*, Revised Edition, San Francisco, Harper & Row.

——. 2001. 'An Irenaean Theodicy' in Davis 2001a, pp. 38–52.

Hopkins, G. M. 1953. *Poems and Prose of Gerard Manley Hopkins*, edited by W. H. Gardner, Harmondsworth, Penguin.

Johnston, M. 2009. *Saving God: Religion after Idolatry*, Princeton, Princeton University Press.

Keller, J. A. 2007. *Problems of Evil and the Power of God*, Aldershot, Ashgate.

Langtry, B. 2008. *God, the Best, and Evil*, Oxford, Oxford University Press.

Levine, M. 2000. 'Contemporary Christian Analytic Philosophy of Religion: Biblical Fundamentalism, Terrible Solutions to a Horrible Problem, and Hearing God', *International Journal for Philosophy of Religion*, 48(2), 89–119.

Lewis, C. S. 1957. *The Problem of Pain*, London, Collins (Fontana).

Mackie, J. L. 1990. 'Evil and Omnipotence' in Adams and Adams 1990, pp. 25–37. Originally published 1955 in *Mind*, 64(254), 200–12.

Manne, A. 1994. 'A Reflection upon Re-entering the World', *Quadrant*, 38(6), 14–25.

McCabe, H. 1987. *God Matters*, London, Geoffrey Chapman.

Moore, A. 2003. *Realism and Christian Faith: God, Grammar, and Meaning*, Cambridge, Cambridge University Press.

——. and Scott, M. (eds). 2007. *Realism and Religion: Philosophical and Theological Perspectives*, Aldershot, Ashgate.

Moore, G. 1988. *Believing in God: A Philosophical Essay*, Edinburgh, T. & T. Clark.

Mulhall, S. 1994. *Faith and Reason*, London, Duckworth.

Murdoch, I. 1991. *The Sovereignty of Good*, London, Routledge.

Neiman, S. 2003. *Evil in Modern Thought: An Alternative History of Philosophy*, Melbourne, Scribe.

Oppy, G. 2004. 'Arguments from Moral Evil', *International Journal for the Philosophy of Religion*, 56(2–3), 59–87.

Phillips, D. Z. 1993. *Wittgenstein and Religion*, Basingstoke, Macmillan.

——. 2001. 'Theism without Theodicy' in Davis 2001a, pp. 145–61.

——. 2004. *Religion and Friendly Fire: Examining Assumptions in Contemporary Philosophy of Religion*, Aldershot, Ashgate.

——. 2005. *The Problem of Evil and the Problem of God*, Minneapolis, Fortress Press.

——. 2007a. 'Pictures of Eternity – A Reply to Mario von der Ruhr', in A. F. Sanders (ed.), *D. Z. Phillips' Contemplative Philosophy of Religion: Questions and Answers*, Aldershot, Ashgate, pp. 75–93.

Phillips, D. Z. 2007b. 'William Hasker's Avoidance of the Problems of Evil and God (or: On Looking Outside the Igloo)', *International Journal for Philosophy of Religion*, 62(1), 33–42.

Pike, N. 1990. 'Hume on Evil' in Adams and Adams 1990, pp. 38–52. Originally published 1963 in *The Philosophical Review*, 72(2), 180–97.

Plantinga, A. 1974a. *God, Freedom and Evil*, New York, Harper Torchbooks.

——. 1974b. *The Nature of Necessity*, Oxford, Clarendon Press.

——. 2004. 'Supralapsarianism, or "O Felix Culpa"' in P. van Inwagen (ed.), *Christian Faith and the Problem of Evil*, Grand Rapids, Mo., Eerdmans, pp. 1–25.

Ramal, R. 2000. '"Reference" to D. Z. Phillips', *International Journal for the Philosophy of Religion*, 48(1), 35–56.

Roth, J. K. 2001. 'Rejoinder' in Davis 2001a, pp. 30–7.

Rowe, W. 1979. 'The Problem of Evil and Some Varieties of Atheism', *American Philosophical Quarterly*, 16(4), 335–41.

Scott, M. 1996. 'The Morality of Theodicies', *Religious Studies*, 32(1), 1–13.

——. 2006. 'How to Defend Religious Realism', *Faith and Philosophy*, 23(3), 314–36.

——. and Moore, A. 1997. 'Can Theological Realism Be Refuted?', *Religious Studies*, 33(1), 401–18.

Stump, E. 1990. 'Providence and Evil' in T. Flint (ed.), *Christian Philosophy*, Notre Dame, Ind., University of Notre Dame Press, pp. 51–91.

Styron, W. 1980. *Sophie's Choice*, London, Corgi.

Surin, K. 1986. *Theology and the Problem of Evil*, Oxford, Basil Blackwell.

Sutherland, S. R. 1984. *God, Jesus and Belief: The Legacy of Theism*, Oxford, Basil Blackwell.

Swinburne, R. 1996. *Is There a God?*, Oxford, Oxford University Press.

——. 1998. *Providence and the Problem of Evil*, Oxford, Clarendon Press.

——. 2004. *The Existence of God*, 2nd Edition, Oxford, Clarendon Press.

Taylor, C. D. 2001. 'Moral Incapacity and Huckleberry Finn', *Ratio (New Series)*, 14(1), 56–67.

——. 2005a. 'Moral Cognitivism and Character', *Philosophical Investigations*, 28(3), 253–72.

——. 2005b. 'Winch on Moral Dilemmas and Moral Modality', *Inquiry*, 49(2), 148–57.

——. forthcoming. *Moralism: A Study in a Vice*, Stocksfield, Acumen.

Tilley, T. W. 2000. *The Evils of Theodicy*, New York, Wipf and Stock.

Tooley, M. 2009. 'The Problem of Evil', *Stanford Encyclopedia of Philosophy* at http://plato.stanford.edu/entries/evil/ (Accessed May 2011).

Tracy, T. 1992. 'Victimization and the Problem of Evil: A Response to Ivan Karamazov', *Faith and Philosophy*, 9(3), 301–19.

Trakakis, N. 2008. 'Theodicy: The Solution to the Problem of Evil or Part of the Problem?', *Sophia*, 47(2), 161–91.

van Inwagen, P. (ed.). 2004. *Christian Faith and the Problem of Evil*, Grand Rapids, Mo., Eerdmans, 2004.

——. 2006. *The Problem of Evil*, Oxford, Clarendon Press.

Vardy, P. 1992. *The Puzzle of Evil*, London, HarperCollins (Fount).

Weil, S. 1977. 'The Love of God and Affliction' in her *Waiting on God*, translated by E. Crawford, London, Fount Paperbacks, pp. 61–76.

——. 2002. *Gravity and Grace*, translated by E. Crawford and M. van den Ruhr, London, Routledge Classics.

Williams, B. 1981. 'Practical Necessity' in his *Moral Luck: Philosophical Papers 1973–1980*, Cambridge, Cambridge University Press, pp. 124–31.

——. 1993. *Shame and Necessity*, Berkeley, University of California Press.

Williams, R. 1996. 'Redeeming Sorrows' in D. Z. Phillips (ed.), *Religion and Morality*, Basingstoke, Macmillan, pp. 132–48.

Winch, P. 1972. 'The Universalizability of Moral Judgments' in his *Ethics and Action*, London, Routledge and Kegan Paul, pp. 151–70.

# Index